Irina Surina (Ed.)

Dilemmas of the Modern Educational Discourse

Dilemmas of the Modern Educational Discourse

edited by

Irina Surina

LIT

Reviewer: Professor Renate Seebauer, University of Education, Vienna

This book is printed on acid-free paper.

Bibliographic information published by the Deutsche Nationalbibliothek
The Deutsche Nationalbibliothek lists this publication in the Deutsche Nationalbibliografie; detailed bibliographic data are available in the Internet at http://dnb.d-nb.de.

ISBN 978-3-643-90512-3

A catalogue record for this book is available from the British Library

Klosbachstr. 107
CH-8032 Zürich
Tel. +41 (0) 44-251 75 05
Fax +41 (0) 44-251 75 06
E-Mail: zuerich@lit-verlag.ch
http://www.lit-verlag.ch

LIT VERLAG Dr. W. Hopf
Berlin 2014
Fresnostr. 2
D-48159 Münster
Tel. +49 (0) 2 51-62 03 20
Fax +49 (0) 2 51-23 19 72
E-Mail: lit@lit-verlag.de
http://www.lit-verlag.de

Distribution:

In the UK: Global Book Marketing, e-mail: mo@centralbooks.com
In North America: International Specialized Book Services, e-mail: orders@isbs.com
In Germany: LIT Verlag Fresnostr. 2, D-48159 Münster
Tel. +49 (0) 2 51-620 32 22, Fax +49 (0) 2 51-922 60 99, E-mail: vertrieb@lit-verlag.de

In Austria: Medienlogistik Pichler-ÖBZ, e-mail: mlo@medien-logistik.at
e-books are available at www.litwebshop.de

CONTENT

FOREWORD

The modern European society is one undergoing constant changes, facing new challenges and presented with opportunities which are as numerous as barriers, tensions and dangers. Political and economic systems are being transformed along with governments, opinions and requirements - and, as a natural consequence, educational system have to change as well. Societies in the process of transformation condition the rise of new (different) challenges which require assuming a new approach to the goals and tasks of education.

In all ages, education served a special purpose. Educational activity is the focus of interest for scientists and researchers from numerous disciplines. Such an interest is determined – on the one hand – by a pseudo-stability of the educational system and, on the other hand, by constant fluctuation which is conditioned by social, political and economic (etc) transformations. Such changes provoke a discussion concerning new challenges that the education is faced with. Education – as an essential factor of the development of societies and individuals - needs to live up to those challenges. According to A. Radziewicz-Winnicki and A. Roter, education can be perceived as an act of "preparing children, young people and adults for their active participation in – frequently unspecified in the scope of its direction – the process of ongoing and frequently surprising changes"

In this world of continuous transformations, new challenges and requirements, teaching and education at every level of educational system has taken on a particular significance. In the context of social transformations, education is considered "the main architect of civilizational changes"[1].

The collected research presented in this book is devoted to the dilemmas of modern education. Its focus – which is both theoretical and practical aspects of educational process and upbringing in different types of schools – reflects the wide range of issues and complexity of the current situation, helps to describe important problems, difficulties, the state of the present educational system as well as certain traits and tendencies characterising the development of education.

This publication is divided into two sections. The first one presents the whole of the system of higher education in its entire diversity through the discussion of selected aspects of the higher education's functioning which inspire an in-depth discussion concerning the present state and the future of the higher education.

[1] A. Chodubski, E*dukacja a wartości cywilizacji współczesnej*, [in:] W. Kojsa (ed.), *Wartości - Edukacja - Globalizacja*, Uniwersytet Śląski, Cieszyn 2002, p.11.

The system of higher education is one which is significantly complex, multi-faceted and multidimensional. Currently, one of characteristic traits of the development of Polish educational system is its steep, multi-faceted competitiveness. It concerns a number of issues which are interconnected. Its competitiveness manifests itself mostly through the diversity of strategies employed by respective institutions of higher education. We can also observe a struggle between not only the public and nonpublic sector of education, but also inside of them – for students, academic teachers, new faculties etc.

Processes taking place in the Polish society are - to a large extent - reflected in higher education. Today one could argue that higher education is one of the most dynamically developing areas of social life; this transformation, however, has a "wave"-like nature. Crucial changes in the system of Polish higher education have been taking place for the last ten years. Currently, there are rapid, profound and multi-faceted changes in progress as well. They will be a consequence of the introduced reforms concerning the implementation of the goals of Bologna Process in the system of European higher education. The Polish system of higher education also (like other social institutions) has its European dimension and progressively begins to resemble in certain areas other systems of higher education in the majority of the EU countries. At the same time, however, it is characterised by a huge internal diversification.

Androulla Vassiliou, European Commissioner for Education, Culture, Multilingualism and Youth, in her preface to the report of Focus on Higher Education in Europe *2010*: *The Impact of the Bologna Process* argues that "the Bologna Process has ensured that national action keeps pace with our European ambition. The Bologna process has been driving forward the most important reforms in higher education in the modern era, and all of the 46 signatory countries have today made significant moves towards establishing the European Higher Education Act. This is vital if we are to provide our continent and its citizens with the levels of education and skills required in a globally competitive, knowledge-based society"[2].

The current situation concerning higher education – which is conditioned mostly by constant changes on numerous levels – requires the scientists and researchers *to stop* and *make an assessment* as well as *conduct a critical analysis* of those changes' directions; it is crucial for them to clearly realise the essence of the ongoing transformations at a given stage of the higher education system's development.

The second section is devoted to considerations concerning a teacher and a student in the expanse of the modern school. School is a special place in the social expanse – it is here that the

---

[2] *Szkolnictwo wyższe w Europie 2010: wpływ Procesu Bolońskiego*. Seria Fokus, Fundacja Rozwoju Systemu Edukacji, Warszawa 2011, p.3-4

intellectual and moral maturing of children and youth has the greatest pace and the process of shaping enlightened minds and noble characters is a priority – a difficult one which does not always end as a success. As E. Murawska argues, "school is a peculiar kaleidoscope of social problems; within its limits appear all kinds of conflicts and crises which plague the modern society – and, therefore, it is an expanse remaining an integral part of its students' everyday life"[3].

Educating and teaching at school – the two fundamental processes inherent in human existence, determining its quality and course – are researched, described and interpreted in a scientific discourse, but also in everyday school practice. It is the school which constitutes an expanse where all those discourses meet.

To summarize, the collective work presented here includes articles which are varied in their methodological approaches, but coherent in describing the chosen aspects of the modern education's transformations. By no means, however, do those texts exhaust the complex range of issues concerning the state of the modern education.

Our reader shall find in this book reflections concerning various areas of educational activity undertaken to meet social challenges and requirements. The diversity of the authors' points of view makes it possible to see education as a complex, multi-faceted and mosaic reality which encompasses various subjects and relations between them.

"In the educational reality – so complex, multicoloured and complicated – one cannot excessively rely on explanations and interpretations which are bipolar in nature: implying that something is either good or bad, efficient or inefficient, proper or improper. Instead, we should rather search for reliable justifications for diversification, plurality of perceptions, models and concepts. Multicoloured manner of thinking about education might lead to a situation that also in educational reality we would be more willing to accept variety and differences which do not divide – but connect" – concludes J.Głodkowska[4].

I sincerely hope that this book shall be equally of interest to educators, academic teachers and researchers of various scientific disciplines dealing with the topic of education.

Irina Surina

[3] E.Murawska, *Wstęp*, [in:] E.Murawska, *Szkoła w dyskursie teorii i praktyki. Wybrane konteksty, CONTACT, Poznań 2013, p. 6.*

[4] J.Głodkowska, *Zamiast wstępu – jak zrozumieć, że nie wszystko jest tylko białe albo czarne*?, [in:] J.Głodkowska (ed.), *Uczeń ze specjalnymi potrzebami edukacyjnymi w szkole ogólnodostępnej*, Wydawnictwo Akademii Pedagogiki Specjalnej, Warszawa 2011, p.6-7.

SECTION I
THE SYSTEM OF HIGHER EDUCATION IN THE CONTEXT OF RAPIDLY CHANGING EDUCATIONAL REALITY

Krystyna Duraj-Nowakowa
Ignatianum University, Cracow, Poland

EDUCATION IN A HIGHER EDUCATION INSTITUTION: REQUIREMENTS AND POSSIBILITIES OF CREATIVE SOLUTIONS TO PROBLEMS

Summary

This article presents: circumstances of impediments in higher education functioning in the light of academic pedagogy; needs of modernization of higher education model in socio-pedagogical and pedeutological contexts; creativity of projects of changes in the pattern of academic pedagogues' work; components and factors of higher education modernization processes; sketch of a model of surmounting obstacles to create progressive effects of academic pedagogues' activity.

Introduction: circumstances of impediments relating to the higher education's functioning in view of the academic pedagogy

After an ongoing reform of the educational system implemented for the purpose of adjusting it to the EU agreements – there has been a change in legislation recorded in *Act on Higher Education* (2010) and its amendment (2011). However, the regulation of rules concerning the higher education's functioning in view of society's opinions and academic pedagogy does not appear to be sufficient [1].

Requirements in this area remain extensive. The knowledge concerning factors and mechanisms of the modern man's development is constantly undergoing changes. The theory of an individual's development in the course of his whole life, various theories concerning autonomy in the process of self-creation and the theory on individual development provide new knowledge which should be taken into consideration by educational processes in higher education facilities. A higher education facility as an educational institution undergoes changes as well. New functions it is supposed to fulfill according to social requirements mean that academic staff will need to possess progressively higher educational qualifications/competences enabling effective

[1] We collectively analysed the highest level of education for the benefit of its lower levels in a critical year. Cf.: K. Duraj-Nowakowa (ed.), *Nauczyciele akademiccy w procesie kształcenia pedagogów u progu reformy systemu edukacji,* Kraków-Łowicz 1999.

work with the highest of educational values: the student and his development[2] towards maturity as well as the shaping of a fully-developed personality.

Therefore, we have high hopes in diverse efforts to improve the quality of higher education facilities' functioning. One of institutions which could significantly contribute to improving quality of such efforts is the State Academic Accreditation Committee.

In addition, there are numerous indicators that in the recent future there will be an increased interest in psycho-educational conditions of the creativity development of all generations, as well as in methods and means to develop this creativity of various age and professional groups. The reason behind it is that Poland needs to make up for its considerable backlog – first, in the sphere of teaching creativity, and then - in its implementation at work and everyday life. To achieve the first goal, an increasingly popular creativity training is employed during classes of higher education facility.

It needs to be observed, however, that academic evaluation in Polish conditions – though it is an element of community accreditation – does not appear in a pure and mature form. More socially relevant in the phase of higher education's development in our country – with its current indicators: massiness and commercialization – is accreditation which, through proper certificates of quality, confirms and guarantees meeting the requirements of proper educating at a given academic facility – which results in a strong position on the market of educational services and its proper social reception.[3]

In Europe, accreditation is the basic method to guarantee quality within state systems of quality assessment which leads to a situation where academic facilities are mostly interested in obtaining this accreditation - and not in quality itself.[4] A similar threat to quality exists in the Polish system of higher education. A significant opportunity for a valid improvement in the sphere of Polish educational quality would result from a strict cooperation of the State Academic Accreditation Committee with community committees. Institutional accreditation offers additional opportunities:

- it allows for a constant monitoring and improvement of the teaching level of academic facilities in Poland,

- it stimulates the creation and development of internal systems of controlling teaching quality,

---

[2] K. Jaskot, *Wstęp*, [in:] K. Jaskot (ed.), *Wprowadzenie do pedagogiki szkoły wyższej,* Szczecin 2006, p.5.
[3] E. Chmielecka, *Akredytacja studiów wyższych w Europie i Polsce – kierunki rozwoju,* [in:] E. Panek (ed.), *Wymiar europejski studiów ekonomicznych w Polsce,* Warszawa, 2003, p.125.
[4] Ibidem, p. 115; Cf.: K. Denek, *Uniwersytet w perspektywie społeczeństwa wiedzy: Nauka i edukacja w uniwersytecie XXI wieku*, v.I, Poznań 2011.

- it enables obtaining or confirmation of the meeting by a facility of threshold requirements in the process of teaching,

- it provides the possibility to compare facilities of the same type in the scale of a town, region or the entire country – as well as the international one; it also enables one to compare majors in the scale of the country or a given region,

- it indicates models to follow (the best facilities) – through its transparent form of evaluation,

- it enables international cooperation in the sphere of teaching and scientific research.[5]

At this point, one can only anticipate considerable implications of the State Academic Accreditation Committee's activity.

1. Necessities to modernize a model of an academic facility in the socio-pedagogical and pedeutological contexts.

A definite obligation – and not merely a need – to modernize higher education results from a gap between ideals of an academic facility and an essence of this kind of teaching in practice.

A fundamental assumption can be seen in ideals of democratization and humanization of social life in Poland's new conditions after the transformation of political system. The educational system – including its higher level – accepts those ideals in its activity in order to prepare graduates for their participation in the construction and development of the whole society according to their spirit.[6]

The concept of humanization encompasses the entire vision of our existence/life activity in the modern world and has a multi-faceted character. Such humanization – drawing from the centuries-old achievements of humanism, starting with the ancient Greece – constitutes a constant process of "humanizing" all human endeavours on the basis of significance, possibilities, achievements and respect for man's subjectivity, dignity of a free individual – working for the common good with communities and remaining in harmony with the nature of the world which we are entitled to transform without disturbing ecological balance.

The very term of humanization is derived from "humanism" (coming from the latin *humanus* – human) and is perceived as a modern implementation of its principles and postulates. The very term of humanism was introduced in order to describe the pedagogical concept in which the achievements of the ancient culture were to constitute the very basis for upbringing and educa-

[5] As it is perceived, for example, by J. Stachowicz, *Troska o jakość kształcenia w szkole wyższej jako przejaw kultury akademickiej – szanse i zagrożenia,* [in:] A. Sowiński (ed.), *Kultura akademicka w oglądzie pedagogicznym,* Szczecin 2009, p.136.

[6] Applications of the problems within pedeutology cf.: K. Duraj-Nowakowa, *Kształtowanie profesjonalnej gotowości pedagogów,* Kraków 2011. The same author: *Nauczyciel: kultura – osoba - zawód,* 2nd edition, Kielce 2002.

tion – which in the German educational system of the 19th century (the epoch of the so-called neohumanism) assumed an extreme form of an apotheosis of the entire ancient culture.

The humanism of Renaissance in the history of civilisation constituted a tendency to revive classical culture, an attitude to life in accordance with its ideals and opposing the theocentric culture of the Middle Ages. Its essence was an interest in the man and human life on the basis of the potential of human mind. Currently, however, it is a school of thought in which a person/human being and their multi-faceted, unlimited development is the priority. One can distinguish varieties of humanism which reflect diverse cultural, philosophical and ideological currents of a given epoch, place and people (just to compare its varieties – evolutionary, Christian, personalistic, Marxist, existential, phenomenological, theocentric, religious, Catholic and evangelical). As we can see, there are versions which absolutize the man and those that make the man's value dependent on his relation with God.

In this fashion, personalism as a current in the modern religious philosophy is based upon the assumption that the highest value of the world – created by God – is a person perceived as an integrated physical, mental and spiritual being endowed with self-consciousness and will.

As a result, we perceive humanism in an extensive sense – as a discipline/set of disciplines which treat human/humanistic understanding of the world as a priority. Hence, humanities deal with properties of humanism (which influence the modern perception of life's humanization, that is - *humanitas*/humanity).

Therefore, humanism in an aspect which is of interest to us – constituting a view or an attitude which, above all, affirms the man's dignity as an assessing relation of a person in reference to oneself and the social and/or professional, class, national (etc.) group they identify with. This philosophical orientation was founded in France in two variations: the first – by Jacques Maritain, strongly theological in nature, and the second – by Emmanuel Mounier, more philosophical and also considered more progressive. Both orientations found a strong reception and continuation in Poland during the interwar period.

In such a personalistic tradition – both in the secular version (for example, Bogdan Suchodolski), professionalism of an educator of an academic facility is understood as a basic indicator of the personal and socio-professional identity with oneself, personal notions concerning the pursued mature personality and requirements of the roles of an educator.

This is why the modern understanding of the goals of an academic facility's pedagogy as a subdiscipline remains so important; a subdiscipline which could support more efficiently the functioning of teachers in general – and academic teachers in particular.[7]

Therefore, it appears convenient to characterize the pedagogy of an academic facility as a theoretical and practical discipline employing output of an experienced researcher who presented his of her own view of the pedagogy of an academic facility as a specific pedagogical science.

"Using my previously specified concepts concerning general pedagogy, methodology of pedagogy, methodology of pedagogical research, academic facility's pedagogy and didactic practice – as well as properly processing and complementing them - I am, however, also taking advantage of the work by other authors – from disciplines such as general pedagogy, methodology of pedagogy, methodology of pedagogical research, pedagogy of academic facility and didacticism - in an attempt to form a construct including the basics of the analyzed scientific discipline".[8]

Thus, we suggest that the pedagogy of an academic facility should be perceived "both as a science having its theoretical and methodological foundations, and a teaching practice realised at the level of vocational academic facilities of first and second cycle, humanistic, technical, artistic, economic and sport-related ones. Both dimensions of this discipline have a cognitive and practical sense and are strictly interconnected; it would prove difficult to imagine a sphere of teaching practice without underlying cognitive, theoretical or methodological assumptions. Pedagogy as a purely theoretical discipline – without any contact with practice which provides it with cognitive and research issues and within which it verifies its theoretical and hypothetical constructs – is hardly constructive".[9]

This study focuses on the essence, subject and structure of the pedagogy of an academic facility. At this point, let us use a characterization we agree with in its entirety:

"Such a specific pedagogical science as the pedagogy of an academic facility does not develop on its own, in separation from the basic disciplines like general pedagogy and didacticism, theory and history of education, and pedagogical thought (pedagogical doctrines); in a similar fashion, it cannot develop in separation from practice defined by the framework of a cognitive discipline. The model of the pedagogy of an academic facility may be derived from the one of general pedagogy. Currently, there is no such thing as one model of generally per-

[7] Cf.: K. Duraj-Nowakowa (ed.), *Modernizowanie pedeutologii akademickiej,* Kielce 2003. – Idem (ed.), *Integrowanie komponentów dydaktyki szkoły wyższej i pedeutologii,* „Studia Pedagogiczne AŚ", Kielce 2003.

[8] A. Palka, *Charakterystyka pedagogiki szkoły wyższej jako dyscypliny teoretycznej i praktycznej,* [in:] K. Jaskot (ed.), *Wprowadzenie do pedagogiki szkoły wyższej,* op.cit., p.12.

[9] Ibidem; Cf. also: I.A. Surina (ed.), *Przestrzeń edukacyjna wobec wyzwań i oczekiwań społecznych,* Kraków 2010 and idem (ed.), *Pedagogika społeczna: współczesne obszary,* Słupsk 2008.

ceived pedagogy, one systematic pedagogy; there is a plurality of perceptions and methods of creating pedagogy – which, on the one hand, might signify richness and pluralism of concepts and, on the other hand, might lead to a state of ambivalence, confusion and uncertainty. Therefore, in our considerations, we need to adopt a precisely specified model of pedagogy – and it shall provide the basis for an analysis of the pedagogy of an academic facility".[10]

For this reason, let us adopt the following approach: "Having taken into consideration concepts and beliefs of educators from the past, the present ones - and my own concept derived from individual cognitive experiences - I am assuming a view that pedagogy is a science concerning upbringing, education and self-education of a human being in the course of their entire life. One might classify as its components both concentric activities: educating and teaching, as well as decentralizing ones – the very process of shaping. The pedagogy of an academic facility is distinguished on the basis of the level of school teaching (next to the early school, school and secondary school pedagogies) - as at the level of an academic facility transpires an important stage in the development of a person entering their adult life. It could be assumed that the pedagogy of an academic facility is a science concerning teaching, education and self-education of youth attending a higher education institutions".[11]

Such a perception of the essence of the pedagogy of an academic institution has a considerable cognitive, research-oriented and practical significance; above all, this discipline is not reduced to teaching – an important element is reinstated in this discipline, namely – the self-development (self-formation and self-education) of studying youth. This fact creates new research areas as well as new and richer solution possibilities - both methodological (cognitive craft) and pedagogy of everyday practice, i.e., teaching/methodology of a professional academic activity.

It results from the definition of "the pedagogy of an academic institution" that within the cognitive scope of this discipline one can distinguish – in my opinion - not three but four following elements: 1) students' education, 2) self-education of students, 3) students' teaching and 4) students' self-teaching.[12]

---

[10] Ibidem, p.13.

[11] Ibidem: Cf. also: K. Duraj-Nowakowa, Chapter 1: *Tło i zarys pedagogiki systemowej,* [in:] also, *Pedagogika społeczna: między integracją w dezintegracją,* Rzeszów 2009, p.19 – 60; Cf. also: E. Gaweł-Luty, *Pedagogika społeczna*, Szczecin 2004.

[12] In this manner we see those issues in individual and collective books – Cf.: K. Duraj-Nowakowa, *Nauczyciele akademiccy w procesie kształcenia...,* op. cit., 1999, part. 1 - 6.

The creativity of the projects of changes concerning the model of academic work of educators

Since needs for social changes require creative projects – then, for academic teachers, problems and tasks related to solving issues concerning these projects constitute the question of how to bring out creative traits of man – beginning with his role as a student.

At the same time, it is assumed that creativity is the man's ability/willingness to create new and valuable output, i.e., more valuable in a certain respect (aesthetic, practical, scientific etc.) than what came before.[13]

In view of that, a creative man is one who is able/ready to generate ideas which contribute to making our world better, more friendly and beautiful – ready to generate/create new output: ideas, methods of action and products.

Training for creativity, on the other hand, consists in a system of individual and/or group exercises used for the purpose of evoking and developing skills/readiness to generate those new and valuable ideas for the purpose of solving cognitive and practical problems.[14]

Creativity training – also referred to as inventiveness (or output-oriented training) – is understood as a training of creative problem-solving as well as creative thinking. Hence, in pedagogy – also in the pedagogy of academic institution – for the practice purposes, we pay attention to three main creative processes and types of creativity that correspond to them:

1) explorations – explorational output – interrogative thinking[15]. Explorations which signify research, investigation, searching for and discovering something in cognitive and practical activities;

2) combinations – combinatorial output - associative thinking through connecting, synthesizing, combining old ideas with new requirements and in new ways through accidental association or noticing similarities, or through mediation, i.e., combining separate elements through an intermediary component;

3) transformations – transformative output – transformative thinking. Transformation, i.e., a process of transformation, modification, metamorphosis leading to a change of content and/or the form of the original by a way of intellectual experimenting. This purpose is served by transforming operations – among which the most frequently characterized and academically useful are the following (let us enumerate them to illustrate the point – as the limited space for the text excludes the possibility for their separate characterization): reintegration,

[13] Cf.: E. Nęcka, *Psychologia twórczości,* Gdańsk 2001; S. Popek, *Człowiek jako istota twórcza,* Lublin 2003.
[14] Cf.: W. Limont, *Analiza wybranych mechanizmów wyobraźni twórczej: badania eksperymentalne,* Toruń 1996, also: Z. Pietrasiński, *Mądrość, czyli świetne wyposażenie umysłu,* Warszawa 2001; Cf. chapters concerning text interpretation: K. Duraj-Nowakowa, *Studiowanie literatury przedmiotu*, Kraków 2012.
[15] Cf.: K. Szmidt (ed.), *Terminy twórczości w szkole wyższej,* Łódź 2005.

multiplication, persuasion (the reverse of multiplication), majorization, schematisation, metamorphosis, animation, colour inversion and conversion.[16]

Creativity of human beings and their projects in the scope of changes concerning the model of academic work of educators is the focus education. Teaching – in order to become an effective process – needs to be active, conscious and full of purpose. Although the traits mentioned above are similar in the sense of content – they are not identical. By the above we emphasize a necessity of clear, unanimous understanding of actions performed by academic teachers and students in the process of education. One cannot expect full activity on the part of students if they only follow instructions and orders of scientific and didactic staff. Such activity happens only when students take part in the educational process as its conscious participants, partners.

Goals of higher education can be graphically presented as: pyramids (its vertex represents the main/principal goal and respective grades are the means to achieve it), trees (its highest point represents the main goal, and respective branches stand for diversified hierarchal stages), constellation (with the central point of reference – with various satellites /goals/ orbiting within its field of gravity), analogues (compounds, atom structure, combinations). One can also analyse them from different points of view (philosophical, praxeological, organisation- and qualification-oriented, pedagogical and others) – illustrating their multifaceted properties.[17]

According to the classical theory of organization, goals form its basis and, at the same time, the foundations of academic facility's activities. Forming an organization begins with the specification of the most fundamental goals, expectations, intentions and visions. They are transferred onto specific goals and a set of tasks from which the scope of activity might be derived. Next, syllabuses and contents are specified which lead to those goals' implementation; also, necessary assets, means, structure and organisational roles are established. Those goals constitute both a challenge – a highly placed bar - and a reference point for the purpose of evaluating results (achieving/completing the goals). Tasks, on the other hand, are specified in a concrete manner, measured according to deadlines through variables and indicators.[18]

---

[16] K. J. Szmidt, *Trening kreatywności,* Gliwice 2008, p. 35.

[17] Cf.: K. Duraj-Nowakowa, *Modelowanie systemowe pedagogiki,* Kraków 1997 ; Idem: *Źródła podejść do pedagogik: zarys problemów*, Kielce 2005; Cf. also: M. Kaliszewska, B. Klasińska (ed.), *Szkice systemowych ujęć pedagogiki*, Kielce 2010.

[18] K. Denek, *Cele edukacji w szkole wyższej,* [in:] K. Jaskot (ed.), *Wprowadzenie...* op.cit., p. 82; Cf. also: M. Kaliszewska, *Funkcje eseju pedagogicznego w dydaktyce akademickiej na tle procesów inkluzji społecznej*, Kielce 2011 and the same author, *Esej pedagogiczny w kształceniu akademickim*, Kielce 2009.

Therefore, it is essential to direct an academic facility towards goals which are logically hierarchized/graded: general, gradual and detailed. If you fail to reach another one, all the previous ones become irrelevant – remaining, after all, in a feedback relation.[19]

The process of perfecting the goals of education requires their optimization in a system-making perspective taking into consideration four aspects: postulative/visionary and causative/action-related, potential/imaginary, i.e., anticipatory and functional/usable.

Goals of education in an academic institution – and we should never underestimate it – need to be characterized by four constitutive features. Each of those goals should be: 1) noticed, distinguished and specified in such a manner that it is possible to establish the state/result of its achieving; 2) feasible, possible to achieve by a given time/deadline; 3) logical, without internal contradictions; 4) substantial, i.e., presenting a synthetic description of what we aim to achieve; 5) measurable, i.e., precise, possible to evaluate.

Components and factors of the processes of modernizing the system of higher education

If we previously established that the needs for modernizing academic facilities are so closely related to the goals of their activity – then there are important reasons for which one ought to consider axiological questions in pedagogy and academic education/pedagogy. Components and factors of the quality improvement in the procedures of modernizing activity of academic facilities are essential here. All the remaining ones – although important (for example, economic) – are of a secondary nature, based on the main (and previously emphasized) idea of humanization of educating students' mature personalities for their activity in a democratic society.

In academic education, values and goals that give meaning to human life are simultaneously given and demanded from a human being. Therefore, such human being is forced to both discover and create them.[20]

In order to specify axiological foundations for establishing the goals of academic education, in the first order, one needs to realize what this academic education and educational axiology really are - and understand those key concepts in the periods of modernism and postmodernism. Subsequently, employing a chosen research perspective – it is necessary to establish consequences

---

[19] Closer characterizations - Cf.: K. Duraj-Nowakowa, *Teoria systemów a pedagogika*, Kraków 1992. Attempts of modern applications of general approaches - Cf.: A. Rogalska-Marasińska, *Humanizm – dialog – tożsamość: edukacja europejska na tle wyzwań globalnych*, Łódź 2010.

[20] J. Gnitecki, *Aksjologiczne podstawy stanowienia celów edukacyjnych szkoły wyższej,* [in:] K. Jaskot (ed.), *Wprowadzenie do pedagogiki....,* op.cit., p. 32-34; Cf. also: A. Rogalska-Marasińska (ed.), *Nauczyciel wobec szans i zagrożeń edukacyjnych XXI wieku*, v. II: *Praktyka edukacyjna w perspektywie wyzwań XXI wieku*, Kraków 2009.

for the theory and practice of forming educational goals of an academic activity (for example, in the vein of work by K. Denek, K. Olbrycht and U. Ostrowska).

In professional literature, we can find numerous definitions of education – including the academic one. Currently, however, academic education cannot be perceived as an adaptational process – in other words, one which adjusts the activities on the part of academic teachers and students to the permanent goals of education which were set *a priori*. Instead, it is more of a dynamic system of activities aiming to reform any hitherto prevailing goals of education and programmes of educational and didactic actions. Such a standpoint results from the belief that the goals of education are dynamically linked to the taught values undergoing changes. Academic education is a symbolic form of communication expressed in a language which enables recognizing, understanding, accepting and respecting values and goals which give meaning to human life. Those values are always grounded in the changing socio-cultural context. Hence, along with such changing context – there follow changes of meaning of taught values as well as any goals of education derived from them. This is why in the conditions of the modern system transformation, another approach is required – one which derives educational goals from educational and taught values[21], as it is taught by axiology and pedagogical teleology.

If we make the above-mentioned assumption that pedagogy/academic education is a symbolic form of communication expressed in a descriptive, predescriptive and symbolic language suited to cognitive, emotional, causative and cultural possibilities and limitations of each human being – that would signify that it leads towards description and explanation, interpretation and understanding, as well as the ability and efficiency of implementing changes in the man's personality in the course of his entire life – in a permanent fashion. This definition emphasizes not only didactic, pedagogical and tutorial aspects, but also rehabilitation-oriented, global, media, interactive, personal and cultural aspects of education, and – in addition – the cognitive, study- and research-related ones. In this fashion, the processes of academic education and research are becoming alike – leading to learning through research. This act of becoming alike has an empirical (description and explanation), praxeological (effectiveness, efficiency of educational activity) and hermeneutical (interpretation and understanding) character. In addition, currently, education is simultaneously perceived in the style of modernity and postmodernity, but also – in a material, and, predominantly, spiritual dimension. In view of that, both the philosophy of education as well as an academic teacher as an

[21] J. Gnitecki, op.cit., p. 32-33; Cf.: K. Duraj-Nowakowa, *Teoria systemów…*, op.cit.

educator change their functions and tasks. An academic teacher as an educator, from the source and transmitter of knowledge, becomes its searcher and discoverer, creator and commentator, interpreter and narrator. This fact opens up a path towards searching for a diversified model of an academic facility[22] which takes into consideration any taught values and goals as well as contents of self-education and education of teachers and our students.

As philosophizing educators, we pose three essential questions in this context. What is the essence of modernity (modernism) and postmodernity (postmodernism) in the modern philosophy of academic science and education, as well as the pedagogy of an academic institution? What assumptions of modernism and postmodernism indicate duality/ambivalence of those two currents in the philosophy of science and academic education simultaneously on the border between modernity and postmodernity?

As a result of in-depth studies, we obtain answers revealing that modernity in the philosophy of science and academic education presupposes generality of discourse, repeatability, but also a certain schematism in the perception of phenomena, recreation of their senses and meanings, explanation of reasons behind certain results, paradigm-like thinking, descriptive language, generality of truths and values, permanence of the cultural context, creating knowledge and unified view of the world, formulating truths and regularities which are general in nature.

On the other hand, postmodernity in the philosophy of science and education presupposes localness of discourse, varied and situation-dependent perception of phenomena, designing senses and meanings, narrative quality of thinking, predescriptive language, textuality, ambivalence, diffusion and – consequently – relativity of truths and values, fluctuating quality of the cultural context, creation of a decentralised and diffused view of the world – and, as a result: impossibility to formulate truths and regularities which are general in nature.

This dissimilarity in the field of principles behind modernity (modernism) and postmodernity (postmodernism) leads to differences in the perception of science and education, as well as the manner in which pedagogical reflection is conducted. In the period of modernity, there are numerous attempts made to generalize the cognitive process, to create unified cognitive structures based on order, necessity and identity. In the postmodern period, however, the diffused structures become prominent – based on chaos, incident and difference.[23] A simultaneous analysis of science and education – currently a quite frequent phenomenon – in the field of modernity and postmodernity, leads to a diversified and balanced perception of those

[22] Cf. Desriptions of three chosen paradigms: K. Duraj-Nowakowa, *Podejścia całościowe do pedagogiki: wybór*, Rzeszów 2008.
[23] J. Gnitecki, op.cit., p. 34.

oppositions.[24] From such a view of science and education result far-reaching consequences in perceiving the pedagogy of an academic institution in the period of modernity and postmodernity – including axiological education and educational axiology, as well as teleology.

Educational axiology is an attempt to define the essence and a manner of man's existence in the categories of the system of values which give meaning to human life in the educational and taught expanse. Educational expanse is filled with essential values (truth, good and beauty). Those values – as it is emphasized by Władysław Stróżewski – have a "supracultural dimension" and this is why they are referred to as supraesthetic values.[25] The man – through his "personal self" - is able to recognize and understand them (as well as accept and respect them), but is unable to create them. The taught expanse, however, is filled with non-essential values – created by the man and already present in our culture (also the pedagogical one). The non-essential values are open to transfer and participation – "self-interaction" – of essential values.

Axiological foundations indicated in this paper which concern the formation of educational goals of an academic facility present the modern educational theory and practice with considerably difficult and responsible tasks. A progressive development of man is dependent on their completion – as well as the protection of the modern civilisation. Whether we can meet those challenges depends only on us. In the current conditions, a particular significance lies in the obtaining by an academic teacher and student of qualifications necessary to unify the non-essential and essential values. That would enable their transfer and participation aimed at both their excess and the reduction of sense.[26] In other words – thinking in a dual/ambivalent manner – it is simultaneously a surplus of reasons and the reduction of this sense's significance.

Conclusion: a draft of the model of overcoming obstacles for the purpose of creating progressive results of academic educators' activity

Whenever I attempt to model in accordance with the systems paradigm – in the first order, I demonstratively make a graph of types of those models,[27] and then I prepare their characterization. (This entire study, incidentally, is based on a paradigm/approach/orientation in accordance with the systems theory and methodology). At this point, I would like to focus on one

---

[24] Cf.: K. Duraj-Nowakowa, J. Gnitecki (ed.), *Epistemologiczne wyzwania współczesnej pedagogiki,* Kraków 1997.

[25] W. Stróżewski, *W kręgu wartości,* Kraków 1992, p. 108-132.

[26] J. Gnitecki, *Aksjologiczne...,* op.cit., [in:] K. Jaskot (ed.), *Wprowadzenie...,* op.cit., p. 51.

[27] Cf.: K. Duraj-Nowakowa, *Modelowanie w badaniach pedagogicznych,* [in:] S. Palka (ed.), *Podstawy metodologii badań w pedagogice,* Gdańsk 2009, p. 139 -152; Cf. idem: *Modelowanie systemowe w pedagogice,* Kraków 1997.

type of thinking model, i.e., the abstract model in its sign (symbolic) meaning. In other words, a model as a sign system interpreted in a specific manner according to a qualitative strategy.

The strategy of qualitative view of a problem combines the topic of this study with an assessment, evaluation, verification of the quality of higher education's functioning. This is why we ought to review the background of a draft of a model of overcoming obstacles for the purpose of creating progressive results of academic educators' activity.

Academic activity since the moment of the system transformation in Poland has remained under the influence of – and taken place on – the free educational market. This is accompanied by the phenomenon of massiness of studying and higher education's commercialization. It is hardly difficult to guess what the character of these phenomena is – and this fact should by no means be ignored. Destruction of academic activity manifests itself also through the lowering of quality and effectiveness of the process of educating students. This phenomenon appears to have a continuous and escalating nature. Hence our worry and concern for the quality of education – both from the institutional and individual point of view – remains valid and actual.

This is why accreditation – along with the evaluation of academic work – should be the proper tool for the purpose of re-establishing of the disturbed order and controlling the academic standards of education. The condition, however, is for the quality of education to become the common concern of: 1) academic facility – through the operating internal systems of ensuring the quality of education and community accreditation; 2) the entire system around such a facility – through setting requirements to be met by academic facilities and using the feedback resulting from the conducted assessment; 3) the state, EU member, willing to make a considerable contribution to the construction of European dimension/area of higher education through perfecting the procedures of obligatory accreditation serving a complementary function in relation to the local one as well as the international cooperation in the sphere of ensuring the quality of academic education of the united Europe.[28]

Let us briefly consider respective viewpoints concerning the chosen range of issues in the context of complications which accompany the process of constructing such model of overcoming obstacles.

Misunderstandings result from the failure to comprehend the nature of accreditation – especially academic accreditation.[29] They can arise in the course of works of a committee

[28] J. Stachowicz, *Troska...* op.cit., p. 136-137.

[29] Guideline cf.. Akademicka Komisja Akredytacyjna, *System oceny jakości kształcenia i akredytacji w szkolnictwie wyższym,* Wyd. Instytut u Problemów Współczesnej Cywilizacji, Warszawa 1997.

itself (internal regulations, evaluation procedures, functioning of expert groups), between an academic facility and a committee (self-evaluation report, inspections of faculties, feedback information for such a facility, potential additional evaluation) or have their origins in academic facilities themselves. This is why it should be noted - before and in the course of a committee's work - that threats resulting from accreditation can be classified in five following categories:

- formalizing and tightening of accreditation procedures employed by committees resulting in their dysfunctionality in the reality of the higher education system;

- failure on the part of a given academic facility to relate obligatory accreditation to the internal system of evaluation of educational quality functioning at a given department or facility;

- treating minimum conditions - the meeting of which is the basis of obtaining (or retaining) accreditation by a facility - as a standard and a level a given facility can treat as satisfactory - to avoid further improvement;

- wrong perception of accreditation as a result of action and not a process of perfecting the quality of education extended in time;

- failure on the part of academic facility to use in practice any feedback information obtained from a committee along with the evaluation of educational quality.[30]

This heightened awareness of academic teachers concerning discussions and disputes in the course of analysing the control shall eventually prevent non-objective and/or inadequate evaluations.

Indicated circumstances probably more clearly point out the necessity of their consideration in everyday work of academic teachers, dealing with those obstacles or – despite such hindrances – searching for/imposing adequate methods of their overcoming by ambitious and responsible persons and, in opposite cases, may lead to passivity, hypocrisy - and even opposition to any progressive changes.

Bibliography

Akademicka Komisja Akredytacyjna, *System oceny jakości kształcenia i akredytacji w szkolnictwie wyższym,* Wyd. Instytutu Problemów Współczesnej Cywilizacji, Warszawa 1997.

[30] For its illustration it would suffice to consult information in – Cf. e.g.: *Działalność Państwowej Komisji Akredytacyjnej w 2006 roku,* PKA, Warszawa 2007; Cf. also: *Autonomia programowa uczelni: ramy kwalifikacji dla szkolnictwa wyższego*, Warszawa 2010.

Autonomia programowa uczelni: ramy kwalifikacji dla szkolnictwa wyższego, Wyd. MNiSzW, Warszawa 2010.

Ciekot K., *Funkcje ewaluacji w zapewnianiu jakości kształcenia w uczelniach wyższych*, Wyd. Politechniki Wr., Wrocław 2007.

Denek K., *Uniwersytet w perspektywie społeczeństwa wiedzy: Nauka i edukacja w uniwersytecie XXI wieku*, t. I, Wyd. WSPiA, Poznań 2011.

Duraj-Nowakowa K., *Kształtowanie profesjonalnej gotowości pedagogów*,Wyd. WSFP Ignatianum i WAM, Kraków 2011.

Duraj-Nowakowa K., *Modelowanie w badaniach pedagogicznych,* [w:] S. Palka (red.), *Podstawy metodologii badań w pedagogice*, Gdańsk 2009.

Duraj-Nowakowa K., *Modelowanie systemowe pedagogiki,* Kraków 1997.

Duraj-Nowakowa K., *Nauczyciel: kultura – osoba - zawód,* II wydanie, Kielce 2002.

Duraj-Nowakowa K., Teoria systemów a pedagogika, Kraków 1992.

Duraj-Nowakowa K. Studiowanie literatury przedmiotu, Wyd. Akademii Ignatianum i WAM, Kraków 2012.

Duraj-Nowakowa K., (red.), *Integrowanie komponentów dydaktyki szkoły wyższej i pedeutologii,* „Studia Pedagogiczne AŚ", Kielce 2003.

Duraj-Nowakowa K., *Pedagogika społeczna: między integracją w dezintegracją,* Wyd. UR, Rzeszów 2009.

Duraj-Nowakowa K., *Podejścia całościowe do pedagogiki*: *wybór*, Wyd. UR, Rzeszów 2008.

Duraj-Nowakowa K., *Źródła podejść do pedagogiki: zarys problemów*, Wyd. ŚSW, Kielce 2005.

Duraj-Nowakowa K., (red.), *Modernizowanie pedeutologii akademickiej,* Wyd. KTN, Kielce 2003.

Duraj-Nowakowa K., (red.), *Nauczyciele akademiccy w procesie kształtowania pedagogów u progu reformy systemu edukacji,* Of. Wyd."Impuls", Kraków-Łowicz 1999.

Duraj-Nowakowa K., Gnitecki J. (red.), *Epistemologiczne wyzwania współczesnej pedagogiki,* Wyd. Nauk. WSP, Kraków 1997.

Działalność Państwowej Komisji Akredytacyjnej w 2006 roku, PKA, Warszawa 2007.

Gaweł-Luty E., *Pedagogika społeczna*, Wyd. WSH TWP, Szczecin 2004.

Jaskot K. (red.), *Wprowadzenie do pedagogiki szkoły wyższej*, Wyd. US, Szczecin 2006.

Kaliszewska M., *Esej pedagogiczny w kształceniu akademickim: teoria, praktyka i ocenianie*, Wyd. UHP Jana Kochanowskiego, Kielce 2009.

Kaliszewska M., *Funkcje eseju pedagogicznego w dydaktyce akademickiej na tle procesów inkluzji społecznej*, Wyd. UHP Jana Kochanowskiego, Kielce 2011.

Kaliszewska M., Klasińska B. (red.), *Szkice systemowych ujęć pedagogiki*, Wyd. UHP Jana Kochanowskiego, Kielce 2010.

Limont W., *Analiza wybranych mechanizmów wyobraźni twórczej: badania eksperymentalne*, Wyd. UMK, Toruń 1996.

Nęcka E., *Psychologia twórczości*, GWP, Gdańsk 2001.

Panek E. (red.), *Wymiar europejski studiów ekonomicznych w Polsce*, PWN, Warszawa 2003.

Pietrasiński Z., *Mądrość, czyli świetne wyposażenie umysłu*, PWN, Warszawa 2001.

Popek S., *Człowiek jako istota twórcza*, Wyd. UMCS, Lublin 2003.

Rogalska-Marasińska A., *Humanizm – dialog – tożsamość: edukacja europejska na tle wyzwań globalnych*, Wyd. UŁ, Łódź 2010.

Rogalska-Marasińska A. (red.), *Nauczyciel wobec szans i zagrożeń edukacyjnych XXI wieku*, t. II: *Praktyka edukacyjna w perspektywie wyzwań XXI wieku*, OF. Wyd. „Impuls", Kraków 2009.

Surina I. A. (red.), *Przestrzeń edukacyjna wobec wyzwań i oczekiwań społecznych*, Of. Wyd. „Impuls", Kraków 2010.

Surina I. A. (red.), *Pedagogika społeczna: współczesne obszary*, Wyd. Nauk. AP, Słupsk 2008

Sowiński A. (red.), *Kultura akademicka w oglądzie pedagogicznym*, Szczecin 2009.

Stróżewski W., *W kręgu wartości*, Wyd. UJ, Kraków 1992.

Szmidt K. (red.), *Trening twórczości w szkole wyższej*, Wyd. WSHE, Łódź 2005.

Szmidt K. J., *Trening kreatywności*, Wyd."Helion", Gliwice 2008.

Irina Surina

Pomeranian University in Słupsk, Poland

THE POLISH SYSTEM OF HIGHER EDUCATION AND THE LABOUR MARKET: CURRENT SITUATION AND TENDENCIES

Summary

The article presented the compatibility considerations for the system of higher education with the labor market in Poland. Characterized the current system of higher education, the demand for occupations in the labor market, the state of unemployment among graduates, the development of educational services market.

Introduction

The rapidly changing globalized world conditions transformations of the modern society, introduces new challenges and brings about threats in all areas of social functioning – it creates a new social reality. This situation also fully relates to the educational system. Recently, one can observe an increased interest in educational problems. J. Szczepański draws a particular attention to the connection between the educational system and social life – stating that the educational system constitutes one of social sub-systems which, on multiple levels, is related to life and functioning of a given society[1].

Education plays an essential role in the process of changes taking place in European countries; in particular, it concerns the implementation of the goals of the Bologna process in the European higher education. Reforming the higher education systems in Europe as an answer to challenges of the globalized world as well as social changes provides an incentive to analyse the essence, structure and characteristic traits of the modern educational expanse and one of its subdivisions – higher education.

The system of higher education – undergoing an intensive and permanent transformation – is still subject to increasing interest: most frequently in the form of scientific research focused on diverse system elements or those of the model of higher education. According to a general understanding, a model "(…) is an instrument of learning, an operator of acquiring knowledge about reality. A model is an object imitating the researched reality. This imitation does not refer to the analogy between the nature of a given model and model object, but rather to

[1] Cf.: J. Szczepański, *Społeczne uwarunkowania rozwoju oświaty*, WSiP, Warszawa 1989.

homomorphism (or isomorphism) between their internal structures. A model is not a copy of reality but an analogue of function, structure and form of this model reality"[2].

In the course of discussing the model of higher education in European countries in recent years, it was assumed that the modern model of higher education is the one specified in the context of the Bologna process.

Processes taking place in the Polish society are also - to a large extent – reflected in the system of higher education. At the time when reforms were introduced in the nineties of the 20th century, a process of expanding the system of higher education was observed – especially in the vocational sphere which was caused by an increase in the number of both public and nonpublic higher education institutions – as well as an increasing competition between them.

In Poland, there are state (public) higher education institutions as well as non-state (nonpublic) ones – created after 1990. Since 1998 also non-state higher education vocational facilities have been created. A tendency – observed in the mid-nineties of the 20th century – of a growing number of academic facilities and their students was noticeable until 2009. As it is manifested by the social reality – an increase in the number of faculties is an attempt to satisfy diverse demands of the present times, i.e., fundamental changes taking place in Polish society.

Polish system of higher education in the years of 2001-2011: condition and characteristics

The currently operating system of higher education encompasses: first-cycle studies (BA or engineering studies), second-cycle studies - MA studies, uniform five year master's studies (at specific majors), third-cycle studies - doctoral and post-graduate studies – other than higher education or doctoral studies forms of education for people possessing higher education diplomas[3].

This system was introduced in 2005. Poland – like remaining member states of the European Union - had to adapt its system of higher education in accordance with accepted rules of the Bologna process, as well as initiate actions which were supposed to stimulate economic growth, increase competitiveness and create more jobs for graduates. As of now, it is impossible to make a precise assessment of this system's efficiency.

[2] Quoted after: K.Duraj-Nowakowa, *Modelowanie systemowe w pedagogice*, Wydawnictwo Naukowe WSP, Kraków 1987, p.79.
[3] *Act of 27 July 2005 Higher eduction Act* (Dz. U. of 2005 No 164, item. 1365, art. 2)

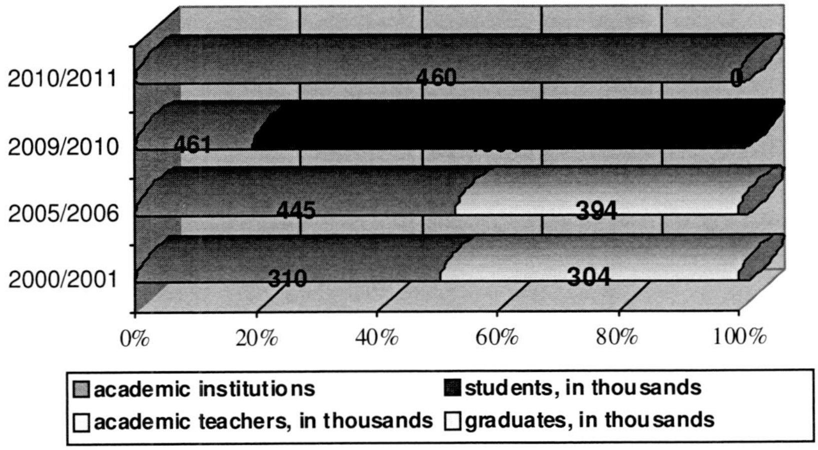

Graph 1. The state of higher education between 2000-2010
Source: own work on the basis of: *Mały Rocznik Statystyczny Polski 2011*, ed. By H.Dmochowska, GUS, Warszawa 2011, p. 235-236

In recent years, an expansion of the higher education system was observed – an increase in the number of academic facilities and students. According to statistical data, in the academic year of 2000/2001 there were 310 higher education institutions with 1584,8 thousand students – however, in the year of 2005/2006 in 445 higher education institutions there were 1953,8 thousand students, and in 2009/2010 – 461 higher education institutions which altogether had 1900,0 thousand students; this number was almost maintained in the academic year of 2010/2011: 460 institutions with 1841,3 thousand students[4].

As it is indicated by an analysis of statistical data, a decisive majority of higher educational institutions is located in the Mazowieckie province (107), the Silesia province (45), the Wielkopolska province (39), the Lower Silesia province (38) and the Łódź province (32). Altogether, they constitute 56,7% of all higher education institutions which are mostly located in the centre and south-west of Poland.

According to the data for 30 November of 2010, in Poland there were four academic centres which had the number of students above 100000: Warsaw, Cracow, Wrocław and Poznań. There were 14 academic centres with the number of students between twenty thousand and hundred thousand – the largest of them were Łódź, Lublin, Gdańsk and Katowice. In eight of the above-mentioned cities (largest academic centres), altogether 58,9% of the total

[4] *Mały Rocznik Statystyczny Polski 2011*, ed. H.Dmochowska, GUS, Warszawa 2011, p.235-236.

number of students were educated (excluding the facilities of the Ministry of Defence and Administration)[5].

It is obvious that new facilities are created wherever organs of the authorities provide support and where it is possible to meet one of the obligatory conditions – a required number of academic teachers for the minimum academic staff complement in order to establish respective majors and be able to conduct MA or BA studies. Such location of academic facilities artificially gives rise to mobility of student candidates.

In recent years, we have been discussing with an increasing interest the phenomenon of demographic crisis. The previous educational boom has been decreasing for the past two years. It is caused by both demographic changes and a healthy competition on the market of educational services. This rivalry for candidates is apparent in traditional academic centres where the greatest number of new schools were formed – and it will only increase. In this case, we are observing one of paradoxes in the functioning of educational system – i.e., regardless of the demographic crisis, the number of academic facilities is increasing.

In the academic year of 2010/2011, in Poland, in 470 higher education institutions – 132 public and 338 nonpublic ones – there were almost 2 million students, which gives Poland one of the highest indexes of schooling rate in the world and the first place if it comes to the number of higher education institutions in Europe[6]. The driving force behind the development of science and higher education are scientists/educators themselves. In the Polish system of higher education, there are 170000 employees, 100000 of whom are academic teachers – employed mostly in public schools (84000), and significantly fewer work in nonpublic institutions (16000)[7].

---

[5] *Academic facilities and their financial situation in 2010 roku,* GUS, Warszawa 2011, p.24

[6] *Statistical data on higher education*, http://www.nauka.gov.pl/ szkolnictwo-wyzsze/ dane-statystyczne-o-szkolnictwie-wyzszym, retrieved on 23.03.2012.
Data concerning the number of academic facilities in the academic year of 2010/2011 presented on the website of Ministry of Science and Higher Education differs from the data included in Concise Statistical Yearbook of Poland for 2011. It is likely a result of the fact that data provided by the Ministry did not include a certain category of academic institutions.

[7] Ibidem

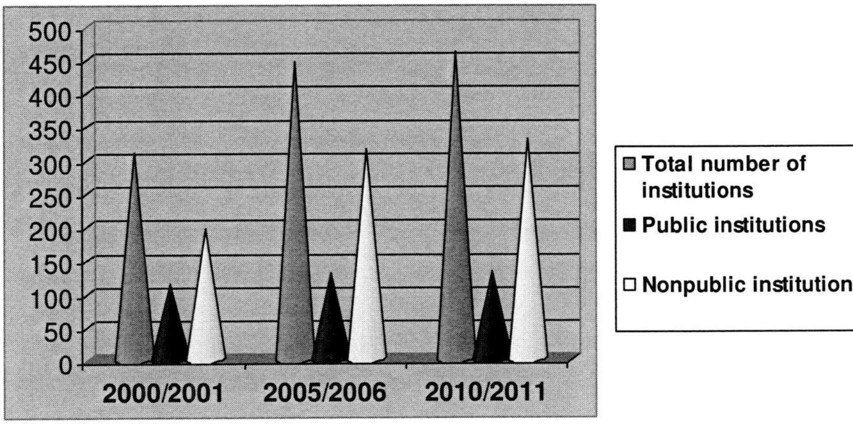

Graph 2. Number of higher education institutions in Poland
Source: own work on the basis of data acquired from GUS

An analysis of statistical data indicates that in the academic year of 2000/2001. the total number of higher education institutions was lower by 50 in comparison with the academic year of 2010/2011. In addition, an increase in the development of the public sector of institutions is stable – there were two new institutions, while the number of nonpublic institutions increased by 133.

It also needs to be observed that while the public sector of higher education institutions is relatively extensive if it comes to educational range, quite stable and clearly specified in its multi-faceted nature (as a result of passed bills) – the nonpublic sector of higher education institutions is - in numerous dimensions - not fixed, but rather flexible.

Public higher education institutions are considerably larger and more versatile – the largest of them possess stable, large staff, material basis and a steady financial situation. Nonpublic ones are significantly smaller and they tend to focus on a limited range of faculties (more than a half of them offer fewer than four faculties) and extramural studies, and are based on outsourcing of assets – staff, teaching content, material basis – which is why they can react in a flexible fashion to demand on which they are entirely dependent [8].

In the academic year of 2010/2011, in 460 higher education facilities of all types, 1841,3 thousand students were educated - including 135 branches and off-campus educational

[8] Cf.: *Szkoły wyższe i ich finanse…*, op.cit.

centers – 93,6 thousand students, and, finally, in 156 off-campus teaching centers and consultation points – 29,8 thousand students[9].

In the academic year of 2010/2011, the number of students at full-time courses amounted to 949,5 thousand, i.e., 51,6 % of the total number of students, while at the extramural studies there were 891,8 thousand of them (48,4 % of the total number of students). At public higher education institutions, the predominant form of studying was the full-time courses (67,5% of students), while at nonpublic academic institutions – extramural type of studying (83,1% of their students)[10].

Numerous nonpublic institutions only conduct education at BA level. Such institutions are frequently located in smaller centers where they constitute the only – and cheaper than studying in university towns – form of studying. In the academic year of 2010/2011, at higher education institutions there were 3,1 % fewer students in comparison with the previous year, while in comparison with the year of 2000/2001 - the number of students was larger by 16,2%.

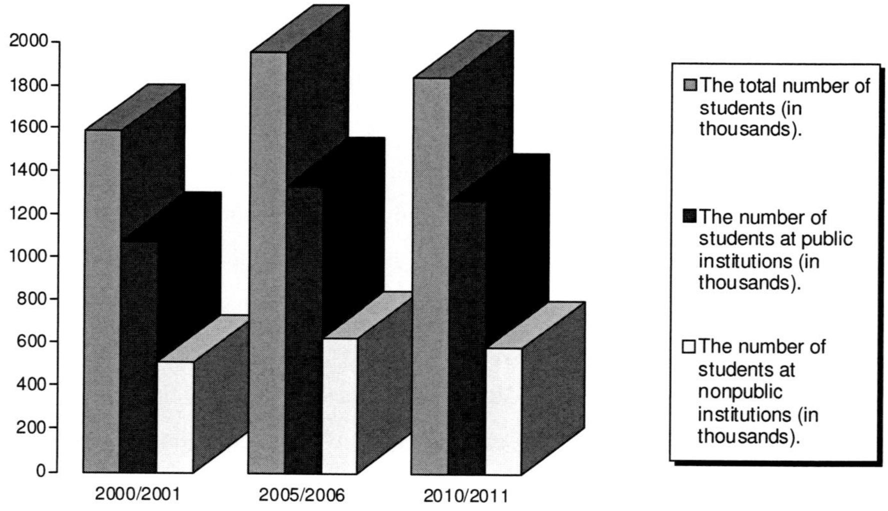

Graph 3. The number of students depending on the type of school, in thousands

Source: own work on the basis of data provided by GUS

In 2009, the Polish system of higher education encompassed over 200 faculties – including the unique and combination majors. The largest number of students was studying at

[9] *Szkoły wyższe i ich finanse...*, op.cit., p.27. The number of academic facilities differs from the one specified by the Ministry of Science and Higher Education, since this publication does not concern facilities in which in November 2010 there were no students or graduates.

[10] Ibidem, p.27-28

economy and administration-related majors– 23%, social – 13,9%, pedagogy – 12%, humanities – 8,8%, engineering and technical – 6,8%, medical – 5,8%. In 2010, according to the data of the Ministry of Science and Higher Education, the most popular BA and uniform MA courses were: business administration – 8,9%, construction – 7,3%, pedagogy – 7,2%, law – 6,4%, computer science – 6,0% and economy – 5,8%[11] (table 1).

Table 1. The most popular majors in 2009 and 2010

2009		2010	
The most popular majors	%	**The most popular majors at the first-cycle studies and uniform five year master's studies**	%
Economy and administration	23,0	Business administration	8,9
Social	13,9	Construction	7,3
Pedagogy	12,0	Pedagogy	7,2
Humanities	8,8	Law	6,4
Engineering and technical	6,8	Computer science	6,0
Medical	5,8	Economy	5,8
Computer science	4,9	Finance and accounting	4,7
Miscellaneous services	3,7	Environment engineering	4,6
Law	3,1	Administration	4,5
Environmental protection	1,4	Psychology	4,49
"Remaining majors"	16,4	"Remaining majors"	40,2

Source: own work on the basis of: Statistical data concerning higher education, http://www.nauka.gov.pl/szkolnictwo-wyzsze

As the above-mentioned statistical data indicates, economy, administration, pedagogy and law-related majors/faculties are still the most popular.

In the academic year of 2010/2011, the largest number of people studied at economy, administration, social and pedagogy-related majors/faculties (also the most popular majors in 2000), while in 1990, the largest number of people studied technical sciences as well as branches of knowledge related to business, administration and pedagogy.

The comparison of popularity of certain majors/faculties in 2010/2011 and 2009/2010 indicates that an interest in economy, administration, pedagogy, humanities, social sciences

[11] *Statistical data concerning higher education*, op.cit.

and computer science is decreasing. On the other hand, those enjoying an increasing interest are majors concerning protection, security and medical services – as well as those related to architecture and construction. One can also observe an increasing interest in studying engineering and technical majors.[12]

A growing demographic crisis, tendencies that manifest themselves on the educational market and labour market lead to a significant decrease in a number of students. Recruitment and the beginning of the academic year of 2011/12 indicate that a decrease in the number of candidates for studying and students is considerable. A struggle to attract candidates is very apparent today in traditional academic regions in which most new institutions function – and in the future this struggle is likely to become even fiercer.

Higher education in the context of the situation on the labour market

One of the tasks of European Higher Education Area is an effort to adapt educational effects to requirements of the market. On the labour market, there are constantly new professions created, the demand for which is still increasing – or will increase – while other lose their demand; the only guarantee of the real success is constant supplemental education/training. The appearance of new professions is connected to the disappearance of others – traditional ones – which are currently becoming redundant and nonprofitable. One can observe a decrease in the demand for marketing and administration specialists – even though this profession appeared to be prospective. The labour market is becoming increasingly demanding and having a diploma of a specialist major no longer guarantees a satisfactory job.[13]

The current situation is such that the labour market is saturated with staff with economy and humanities-related major diplomas. There is a demand for engineers, doctors, children and elderly people carers, as well as construction workers, designers, IT specialists and network administrators. Accountants are also among the sought-after professions along with persons working in logistics and consulting. The worst situation faces the graduates of humanities – 71% out of whom feel useless, and over 50% see no chance of having a career in our country. Taking into consideration geographical criterion – the most privileged graduates are those from the Mazowieckie province, Silesia province, the Zachodniopomorskie province

[12] *Academic institutions and their finances…*, op.cit., p.29

[13] P.Łysak, *Zawody przyszłości*, http://www.jobs.pl/artykuly/zawody_przyszlosci, retrieved on 04.02.2012.

– and the least privileged those from the Podlasie province, Lublin province, Subcarpathian province and the Malopolska province[14].

48% of employers in Poland declare they have difficulty finding staff due to the shortage of candidates with proper qualifications. According to a report published by Manpower Polska on the most sought after professions, it is apparent that in Poland it is most difficult to find qualified physical workers, project managers, as well as sales representatives. The results of the study indicate that the largest number of employers declaring difficulties finding proper candidates can be found in Romania and Taiwan (62%), in Peru (56%), Japan (55%), Australia (49%), the republic of Costa Rica and in Poland (48%). It is easiest to find employees in Ireland (5%), Spain (8%), Great Britain (11%), China (15%) and the Czech republic (17%). The results for the EMEA region (Europe, Middle East, Africa), in which over 15 000 employers were polled indicate that 25% of them have difficulty with finding proper employees. The largest problems are reported by: Romania (62%), Poland (48%), Greece (37%), Switzerland (36%), while the smallest - by Ireland (5%), Spain (8%) and Great Britain (11%). Those are also the same countries which report the smallest problems in a global scale. The list of the most sought after professions includes qualified physical workers, sales representatives, technicians (of production, production process and maintenance) and engineers[15].

It is worthwhile to note that Polish companies have had problems with finding proper engineers-specialists since 2007. In the future, the shortage of engineering staff will only become more significant. Paradoxically, the most sought after specialists are people having higher technical education diplomas. The shortage of engineers concerns over 60% of enterprises[16]. As a result, we experience the so-called "wave effect", a situation in which the shortage of engineers on the labour market (after 10-15 years after the profession of engineer lost some of its prestige) determines a renewed increase in the number of students at engineering-technical faculties which, subsequently, has the effect that the prestige of the engineer's profession is rapidly growing.

The situation on the labour market leads to the fact that professional competition is so high that an increasing number of young people after graduation have problems with finding jobs – which, as a result, forces them to take advantage of unemployment benefits. Every sec-

---

[14] *Młodzi i bezrobotni. Coraz większa liczba absolwentów pozostaje bez pracy*, http://www.gazetaprawna.pl, 2010-09-08, retrieved on 25.04.2011.

[15] *10 najbardziej poszukiwanych zawodów w 2009 roku*, http://www.studia.net, published on 22.11.2009., retrieved on 10.05.2011.

[16] *Rosnące zapotrzebowanie na inżynierów-specjalistów*, http://www.rynekpracy.pl, published on 03.06.2008, retrieved on 10.05.2011.

ond graduate has difficulties finding employment and only 10% of graduates have a chance of finding job in their profession[17].

Such a situation results in the fact that in the process of development of the current system of higher education there is a clear paradox with unforeseeable social consequences – one of "the unforeseeable professional career of higher education institutions' graduates". This paradox is built upon a contradiction between students' motivation to study at an academic facility and a real unemployment rate among youth in our country.[18]

The unemployment rate in Poland (for 31 December of 2011) averages 12,5% and this unemployment mostly affects youth. Its rate, in the case of youth below 24 years, averages 26,5% of the total number of newly-registered unemployed – 46,5% were men and 53,5% - women[19]. Higher education no longer prevents one from the possibility of becoming unemployed. Since 2007, the number of unemployed has increased by 70,4 thousands. Currently, graduates of higher education institutions constitute 10,5 percent of the total number of the unemployed[20]. This indicates that almost one in ten of the unemployed has a diploma of a higher education facility.

The shortage of job vacancies in Poland leads to a situation where more and more members of the unemployed youth are forced to choose emigration and mobility for profit.

According to "The first steps on the labour market" study conducted by Deloitte, a consulting company, and AGH University of Science and Technology (n= 3618 students from Poland, Czech republic, Lithuania, Latvia and Slovakia), most of respondents see no problem in the necessity of changing their place of residence for work-related purposes. Readiness to move to another city is declared by 69% of them and 59% is ready to move abroad. 60 percent of Polish students believe that academic institutions do not adequately prepare them for the future job and negatively assess any preparation received from such institutions for the process of looking for employment. Polish students are ones with the highest demands. At the initial stage of their careers, they expect a salary of 3000 PLN – which is 1000 PLN more than those from Lithuania and Latvia[21]. It mostly results from a low remuneration for gradu-

---

[17] K.Zamana, *Młodzi ludzie na rynku pracy*, http://www.sld-zowsze.pl/index.php?show =18&id=101, 1.08.2010, retrieved on 04.05.2011.

[18] I. Surina, *Paradoksy rozwoju systemu kształcenia wyższego*, [in:] A.Karpińska (ed.), *Edukacyjne obszary „głębokiej zmiany" w dialogu i perspektywie,* Trans Humana, Białystok 2005, p.292.

[19] *Mały Rocznik Statystyczny 2012*, Główny Urząd Statystyczny, Warszawa, p. 159-164.

[20] A.Baranowska-Skimina, *Rośnie bezrobocie wśród absolwentów*, http://egospodarka.pl, 20.03.2011, retrieved on 04.05.2011.

[21] *Studia są bez sensu? Polacy krytykują szkolnictwo wyższe*, http://www.natablicy.pl, 15.04.2011, retrieved on 10.05.2011.

ates – for example, at the so-called state-subsidized internships they only receive about 860 PLN (gross amount)[22].

Let us point out the fact that the European countries specified in the study are ones with the lowest minimum salaries (also Bulgaria, Romania, Estonia, Hungary, Turkey and Croatia) – ranging from 100 EURO to 400 EURO per month[23]. The minimum statutory remuneration in Poland in 2011 was 1386 PLN[24], and according to the data provided by GUS – the average state remuneration in the IV quarter of 2011 was 3586,75 PLN[25] - which, respectively, averages 334 EURO and 864 EURO for 15 August in 2011.

A research conducted in Poland indicates that the part of youth willing to go abroad in search of work consists of those who have never worked or are unemployed. This group of young people believes that going abroad is their only solution to unemployment and a chance to settle their life. After Poland's inclusion into the EU - and due to the already existing integration with the European Educational Area - a certain part of graduates believe that they will have an opportunity of a faster career development and obtaining a higher salary.

Finding work abroad according to one's qualifications is not only difficult – but practically impossible since a Polish diploma (and qualifications) is only respected in a few countries with which Poland signed bilateral agreements and so, in such a situation, our graduates are not helped by their academic mobility during studies. The result of such an inadequacy of the system of higher education and the labour market is that, currently, the Polish system of higher education prepares professional specialists for other countries in which they constitute "cheap labour force".

The development of the market of educational services is conditioned by numerous factors out of which the most difficult ones are: the given academic institution's prominence on the local/country-wide educational market, its status and the quality of academic staff. Those factors are conducive to creating new majors/specialties and result in increasing competitiveness of a given institution on the educational market in the regional and country-wide scale. Generally, the so-called "flagship-like institutions" are favoured – while the regional institutions are in a more difficult situation. In most cases, creating such majors/specialties is not compatible with the needs of respective sectors of economy. Even if there exists such a compatibility, anyone who has ever tried creating a new major/specialty knows that from the

---

[22] *Młodzi i bezrobotni...*, op.cit.
[23] Statistical data concerning minimum salaries (retrieved in August of 2011 roku), http://epp.eurostat.ec.europa.eu/statistics_explained/index.php/Minimum_wage_statistics/pl, 03.02.2012 r.
[24] Regulation of the Council of Ministers of 5.10.2010 on minimum salary for 2011 (Dz.U. No 194, item 1288)
[25] The research results were published in 2011. Therefore, both minimum salary and average remuneration is given according to GUS data for 2011.

moment of submitting an application and the time when there appear first graduates with specific skills - at least 4-5 years need to pass.

One solution to such a situation is the "Ordered specialties" program implemented by the Ministry of Science and Higher Education. Its purpose is to increase properly qualified graduates of majors/specialties crucial to the development of competitive and innovative economy; this project, however, is only implemented at selected institutions and the percentage of such specialties' graduates is rather insignificant. Consequently, for the present moment, it does not solve the problem of finding employment for graduates of higher education institutions in the scale of the whole country.

Fion Harvey, chief growth officer of CIMA (Chartered Institute of Management Accountants) believes that an opinion grows more and more popular that "the Polish system is excessively academic and this may signify that syllabus is not properly suited for the expectations and requirements of the labour market. As a result, despite the fact that the number of MA graduates in Poland is one of the highest in Europe, it is precisely this social group which has an increasing problem with a smooth transition onto the labour market and is frequently forced to undergo professional retraining and acquire new knowledge"[26]. The main reason behind such a situation is the incompatibility of majors/specialties and syllabuses with current demand on the labour market.

Conclusion

We may conclude today that higher education in Poland is one of the most rapidly changing areas of social life – but this development has a "wave-like" nature. In the course of the last twenty years, this system has undergone rapid changes – and, yet again, it is in the state of transformation. The Polish system of higher education is becoming increasingly different from systems in developed countries of the European Union, but it also has huge internal differences.

Currently, one of characteristic traits of the Polish system of higher education is a considerable, multi-faceted competitiveness which concerns a number of interconnected problems. This competitiveness manifests itself mostly through the diversity of strategies employed by respective academic facilities. We can also observe a struggle not only between public and nonpublic sectors – but, additionally, within each of them – for students, academic teachers, new majors/specialties etc.

[26] Ibidem.

On the basis of conclusions made in the report concerning the diagnosis of the higher education in Poland prepared by Ernst &Young and the Institute of Research on Market Economy – the traits which distinguish the Polish system of higher education are, among others:

- prevalence of higher education in Poland. The level of commonness of higher education is among the highest in Europe,

- emerging polarization within the system of higher education in Poland – mostly on the basis of the property form: public and nonpublic institutions. Public institutions are large and they conduct their educational process in a variety of disciplines; nonpublic institutions are generally small and focus on low-cost extramural studies in the disciplines related to "education" and "social sciences, commerce and law",

- disproportion of a number of academic teachers in relation to the number of students in respective disciplines. The nominal proportion of the total number of academic teachers to a number of students is at an average European level, but disproportions between the academic staff number to that of students at respective disciplines are a serious problem,

- low mobility of students – which is a weakness of the system of Polish higher education. A possibility to conduct a portion of one's studies at a different institution (both in Poland and abroad) is not sufficiently taken advantage of[27],

- and, finally, inadequacy of majors/specialties regarding the demands of the labour market[28], which means that the current system of higher education is not fully compatible with the labour market.

Bibliography

10 najbardziej poszukiwanych zawodów w 2009 roku, http://www.studia.net, data publikacji 22.11.2009 r.

Baranowska-Skimina A., *Rośnie bezrobocie wśród absolwentów*, http://egospodarka.pl, data publikacji 20.03.2011.

Dane statystyczne dotyczące płac minimalnych (dane z sierpnia 2011 roku), *http://epp.eurostat. ec.europa.eu/statistics_explained/index.php/Minimum_wage_statistics/pl.*

Dane statystyczne o szkolnictwie wyższym, http://www.nauka.gov.pl/ szkolnictwo-wyzsze/ dane-statystyczne-o-szkolnictwie-wyzszym.

---

[27] *Diagnoza stanu szkolnictwa wyższego w Polsce. Raport*, Ernst & Young Business Advisory, Instytut Badań nad Gospodarką Rynkową, Warszawa 2009, p.6-8.

[28] *Strategia rozwoju szkolnictwa wyższego w Polsce do 2020 roku…*, op.cit., p.28.

Diagnoza stanu szkolnictwa wyższego w Polsce. Raport, Ernst & Young Business Advisory, Instytut Badań nad Gospodarką Rynkową, Warszawa 2009.

Duraj-Nowakowa K., *Modelowanie systemowe w pedagogice*, Wydawnictwo Naukowe WSP, Kraków 1987.

Łysak P., *Zawody przyszłości*, http://www.jobs.pl/artykuly/zawody_przyszlosci.

Mały Rocznik Statystyczny 2012, Główny Urząd Statystyczny, Warszawa 2013.

Mały Rocznik Statystyczny Polski 2011, red. H.Dmochowska, GUS, Warszawa 2011.

Młodzi i bezrobotni. Coraz większa liczba absolwentów pozostaje bez pracy, http://www.gazetaprawna.pl, data publikacji 2010-09-08.

Rosnące zapotrzebowanie na inżynierów-specjalistów, http://www.rynekpracy.pl, data publikacji 03.06.2008.

Rozporządzenie Rady Ministrów z dn. 5.10.2010 r. w sprawie wysokości minimalnego wynagro-dzenia za pracę w 2011 r. (Dz.U. Nr 194, poz. 1288)

Studia są bez sensu? Polacy krytykują szkolnictwo wyższe, http://www.natablicy.pl, data publikacji 15.04.2011.

Surina I., *Paradoksy rozwoju systemu kształcenia wyższego*, [w:] A.Karpińska (red.), *Edukacyjne obszary „głębokiej zmiany" w dialogu i perspektywie*, Trans Humana, Białystok 2005, s.292.

Szczepański J., *Społeczne uwarunkowania rozwoju oświaty*, WSiP, Warszawa 1989.

Szkoły wyższe i ich finanse w 2010 roku, GUS, Warszawa 2011

Ustawa z dn. 27 lipca 2005 r. Prawo o szkolnictwie wyższym (Dz. U. z 2005 r. Nr 164, poz. 1365, art. 2)

Zamana K., *Młodzi ludzie na rynku pracy*, http://www.sld-zowsze.pl/index.php?show=18&id=101, data publikacji 1.08.2010.

Bogdan Gębski

Pedagogical University of Warsaw, Poland

DEMOCRACY IS BAD FOR STUDENTS – CONTEMPORARY PATHOLOGIES OF NORMALCY IN EDUCATION

Summary

The reflection on the quality of higher-education was directly inspired by an excessive pace of changes to the educational structures that are subject to regulations imposed by the Ministry of Science and Higher Education. In academic practice, significant changes have been made in every year in the past decade. During the first 15 years of Poland's democracy, the number of college/university students exploded and establishing competitive, non-public higher-education institutions was easy. Non-public higher-education institutions have been offering courses in fields and areas with low capital intensity: social, economic and legal sciences. The quantitative growth of higher education, with its apogee in 2005, was a two-way process: public higher-education institutions (in circles with academic traditions) developed their premises and increased their limits for the number of students admitted to university, while non-public higher-education institutions, within those circles, satisfied the demand for higher-education courses and were setting up branches or appearing as new educational institutions without academic traditions. This is a positive aspect of cultural influence on the circles. The increase in the number of students from 400 thousand in the early 1990s to almost 2 million in 2005 was not parallel to an increase in the number of academic teachers, especially those with PhD degrees and professorships. The exponential increase in the number of students – the nature of exponential processes – manifested itself in a considerable decline in the quality of education and in the "teaching discouragement" of academic teachers, who – while working in a number of jobs at the same time – neglected the quality of their lectures and seminars. After 2005, the law on higher education began to regulate the already established bad academic practices in the specified areas of study. Following its amendment in 2011, many previous requirements, for example regarding personnel, were loosened. The ongoing period of population decline may modify the problem of educating students at the higher level. Currently, the pathology of normality in education manifests itself in attempts to attract students even with very low intellectual potential. Every student, if considered in these terms, is seen as registered income for his or her university, especially if its operation is based on commercial principles.

Introduction

The above-mentioned way of formulating the problem which is the subject of consideration, by no means aspiring to become its full analysis, is a joint effect of reading a short article by Leszek Kołakowski[1], which reveals the weaknesses of democracies compared to different forms of *monocracy* and Erich Fromm's[2] written lectures from the 50s, published as a monograph in German-speaking culture area forty years later (1991), only to appear in Polish after next twenty years (2011). Complementary to the circumstances which motivated me to sharing the afterthoughts presented in this work is my own 20-year experience in shaping higher education during the time of political changes in Poland. Not entirely insignificant was also the introduction of Higher Education Act and its currently implemented amendments[3]. Among others, the emphasised modifications from 2005 to 2011 were: extension of student rights, simplification of academic career path (significantly shorter procedure of granting the degree of habilitation) and integrating academies with the economy, which gave considerable opportunities of development and obtaining funds at technical universities. For students, the essential forms of financial aid are, among others, merit-based and need-based scholarships. Academic staff members have considerable opportunities to obtain grants, write and carry out research projects by means of invitation to tender.

Democratisation of Academic Life and its Economic Efficiency

It might be stated that democratisation of academic life had been formed for 15 years, until the introduction of Higher Education Act. The new political conditions of young Polish democracy after 1989 favoured uninhibited development of higher education by introducing rules *post factum*, without general system solutions. In many academic circles being able to decide upon their own development strategy, set new directions for education, organise the so-called Regional Branches (Zamiejscowe Ośrodki Dydaktyczne, ZOD), or even create new academies in towns and cities without academic tradition was seen as a hallmark of an enterprise, with business incentive and financial consequences. They quickly realised that organis-

[1] Kołakowski L., *Nasza wesoła apokalipsa. Wybór najważniejszych esejów,* Wydawnictwo Znak, Kraków 2010.
[2] Fromm E., *Patologia normalności. Przyczynek do nauki o człowieku*, vis-à-vis/Etiuda, Kraków 2011.
[3] Dz. U. no 84, item 455 – Higher Education Act, consolidated text of Act of 27 July 2005 valid until 1 October 2011. The current law is regulated by an amendment of an Act included in Dz. U. no 164, item 1365, as amended

ing education is easiest in social sciences, especially variations of pedagogics and economics, banking, as well as sociology, political sciences and, to some extent, a new field connected with social work, social services and career counseling as a response to increasing unemployment and deepening social poverty. In the changing political conditions of the 90s, these fields of education filled the niche for new skills. Business activity and rapidly developing commercial service sector contributed to the conviction that receiving higher education provided professional opportunities. In the early years of Polish democracy, highly educated people were rarely unemployed, hence the great popularity of economy-related faculties.

Another aspect of economic efficiency in higher education is a relatively low cost born by the organisers of studies. The proverbial chalk and board, rented classroms in a secondary school and relatively well-paid professors/educators on a contract for specific work were sufficient. Suffice it to say that in 1996 a doctor received a gross rate of approximately 120 PLN for a teaching hour and after 10 years this rate dropped to 70-90 PLN. For many professors, who were heavily burdened with teaching hours, especially at weekends, these were good times in terms of finances. The number of teaching hours did not go together with the quality of teaching[4]. Naturally, after the year 2000 many professors suffered from professional burn-out. The symptoms included reluctance to teach groups of over thirty students during practical classes and even several hundred during lectures. And, as usual, the greatest burden of conducting classes fell on academic teachers with MA or PhD[5] degree. Many senior academic staff members agreed to conducting lectures and proseminars. The increase in the numer of extracurricular students (at both public and non-public academies) generated a considerable number of teaching hours and seminars. Senior academic staff members preferred seminars and some of them, after several years of work, were only willing to conduct classes in a few seminar groups. Commercialisation was prevailing, qualities of academic institutions were deteriorating.

Quantity development of higher education

The tremendous growth in the number of students from 400 thousand in 1990 to 1 million 953 thousand in 2005 and significantly slower and disproportionate increase of the number of academic teachers equaled over 99 thousand in 2005 - the student-teacher ratio equal

[4] Gębski B., *Definicja jakości życia studentów szczecińskiej humanistyki*, [w:] *Zrozumieć społeczeństwo. Szanse i zagrożenia w sferze mentalności, kultury i gospodarki w przededniu wejścia Polski do Unii Europejskiej*, ed. J. Leoński, Zachodniopomorska Szkoła Biznesu, Szczecin 2004, p. 64-70.
[5] Cf.: Gębski B. and others, *Sytuacja młodych pedagogów w Polsce. Determinanty rozwoju naukowego młodszej kadry naukowej nauk pedagogicznych w Polsce*, „Rocznik Pedagogiczny" 1989, no 12, p. 29-112.

on average 20:1 – was, naturally, bound to cause a discomfort in academic work and create pathologies. High demand for senior academics caused a practice of 'multi-jobbing' and thus, inevitably, numerous substitutions. Some limitations were introduced by the administrations of several non-public academies. However, the most important issue was to show the number of professors even if hired only on a contract for specific work. This dynamic development was recognised as a norm. There were no instruments to limit the number of students. In the first half of the 90s the development of institutions of tertiary education was pleasing; there was considerable freedom of making investments in the academic institutions from the funds obtained from tuition fee paid by students. The mentions of commercial studies and hours were even made - academic circles in Szczecin used an expression „I'm going to work for dollars now" („teraz idę pracować za dolary"). The advantage of this practice was, after years of crisis in the former political system, the possibility to obtain funds for making investments, which contributed to modernising didactic resources of departments of social sciences and economics, where there were available funds from tuition fees. Academics in natural and exact sciences were in significantly worse spirits.

In this current of reflection, the extraordinary quantitative development in law studies/departments should be emphasized. In the 90s, hundreds of students enrolled in the first year of studies in many public institutions of tertiary education. Students themselves commented on this state of affairs briefly: "there is lawlessness in law departments", among other similar criticisms regarding the organisation of such departments/studies. Students, in order to receive credit or pass an exam, stood in lines one day earlier and camped out around professors' offices. Vast number of graduates affected the quality of teaching law and the effects are visible. Various types of verification in the form of exams enabling further career advancement of graduates are a sign of their low legal qualifications.

Departments of mathematical and natural sciences were facing a crisis due to small number of enrolling students. Polytechnical departments were also going through a financial crisis. The teaching staff lacked the "opporunity" to conduct the well-paid, extra classes. Some primarily engineering institutions of higher education started to organise quasi-humanistic major courses (*curiosum*: Agricultural University created postgraduate Master's degree programme in pedagogics). Currently the financial situation of these institutions is improving thanks to systemic solutions, numerous scholarships awarded to students for the mere fact of studying mathematics and intensified cooperation with the more and more modern technical infrastructure of companies. The economy forces the demand for well qualified engineers with managerial skills.

Resuming the topic of quantitive aspect of development in higher education institutions, we notice the following pattern: after five years of their activity, the number of students doubled (795 thousand in 1995) and then doubled again after another five years (1 mln 585 thousand in 2000)[6]. The number of students increased by one-fourth (0.232) in the next 5-year period. In the first 15 years of democracy, the increase in the number of students was of exponential character. It is a known fact that every process developing exponentially leads to a collapse. Recent years have been a period of significantly lower quantitative growth in the number of students in Poland. A decrease in this number was observed after 2005. For the last five years the drop amounted to 100 thousand (from 1954 thosand in 2005 to 1841 thousand in 2010)[7]. This process has caused anxiety in self-funded (non-public) institutions of higher education and prompted increased activity in obtaining European funds from the Human Capital Operational Programme 2007-2013. A change in the form of obtaining funds by means of inviting tender is already observable. Już obserwuje się zmianę form pozyskiwania środków za pośrednictwem ogłaszanych przetargów.

It should be stressed that the increase in the number of academic teachers is disproportionate to the number of students. In 2000 there were 80 thousand academic teachers, in the following five years this number grew by 20 thousand and by 4 thousand in yet another 5-year period, despite the drop in the number of students. As a result, in academic year 2010/2011 we had 1,841,251 students and 103,500 academic teachers[8]. How were these students admitted to the structures of a higher education institution? The following table shows two trends in the changing numbers of higher education institutions: a moderate one regarding public facilities and a growing one in the non-public sector. Public (state) institutions of tertiary education developed by extending their premises, especially in departments of social sciences and humanities, as well as creating Regional Branches (ZODs). Founding non-public institutions in various municipalities in many cases resulted in establishing academic tradition, which, regardless the pessimistic tone of my reflections, is very valuable for local communities, especially for these students who could not afford to study in an academic city. Particularly positive were the effects on the service sector and administration.

[6] Data from statistical yearbooks of GUS.
[7] One could menton that the Polish percentage of higher education amounts to 5% and is the highest in Europe. Norway has similar results (4,7%) with 210 thousand students. Germany, on the other hand, has significantly fewer students (1600000), which constitutes 2% with four times as large expenditure per student. We are still far removed from the increase of the index (0,38) of resources allocation from GDP to at least 1% - like in most European countries. This index even in Spain averages over 1.5%.
[8] *Mały rocznik statystyczny,* GUS, Warszawa 2011, p. 235.

After comparing the growth rates of the number of tertiary education institutions (tabel 1) we notice that the increase in the number of public (state) institutions is small with a tendency to stabilise. On the other hand, the growth rate of the number of non-public facilities displayed extreme dynamics in the first five year period of democracy. This phenomenon resulted from the fact that it was relatively easy to found a non-public higher education facility. It was sufficient to deposit the required amount of money in a bank, present documents stating that teaching staff is available, describe the location of the facility (usually in the premises of various secondary schools), obtain the ministry's permission to operate such an institution and announce its existence in the available media. To put it simply, this course of action allowed in a relatively short time to start academic activity oriented to „stress-free" admission of candidates. Therefore, the requirements for candidates significantly changed compared with public higher education institutions, where the so-called admission interviews were a common practice. The only requirement to be admitted to non-public higher education institutions was to file documents and sign up, which was one of the factors contributing to the growing number of higher education students; the number of students who applied was the number of students accepted. Accidentality of studying was reflected in the so-called personal culture of students. Authorities of public higher education facilities quickly realised that the sector of non-public higher education is governed by the laws of business (demand – supply). As a result, public institutions of higher education increased the number of students admitted to full-time, evening and extramural programmes, so that the admission limits in commercial studies (evening and extramural programmes) could be determined in line with the level of popularity of a particular major or specialization.

Table 1. The growth dynamics in the number of higher education institutions in Poland

Academic year	The number of higher education institutions			Growth rate	
	total	public	non-public	public	non-public
1992/93	124	106	18	0.00	0.00
1995/96	179	99	80	93.40	444.44
2000/01	310	115	195	116.16	243.75
2005/06	445	130	315	113.04	161.54
2008/09	458	132	326	101.54	103.49
2010/11	470	132	338	100.00	103.68

Source: www.nauka.gov.pl/szkolnictwo-wyzsze (retrieved May 5, 2012)

Generally speaking, in the second half of the twentieth century, higher education institutions, which had been formed for hundreds of years, underwent a serious metamorphosis. The petrified structure of higher education institutions was blurred, especially in the american culture area after 1945. The times after World War II favoured close relations between higher education and industry, which was a result of many significant factors. There was a famous saying that $1 invested in education yields a $4 return after a successful investment, which was an incentive for business activity in the field of higher education. One can receive an impression that the development of higher education in Poland follows the same path. The trends characteristic of the relations between science and economy appeared only after 2000 and since then higher education institutions have become serious beneficiaries thanks to R&D (Research and Development) programs managed extraneously by the EU. Significant links with businesses (most frequently banks and new manufacturing companies) are also visible in economic sciences. After the year 2005, however, pedagogics, political science, sociology, and similar faculties suffer a decline in popularity.

Formation of new institutions and forms of teaching

Since 2004, intensive advertising and marketing activities of non-public higher education facilities have been undertaken. The non-public institutions encouraged pleasant studying and offered „novelties", e.g. cosmetology (instead of the former hairdressing taught at the level of vocational school), hospitality and hotel management, tourism and similar specialisations. It could be argued that some professions have advanced through the process of education. In the following years, another novelty appeared: distance education via a television station EduSat located on the premises of The Warsaw School of Social and Economic Studies (WSSE). EduSat contributed to popularization of distance education on a global scale by broadcasting recorded lectures via geostationary satellite. WSSE established cooperation with Pedagogical University of Warsaw, WSP TWP /society of public knowledge/. WSP TWP has operated distance education since 2008 and has gathered a significant number of students. Numerous incentives, such as a smaller number of sessions in an academic year, a lower tuition fees, the possibility to watch lectures on the Internet at any convenient time, are attractive to students. The results of this form of teaching are monitored by the University's authorities. Many students, however, value classes taught "live", in direct contact. I, also, am a believer in traditional academic values, although I popularise lectures via Internet channels for Pedagogical Universities.

Introducing by the Ministry of Science and Higher Education certain staff requirements (minimum academic staff complements) and visitations of The State Accreditation Committee became a factor limiting "didactic freedoms", which resulted in reduction or suspension of evening and extramural programmes in public tertiary education institutions. Nowadays, admission limits for full-time studies are higher than the number of candidates. Public higher education institutions are also headed towards distance education. The major obstacle to conducting such classes lies in psychological factors of lecturers. The difficulty lies in finding enthusiasts of recording their lectures, classes and seminars. The presented problem is of a very complicated and delicate nature. Suffice it to say that in public higher education institutions there are professors who are bored with their own lectures and manage to find other forms of spending time than fulfilling their teaching load (sinecure).

In relation to the growing number of non-public tertiary education institutions, it might be pointed out that, historically, the process of founding new facilities was encompassing a growing geographical area. Local authorities of Polish cities and towns without academic tradition came to a conclusion that it was only appropriate to have a facility with academic status in their area. There even were cases of rivalry between two municipalities over which one was to found a higher education institution, which was connected with various incentives pointing to the attractiveness of a given municipality. For instance, in Tyczyn near Przemyśl, a higher education institution received, apart from attractive premises, over a dozen hectares of land to develop the facility; another example is Dębno, a small town in Zachodniopomorskie province, which competed in 2000 with another town, Chojna, whose municipal and commune authorities donated to Uniwersytet Szczeciński (Szczecin University) a building for didactic purposes along with small hotel and gastronomic infrastructure and the use of the premises of a local school. Kętrzyn, a border town, also eventually became an academic centre.

Academic centres emerging in small towns positively influenced the life of local communities in terms of culture. The research showed that, for many students, studying in large academic centres would be too expensive. Since unemployment is more severe in smaller social communities, a chance to study in one's home town, with significantly lower living expenses, is a circumstance contributing to cultural advancement of inhabitants.

The present state of higher education

In the academic year 2010/2011, according to the ministerial data, there are 470 tertiary education facilities operating in Poland, including 338 non-public ones. Currently, the number of these facilities has slightly declined. Introduction of the Law on Higher Education caused a reduction in the number of regional branches (ZOD) of public schools which were unable to muster the required number of academics (minimum academic staff complement). The State Accreditation Committee heavily revised the state of public education.

Table 2. Percentage share of academic centres

Municipality	Number	%%	Municipality	Number	%%
Other municipalities	**235**	**50,0**	Kielce	9	1.9
Warszawa	60	12.8	Konin	5	1.1
Katowice and others	19	4.0	Częstochowa	4	0.9
Poznań	19	4.0	Olsztyn	4	0.9
Trójmiasto	18	3.8	Opole	4	0.9
Łódź	17	3.6	Przemyśl	4	0.9
Wrocław	17	3.6	Rzeszów	3	0.6
Szczecin	14	3.0	Toruń	3	0.6
Kraków	11	2.3	Elbląg	3	0.6
Bydgoszcz	10	2.1	Koszalin	2	0.4
Białystok	9	1.9			
			Total	**470**	**100.0**

The overall number of higher education institutions decreases year by year. In 2012 there were 131 public facilities and 326 non-public ones. The data presented in Table 2 takes into account the concentration of higher education in bigger academic centres. There are currently 156 cities and towns with operating higher education institutions, branch faculties and regional branches (ZOD). These academic environments are located primarily in county towns and cities. The demographic decline plays a significant part in this process. Rectors of some tertiary education institutions view this process as advantageous to the quality of teaching. The decline in the number of evening and extramural programmes hardly means restoration of the disturbed proportion between the number of full-time and part-time students. Non-public higher education facilities were virtually forced by the ministry to run full-time programmes (day programmes) if they want to sustain the right to teach at master's level (second-cycle studies).

The ministry notices the problems of the rapid quantitative development of higher education in the past decades[9]. There is a possibility that the population decline will contribute to the reduction of many academic communities based on non-public (self-financing) higher education institutions. These institutions are the first in line to be reduced as long as they rely

[9] Interviews and studies published in "Gazeta Prawna" prove that increasing educational problems at the academic level are not ignored by representatives of the Ministry of Science and Higher Education.

on candidates for such departments as social science, law, economics. One such faculty is political science, which for the last several years has experienced a drop in the number of candidates resulting in cessation or suspension of didactic activity. There are reports that social rehabilitation education, which has been popular among students for years, has "saturated" the market with its graduates.

Table 3. Students according to forms of teaching

	total	women	programmes			
			Full-time		**Part-time**	
			total	**women**	**total**	**women**
Total number	1,927,762	1,098,351	928,133	520,026	999,629	578,325
Public	1,268,366	708,178	807,615	449,039	460,751	259,139
Non-public	659,396	390,173	120,518	70,987	538,878	319,186

Source: www.nauka.gov.pl/szkolnictwo-wyzsze (retrieved May 5, 2012)

Manifestations of pathologies of normalcy in education

The titular *pathology of normalcy in education* generated by democratic freedoms of founding new higher education institution, as well as liberalisation of the terms and conditions of admission appear in statements of higher education experts. The content of Table 3 is present in opinions of experts who represent the stance of the Ministry of Science and Higher Education. The ministry commissioned formulation of a development strategy of Polish higher education institutions to the Ernst & Young consortium and the Institute for Market Economics[10]. The practice of "weekend studying" of part-time students, who constitute over a half of all students, was considered abnormal. Similarly viewed is the concentration of didactic hours (20 and more) in only two days with two or three week interval between sessions and the large number of students per profesor. It was calculated that, in pedagogical departments, the student-profesor ratio is 600:1 and in departments of law and economics it is 300:1. The conclusion is unequivocal: according to experts, employees with a doctoral degree and senior academic staff members are unable to perform their duties well, which was apparent in the first five years of democracy. The present state of education is connected with the fact that the increase in the number of part-time students entails an increase in the number of teaching hours set forth in ministerial provisions. I observed the phenomenon in the early 90s, when the number of hours at bachelor's level within part-time programmes increased from

[10] Cf.: opinion of Jerzy Thieme in „Gazeta Prawna" on 19 February 2010.

approximately 1,000 to almost twice this number. This process caused considerable didactic overload on the part of both students and employees. Currently, there are postulates to reduce by 20% the number of hours in non-public higher education institutions and put emphasis on self-teaching as well as increase the consulting duties of teachers.

In this context, the inspiration to reflect upon the quality of teaching students are rapid changes in the structure of education regulated by provisions made by the Ministry. Significant alterations in academic practice were made every year for the past decade. For instance, students who take dean's leave must make up for "curricular differences" after their return. A minor alteration in the name of a subject causes new consequences in the teaching process. Only some of the dysfunctional circumstances of the forming model of higher education are: lack of relative stabilisation of academic life, overinterpretation and sometimes even literal interpretation of the changing Law on Higher Education, fading academic tradition, explosion in the number of students, excessive didactic duties and requirements regarding academic advancement of the younger academic staff members. The subject of the reflection is also excessively beaurocratic management of the subtle, cultural in its nature, system of a higher education institution as well as the consequences of control, which manifest themselves in the form of various "parametrisations" relativized by the amount of subsidies. I will refrain from mentioning the rankings of higher education facilities published by the "Wprost" magazine and other research, including "webometrics". It is sufficient to emphasise that in the early 90s 0.88% of GDP was allotted to higher education, whilst currently this amount equals merely 0.38%. The salaries in higher education institutions for the last ten years have been nominally constant and oscillate around the national average, and in the case of assistant professors, as usual, below the national average.

These are the selected aspects of the state of Polish higher education institutions, whose mission is scientific development and educating academic youth. In the students' experience, studying conditions fossilise cultural stereotypes as a constituent of the received education. The eternal dilemma "to be or to have", expressed in the report on the state of education by Jan Szczepański (1973), is vividly present in the 70s in Poland. Contemporary students want (or sometimes have to, as in the case of court administration employees, who are obliged to obtain a master's degree) to have a degree and various certificates attesting their skills, which altogether should ensure success on the labour market. Students, however, are less interested in being educated. Due to easy admission, students are not interested in studies and treat them instrumentally. They want to "check them off", since, in their opinion, it is a requirement of the labour market. Recently, it has been indirectly implied that a doctoral degree is prerequisite to take up prestigious administrative posts such as directors and executives.

This grim picture is only a reflection, a result of studying. I have an impression that contemporary students, both full-time and part-time, lose the ability to read and write. This opinion is based on many years of conducting seminars. Great kindness needs to be shown to students in order for them to unblock and be active during the seminars. Half of them open up and the cooperation assumes the form of a regular discussion aided by handwritten notes or edited texts. Many seminarists think they can "catch up" and consider listening to fellow students a waste of time. There is little to be done in terms of administrative measures. In a public higher education institution it is possible to let a student go after one term. Often bad manners and irresponsibility create a barrier in cooperation. The reported difficulties result from the practice of knowledge consumption during lectures (it is possible that students listen) and class conducted in a form of a "presentation", with little contribution on the part of students. Printing information from the Internet, often without reading, becomes an illusory basis for getting credit. It is not a rule, it is a regularity.

We live in the world invaded by TV information and easily-digestible Internet content. Contemporary students were raised and socialised in the environment filled with intrusive information of low cognitive value, quick and stress-free success and consumerist attitude. Let us imagine two days without television. What could fill this void? Such silence? Why, conversation.

I noticed an increased process of linguistic vulgarisation of the youth. Especially among women, which could be seen as alarming. Let us consider this telling scene: one evening I see four female students standing on a lawn near a wide campus pavement, gesticulating wildly and using extremely vulgar and illiterate expressions. Not only students are afflicted by the progressive vulgarisation of academic culture. It is also characteristic of academic employees. Slovenliness of language during class and in other situations is becoming a norm of linguistic behaviour.

Expressions on lecture rooms desks are another token of the cultural quality of a contemporary student. Until recently, toilets were such a "forum". We no longer read there quasi-poetic confessions of love, but various obscenities, such as the famous four-letter word, frequently accompanied by a vulgar drawing - used as a commentary of the lecture. *O tempora, o mores* – to quote Cicero.

One of the dimensions of human quality is *conscientiousness*. For many students, this "archaism" is valueless, although it is one of the major problems exhibited by students. Especially during seminars, when students display almost no sense of responsibility for the content of their theses. Symptomatic is the fact that students are being "threatened" with anti-plagiarism software; so is the requirement to sign a declaration that "the student is aware (...) - with the consequence of cancelling the certificate of graduation". Students infrequently come with their own handwritten notes, wich is a sign that the discussion is going to be substantive. The text proposals are usually in a printed form. Such texts often include passages copied directly from the Internet. It is easy to recognise such allegedly original texts by examining the following features: (1) the opening quotation mark is different than the closing one. (2) random letters in bold (3) foreign letters out of the set of tags controlling the typographic layout of the text (4) a different font and odd spacing in references (5) concentration of long words on a page, which indicates considerable experience in writing, a feature I failed to observe in students. Buying papers on the Internet is also commonplace (for example, at pracenaukowe.net.pl). A 100-page paper costs over 400 PLN. The problem lies in the fact that I prefer empirical theses, in which, after a methodological part, the empirical part is written before researching literature on the subject. This way I probably prevent students from wasting money.

In order not to offend authors (and prevent them from experiencing a trauma) of notes or longer passages, I tell them that the text is a set of notes and not the final version of the thesis and that these notes display many of the above mentioned features. I stress the fact that the notes are private and they are not subject to my ethical evaluation. This course of action at the first stages of cooperation usually leads to understanding on the part of the student. Few of them, to my relief, ask for a change of the thesis promoter. Furthermore, unconscientiousness in manifested in poor attendance at seminars, forgetting to bring the allegedly prepared notes and seeking extenuating circumstances or a person to blame. One could say that the closer the deadline for handing in the theses is, the more frequent are failures of computer equipment needed to write and print the paper.

The issue of openness to new experience

Why are social science students not interested in the subject of their studies? It could be assumed *ex cathedra* that a student is a human being open to gaining new experience in academic environment. Aside from the so-called standard way of gaining knowledge in the course of studies, a student can enrol in various short postgraduate studies, in order to gain additional qualifications documented with certificates, which is sometimes encouraged by academic authorities and teachers. Most second-cycle students are aware of the value of such additional certificates, aside from the Bachelor's degree, on the labour market.

Limited perception of the experienced world might be illustrated by this example: I conduct a class on *Changing dynamics of modern Polish society* in the course of sociological studies. I often emphasise the impact of various positive (for example, development of the construction industry, architectural changes improving the image of cities etc.) and negative phenomena which dynamise social changes in Poland. At the end of the lecture course, students are asked to provide any two phenomena influencing social change. I should also mention that the closer the end of the term, the larger the students' attendance at a particular course (lectures, seminars). The results of the students' perception of social phenomena are illustrated in Table 4. The impression of the limited nature of discerned classes of social phenomena is striking. The provided phenomena are trivial and obvious and possible to think of without attending the lectures. It is a disappointing picture, seeing as all the lectures were held. Even the few students who attended the lectures regularly failed to include positive phenomena. A possible explanation is the functioning of a stereotype that a social phenomenon is intrinsically pathological. This view is confirmed by the media. No pathology means no sensation or, as it is put by those who mould public opinion, good news or a cultural event is no news.

Table 4. Social phenomena discerned by students

Class of phenomena	%%
Unemployment	22,97
Poverty	12,16
Alcoholism	12,16
Domestic violence	6,76
Drug abuse	6,76
Disability	5,41
Juvenile agression	5,41
Homelessness	4,05
Suicide	2,70
Euro-Orphanhood	2,70
Social exclusion	2,70
Parental ineptitude	2,70
Demoralisation	2,70
Professional burnout	2,70
Prostitution	2,70
Nicotine dependence	2,70
Social violence addiction and the sense of agency of an addict	2,70
Total	100

Conclusion – typology of student behaviours in interaction with academic teachers

The following section presents a typology of student behaviours in interaction with academic teachers. In line with a certain human tendency: one case of inappropriate behaviour beclouds numerous examples of positive experiences. Just as negative cases accumulated during years of academic work form a certain regularity, less frequent cases of intensive intellectual cooperation with students justify continuation of academic activity.

What about the remaining majority of students? As in every process, regardless of its nature (physical, social), there must be the so-called *critical mass*[11], which conditions functioning of a phenomenon. With such a large number of students, averageness is a norm and it is difficult to dynamise it, orient it towards set goals. In many higher education institutions compulsory courses on a given faculty are specified by resolutions of department boards. Students with a developed sense of responsibility are present and constitute the aforementioned critical mass. Many times I practiced "voluntary compulsion" to attending the class in full-time studies. The procedure presented as follows: after a lecture, as he or she was leaving the lecture room, every student put on the desk a small piece of paper with their full name on it. I did not make so-called attendance lists. Folded pieces of paper eliminated any undignified intentions of students. Then followed some effort on my part to update the attendance register in e.g. a spreadsheet application (Excel) and to calculate the attendance mean which resulted in an over 70% attendance rate. Not all lectures followed this procedure for I needed to reveal whether in similar circumstances (the same lecture in the same year of studies, but in different academic years) such undemocratic measures ("voluntary compulsion") exceeded the sense of democracy in students. They, in fact, did not object to my style of academic work.

There is one more tendency in the rates of attendance. In many years of my didactic experience in many departments and in both MA and PhD studies, I observed a regularity concerning a high or low level of mathematical content in the structure of taught subjects. The more mathematics in the process of studying, the stronger is the students' discipline. For instance, characterisation of a sigmoid course of some social processes (logistic functions) hardly causes any difficulties in understanding among students of economics; students of social science, however, experience insuperable problems. Even a minor digression of mathematical or statistical nature causes in them an "intellectual allergy". As a result, it comes as no

---

[11] Ball P., *Masa krytyczna. Jak jedno z drugiego wynika. Badania wzajemnych zależności między przypadkiem a koniecznością w powstawaniu kultury, zwyczajów, instytucji, współpracy i konfliktów między ludźmi* (trans.: M. Brzozowska, T. Brzozowski, Redaktorzy, W. Turopolski), Wydawnictwo Insignis, Kraków 2007.

surprise that the data analysis part of their diploma theses abound in, to use a euphemism, "percentology".

Let us now proceed to the aforementioned typology of student behaviours.

Demanding attitude – students know what their rights are, but they somehow forget about their primary duties. If a student has a question or a matter to discuss with an academic teacher, the former should be at his or her immediate disposal. Whether the teacher is busy or engaged in a conversation is immaterial. Only the students' problems seem to matter, which is a result of complete ignorance of the rules of savoir-vivre. This instinct is especially well-developed in homilopathic personalities (of various intellectual deficiencies; although I do not refer here to spiritually brave persons with physical deficiencies). It is typical, for example, for certain students to believe that an academic teacher should be available to them whenever they need it, everyday.

Surprise – a student comes to make up for curriculum differences or to take an exam and is deeply agitated and surprised to learn that, in order to pass, they have to display some knowledge. They usually expect only to collect a signature. For several years, students have not bothered to distinguish between courses ending in an exam and a graded credit. In this obvious situation, they still need to be persuaded into putting in any intellectual effort. It is a result of some irrational conviction that the mere act of approaching the teacher should be sufficient for getting a credit. Some state, as I once heard, "I am under such influence of alcohol that I am running out of rational thinking".

Poor hygienic awareness – I often hear that male students fail to wash their hands after a visit in the toilet. My conversations with female students reveal great insouciance about using the facilities. Toilets expose personal etiquette of a statistical citizen, which, in turn, reflects personal behaviours standards of a given society. It seems, therefore, impugnable that academic *ethos* will recover

Heading for averageness – (*regressus ad infinitum*) *nota bene* the process of heading for averageness is always present. It usually entails determining the the level (setting the value) of this averageness, intermediateness. Classic examples are defined standards of studying, unnaturally constructed ECTS parameters, framework teaching standards. Another matter is prescribing standards, which for years have been very general, even blurred. To illustrate, let us consider the operating framework teaching standards. These measures, apart from constructing a curriculum and presenting a syllabus for a given subject, are, in fact, an administrative interception of control over the work of academic teachers.

Neurotic behaviour – in the course of full-time studies, students tend to take up various jobs, in order to prove their value before the employer and gain experience attested with a document. In this situation it seems as though studies interfered with work and their organisation was "defective". One of curiosities is the practice of granting students permission for an individual timetable of studying. As a practical implication, students seem to think that they are exempt from various contacts with their higher education institution. However, with commencement of the examination period, problems arise. Then, which is symptomatic, the student, in his or her "infinite graciousness", offers (offers!) to write a paper, send it via e-mail and...to use a colloquialism, it is all over and done with. In such circumstances I emphasise that a subjective discussion on the subject matter covered in the course of lectures and in the suggested literature is essential. "I regard those virtually telepathic contacts via the Interned medium as impossible."

Unconscious crassitude – students often think that in academic environment, which is devoid of defined conventions of behaviour, they can follow the behavioural patterns characteristic of secondary school; that his or her intelligence, cleverness and resourcefulness are more than enough to meet the academic teacher's requirements. Tolerating attempts at cheating is, in fact, a lack of respect for the student. Such situation is reprehensible on the part of both the student and the teacher. It is common that first year students come to their first class and manifest their presence by behaviours hampering the lecture (clowning etc). I have practically proved the effectiveness of my response to such incidents. After the usual greeting of students with the words "good morning", I wait a brief while for silence. Some more submissive students usually call out "Be quiet! Order!", which results in silence. Then one should thank these students and stress their commendable respect for the lecture (and intermediately for the lecturer). After several minutes, however, some individuals deem it necessary to manifest their presence yet again by talking to one other. One should immediately look their way and stop talking. Such measure can be taken only one more time. Then, one must announce a short break, after which only real students should remain in the lecture room. Individuals unworthy of being called a student have a chance to correct their mistake. The technique is so efficient you could hear a pin drop.

Limited trust – monitoring systems in dormitories are supposed to prevent uncontrolled alcohol-induced behaviours. It is one of the manifestations of *controlled democracy*, which, in fact, is not far removed from autocratically defined forms of behaviour.

Students seemingly well-developed intellectually – in the course of seminars I point out to students how important these meetings are. I stress that they constitute 50% of the curriculum of first-cycle studies and 100% of the second-cycle. The result of being present at the seminars is a ready dissertation whose weight equals 25-30% as a component of a grade average (50%) and diploma examination is 20-25%. One could say that studies measured with an average are half of success – expressed by a grade in a diploma. The remaining half is student's individual work (including exams). It is almost a rule that the higher the general average of grades, the lower the grade from diploma exam. In few cases an examined person has serious problems commenting excerpts of his or her diploma paper. Therefore, we should focus our attention on mechanisms leading to such suspiciously high grades at tests and exams. Perhaps, it is a positive phenomenon that certain types of classes are evaluated by students (by the power of their organisations). And one could end the above discussion with a bitter observation: "Dear colleagues in the academic profession! The process of reducing democratic liberties has begun. Now is the time to invest in prestige…".

Note: it is possible to classify other typologies of student behavioural patterns.

Bibliography

Ball P., *Masa krytyczna. Jak jedno z drugiego wynika. Badania wzajemnych zależności między przypadkiem a koniecznością w powstawaniu kultury, zwyczajów, instytucji, współpracy i konfliktów między ludźmi.* (tłum.: M. Brzozowska, T. Brzozowski, Redaktorzy, W. Turopolski), Wydawnictwo Insignis, Kraków 2007.

Fromm E., *Patologia normalności. Przyczynek do nauki o człowieku, vis-à-vis/Etiuda*, Kraków 2011.

Gębski B. i inni, *Sytuacja młodych pedagogów w Polsce. Determinanty rozwoju naukowego młodszej kadry naukowej nauk pedagogicznych w Polsce*, „Rocznik Pedagogiczny" 1989, nr 12.

Gębski B., *Definicja jakości życia studentów szczecińskiej humanistyki*, [w:] *Zrozumieć społeczeństwo. Szanse i zagrożenia w sferze mentalności, kultury i gospodarki w przededniu wejścia Polski do Unii Europejskiej*, red. J. Leoński, Zachodniopomorska Szkoła Biznesu, Szczecin 2004.

Kołakowski L., *Nasza wesoła apokalipsa. Wybór najważniejszych esejów,* Wydawnictwo Znak, Kraków 2010.

Mały rocznik statystyczny, GUS, Warszawa 2011.

Prawo o szkolnictwie wyższym, ujednolicony tekst ustawy z dnia 27 lipca 2005 roku /Dz. U. nr 164, poz. 1365 z późniejszymi zmianami.

Karolina Zaniewska

Pomeranian University in Słupsk, Poland

SIGNIFICANCE OF VALUES IN THE MODERN ACADEMIC EDUCATION

Summary

The article discusses the problems of space and place "for the" value in contemporary higher education. Values "give meaning to human life in the educational area. We can't talk about education without talking about values. Is the university a place that should educate, if so, what values" should we give young people to have a chance to reach its full potential. Perhaps more valuable is to move away from specific theories of education for the recognition process of education as an axiological act of human development, especially the young generation of XXI century is preparing to take up social roles.

Introduction

Education is a key area of shaping the European community. It is both a centre for the development of European identity and an instrument which increases opportunities to lead a life at a suitable level. Numerous countries – especially among those which are highly developed – implement a number of actions which are to increase the quality of education at respective levels of the process. One of the main tasks – according to M. Czerepaniak-Walczak – is "such coordination of educational effects so that it is possible to achieve the real purpose of intergration – creating conditions for self-realisation for every citizen of Europe"[1]. This article is devoted to issues regarding academic education and axiological dimension of education.

J. Gnitecki defines academic education as a symbolic form of communication expressed in a language (descriptive, predescriptive and symbolic) "suited to cognitive, emotional, causative and cultural possibilities and limitations of each human being and aiming to describe, explain, interpret and understand - as well as effectiveness and efficiency of implementing changes within this human being's personality in the course of the whole life"[2].

While discussing education/teaching one cannot forget about values since "at the basis of educating tendencies there usually lies a specific concept of values and human being" –

---

[1] M. Czerepaniak-Walczak, *Uczenie się czy studiowanie? Niektóre aspekty procesu bolońskiego*, [in:] K. Jaskot (ed.), *Wprowadzenie do pedagogiki szkoły wyższej*, In Plus Oficyna, Szczecin 2006, p. 415.

[2] J. Gnitecki, *Aksjologiczne podstawy stanowienia celów edukacyjnych szkoły wyższej*, [in:] *Wprowadzenie do pedagogiki szkoły wyższej*, [in:] K. Jaskot (ed.), op.cit., p. 33.

writes W. Cichoń [3]. The issue of values is the topic of general and specific axiology which is an expression of respective disciplines' interests. The range of issues related to pedagogical axiology is one analysed by K. Denek, K. Olbrycht, J. Półturzycki, W. Zaczyński and other educators.

Axiology is expected to provide theoretical rules behind the system of values which are to be operating in the area of educating processes as well as to specify the rules of ideology and politics for the purpose of justifying the choice of a specific social program. Its another task is to influence the development of humanities and social sciences – including assistance in the process of solving human conflicts[4]. Educational axiology – according to J. Gnitecki - "is perceiving the essence and manner of human existence in the categories of the system of values which give meaning to human life in the educational and taught expanse"[5]. T.W. Nowacki while defining pedagogical axiology made an observation that it concerns "systems of values" which control pedagogical activity"[6]. Axiological range of issues is present as soon as the stage of creating pedagogical concepts; it can be observed in a projection of a personal role model having its reflection in educating activity. J. Półturzycki voices a similar opinion – stating that "without axiology there is no education and it is impossible to construct its theory"[7]. The system of values constitutes the essence of the role model. A student should cultivate, strenghten and multiply those values.

The essence and definitions of values

Representatives of numerous sciences attempt to grasp the essence of values. For J. Szczepański, a sociologist, value is "an arbitrary material or ideal subject, idea or institution, imagined or real object in relation to which individuals or collectives assume an attitude of respect, ascribe an important role in their life and perceive endeavours to achieve it as an obligation"[8]. For M. Tyszkowa (representative of psychology), on the other hand, a value "in the first order constitutes what is important for human existence, activity and development in various stages of man's life – and, in addition, individual's perception and conviction on what is important, desirable and/or possible to achieve – what has a meaning in life, activity and development"[9]. In psychology, the theory of Rokeach is one of the more popular concepts of

---

3 W. Cichoń, *Wartości, człowiek, wychowanie*, WUJ, Kraków 1996, p. 7.
4 Ibidem, p. 15.
5 J. Gnitecki, *Aksjologiczne …*, op.cit., p. 34.
6 See: T. W. Nowacki, *Leksykon pedagogiki pracy*, ITE WSP, Radom 2004.
7 J. Półturzycki, *Potrzeba rekonstrukcji aksjologii w pedagogicznych studiach akademickich*, [in:] J. Kostkiewicz (ed.), *Aksjologia w kształceniu pedagogów*, Impuls, Kraków 2008, p. 61.
8 J. Szczepański, Elementarne pojęcia socjologii, PWN, Warszawa 1972, p. 38.
9 M. Tyszkowa, *Kultura symboliczna, wartości i rozwój jednostki*, [in:] M. Tyszkowa, B. Żurawkowski (red.), *Wartości w świecie dziecka i sztuki dla dziecka*, PWN, Warszawa – Poznań 1984, p. 26.

psychological interpretation of values; according to Rokeach "a value is a permanent conviction that a given manner of acting or a final state of existence is personally or socially preferred in relation to an alternative manner of acting or a final state of existence"[10]. Ethicist perceive value as "everything which is valuable and desirable; everything that constitutes a final purpose of human endeavors"[11]. K. Denek, on the other hand, makes an observation that the concept of "value" is by humanities most frequently referred to what a human being or a social collective perceive as something most valuable – what they consider as important and live it out as such – and beliefs and manners to live them out serve as those values' distinguishing[12]. As G.Kloska states - "values constitute a category of man's existence connected with a way of living specific to human being. All human activities exist in relation to values. We perceive them as objects or state of things with a certain significance which is felt subjectively"[13]. Values force us to be active, lend meaning to our life and make it possible to put all actions in a proper perspective/order; owing to them we orient ourselves in the world and are able to make assessments and put the perceived world in order. Values are essential in the process of decision-making – especially when we encounter conflicts of motives and arguments; according to K. Denek, they can also be a source of satisfaction[14].

J. Półturzycki points out that the culture in which a man is brought up is responsible for his acquisition of values - and the language, manners of behaviour, literature, customs, sign systems and art are carriers of values[15]. In the modern world – influenced by social events, economic transformations and processes one can observe the phenomenon of questioning and rejecting fundamental values which have provided order in the world for thousands of years. Changes in a traditionally perceived family, acceptance of liberties and rejecting obligations, mass consumption and its influence on character along with disdain for authorities and honest work – give rise to consequences in one's system of values which, in turn, results in a number of consequences in education.

Values in the educational process in a higher education institution

A key question is then the significance of values in the modern education which faces a complicated state of the moral and ethical reality. Pedagogy needs to enter into discourse with philosophy, ethics and sociology of morality as well as focus on the axiology of

[10] Quoted after: W.W. Szczęsny, *Edukacja moralna*, Żak, Warszawa 2001, p. 71-72.
[11] S. Jedynak (ed.), *Mały słownik etyczny*, Branta, Bydgoszcz 1999, p. 281.
[12] K. Denek, *Aksjologiczne aspekty edukacji szkolnej*, Adam Marszałek, Toruń 2000, p. 27.
[13] G. Kloska, *Pojęcia, teorie i badania wartości w naukach społecznych*, PWN, Warszawa 1982, p. 74.
[14] K. Denek, *Kształci i wychowuje*, „Forum Akademickie" 6/2009, .29.
[15] J. Półturzycki, *Potrzeba rekonstrukcji...*, op.cit., p. 48.

education. Is an academic institution a place where a student should be brought up – one where an individual is educated is such a manner that he or she obtains a correct, universal system of values?

Academic community – in a wide definition of the term – was for many years considered a significant educational and socialization system. According to J. Modrzewski, it can be perceived in three complementing dimensions as: one of typical educating environments generating phenomena and educational and socialization processes in basic structural elements of studying processes (contents, forms, patterns etc.); environment of secondary socialization of academic youth (different from primary environment of socialization); socio-cultural system mediating in the transfer of global cultural output (fulfilling functions in the scope of enculturationi)[16]. K. Jaskot, on the other hand, distinguishes internal functions of an academic institution among which he classified functions such as: didactic, educational, supporting students' development and compensation-related[17]. Among essential functions of an academic institution, didactic function was usually perceived as a priority since an academic facility is an institution which is supposed to educate and hence – its main task is to provide students with scientific knowledge and qualifications. However, especially in case of universities, this belief is not predominant as –both in the past and in the present times – the most important task of an academic institution is to create knowledge and seek truth[18].

As long as – in its socialization layer – this system did not provoke any doubts – the education-related questions inspired numerous reservations. Arguments regarding educational functions of an academic institutions had various causes. One of them was the fact that specific educational doctrines at the academic level stated that "students are people with a considerably developed personality and there is no need to exert pedagogical influence on it"[19]. An important argument was also that the nature of conducted didactic classes in an academic institution limited to a certain extent the implemenation of educational functions.

This problem is also valid nowadays since it appears that from a viewpoint of modern problems, educational functions of an academic institution are analysed to a smallest extent – and academic teachers are not significantly preoccupied with them. Understanding the essence of educational function of an academic institution is inconsistent and this is why it is so necessary to specify the concept of education. W. Cichoń believes that education is, above all,

[16] J. Modrzewski, *Środowisko społeczne młodzieży studiującej*, Poznań 1989, p. 34-35.
[17] This category encompasses, according to K. Jaskot, entirety of academic tasks directed towards students, Cf.: K. Jaskot, *Wprowadzenie do pedagogiki szkoły wyższej*, Szczecin 2006.
[18] K. Jaskot, *Funkcje szkoły wyższej jako instytucji edukacyjnej*, [in:] K. Jaskot (ed.), *Wprowadzenie do pedagogiki szkoły wyższej,* In Plus Oficyna, Szczecin 2006, p. 404.
[19] E. Kubiak- Szymborska, *Podmiotowość młodzieży akademickiej*, WAB, Bydgoszcz 2003, p. 250-251.

"realisation of personal values in the creative development of students. Development of a full person requires an understanding of human nature and an internal potential of a human being"[20]. J. Półturzycki emphasises that "the processes of teaching and education are – in the most general sense – a way to introduce people to national, regional, family-related – and interpersonal – culture. It is a process inspired by values that are accepted in those contexts"[21], while K. Jaskot distinguishes two approaches to education. The first – "accepts the wide definition of the term of "education" and as educating classifies all influences and interactions as a result of which human personality is formed"[22], the second approach defines "education" in a narrow sense: "education only concerns intended influences directed at emotional and motivational sphere of human personality"[23]. H. Muszyński defines education in a higher education institution as "all the activities which aim to form in a student's personality the emotional and volitional sphere – equipping him with a system of attitudes, ideals, values and rules which indicate his or her approach to the world"[24].

One needs to place sufficient emphasis on an institution's educating functions because of two aspects. The first is connected to an individual development of the studying youth - the personality of which is a work in progress – as "the academic years constitute a crucial educating moment in the life of a young person"[25], when the final personality dispositions are formed – deciding about one's ideals, values and life goals.

The second aspect concerns the fact that this is the time when a young person has the greatest possibilities to create his or her relations with external environment and his or her own "self" in relation to other people – as at this stage reflective self-awareness is achieved. K.Jaskot made an observation that students' personality is created not only under the influence of external factors, but also due to personal, independent action undertaken with an intention to move closer to "ideal self"[26].

Academic facility fulfills an educating function – if actions it undertakes lead to changes in student's personality, especially in the emotional and volitional sphere; the essence of this function then is intentional shaping and transforming in the studying youth – and with their participation – of "systems of values, life goals, attitudes, convictions, motives and

[20] W. Cichoń, op.cit., p. 8.
[21] J. Półturzycki, op.cit., p. 48.
[22] K. Jaskot, *Funkcje…*, op.cit., p.406.
[23] Ibidem, p.406.
[24] H. Muszyński, *Kierunki i formy realizacji celów dydaktyczno-wychowawczych w szkole wyższej*, „Życie Szkoły Wyższej" 1997/9, p. 19.
[25] M. Partyka, *Afirmacja osoby jako podstawa edukacji aksjologicznej w szkole wyższej*, [in:] J. Kostkiewicz (red.), *Aksjologia w kształceniu pedagogów*, Impuls, Kraków 2008, p. 192.
[26] K. Jaskot, *Funkcje…*, op.cit., p. 407-408.

needs – those elements which are decisive in the areas of graduates' aspirations, tastes, goals – and how they will take advantage of general and specialist qualifications acquired in the course of education in a higher education institution"[27].

Values serve the function of inspiring creative activity at the level of constructing oneself and the surrounding world. They have a hierarchal construction – which, according to D.Luber, signifies that "some of them are higher, some – lower; some of them oblige a man above anything else and some - a little less"[28]. W. Cichoń makes an observation that "values usually appear in combination with other values; appearance or existence of certain values tends to leave an impact on other ones. In the world of values there are certain regularities based on interrelations between values"[29]. S. Głaz, on the other hand, adds that "no accepted value can be implemented in separation from other ones"[30]. A human being existing in the world of values is forced to take a standpoint in relation to them – either choose them and live accordingly, or reject them and select other ones as goals. The world of values surrounds a human being who is a part of it – subject to some of those values and a creator of others. This does not, however, influence their axiological significance. Values manifest their objective reality, felt subjectively by a human being in a direct interaction with them. Values are an essential component of the objective reality regardless of the manner of its metaphysical explanation[31].

Today it is essential to search for a diversified model of a higher education institution – not only in the aspect of the taught values but also the goals of educated content[32]. W. Cichoń emphasises that "it should be a model which in an epoch of the crisis of values shall show to the young people the purpose and meaning of life. Significance of axiology is growing if we realise the immediate presence of the world of values and its role in solving conflicts and challenges brought by the current reality"[33].

Academic education in the axiological context

In the 21st century it is particularly desirable and important to develop in a human being – during all stages (also the one of academic institution) – essential, universal values and individual properties which reflect the non-cognitive development. Modern reality is so complex that it is no longer sufficient to transmit knowledge and skills in the cognitive sphere to

---

[27] Ibidem, p. 406.
[28] D. Luber, *Pedagogia osoby w aspekcie antropologicznego kontekstu nauczania Jana Pawła II*, [in:] Z. Matulka, M. Wójcik (ed.), *Wybrane problemy współczesnej pedagogiki społecznej*, WPS, Mysłowice 2008, p 153.
[29] W. Cichoń, op.cit., p. 35.
[30] S. Głaz, op.cit., p.55.
[31] W. Cichoń, op.cit., p. 32-33.
[32] J. Gnitecki, *Aksjologiczne* …, op.cit., p . 33.
[33] W. Cichoń, op.cit., p. 7.

ensure correct functioning. To make sure one does not get lost in such a world, it is essential to draw from universal values – general and timeless – connected with human life and the man himself; those values should originate from the trinity of the Truth, the Good and the Beauty[34]. Those are essential values which fill the educational expanse, have a dimension that surpasses culture and are referred to as supraesthetic values. "A human being – through his or her "personal self" can recognize, understand, accept and respect them in life – but is unable to create them."[35]. The taught expanse, on the other hand, is filled with non-essential values created by the man; those taught values are ones of the truth, good and beauty perceived in a diversified cultural context. After the phase of integration of values by "the personal self", non-essential values "open up to the transfer and participation of essential values"[36]. Educational values are a signpost for the didactic and educational activity of the higher education institution while the taught values create the potential of their implementation[37]. The truth perfects the intellect, the good develops the will and the beauty shapes emotions. Those values have an autotelic nature – they are universal and are based on the good in the absolute sense[38].

The truth is to constitute the foundation of free and responsible actions and decisions on the part of a human being. Human activities should be conditioned by kindness and acceptance of another person. All values that are considered as principal – freedom, good and love – live in the expanse of the truth which is not an objective value: it is superior to all of them[39]. "Truth is the value forming a component of the science conducted in freedom"[40], hence the truth needs to constitute one of the most important pillars on which the process of shaping academic youth in a higher education institution is to be based. Also J. Gnitecki sees the necessity of "education in an academic facility for the truth and in the truth"[41], and J. Winnicka-Gburek states that "honest search for the truth for itself should be undertaken jointly by professors and students. Respect for it conditions the need to exchange observations with the participation of critical reflection in the course of discussion - dialogue"[42], which has to be free and result from an internal need of its participants.

[34] A. Krajewska, *Jakość kształcenia w szkole wyższej*, [w:] K. Jaskot, *Wprowadzenie* … op.cit., p. 284.
[35] J. Gnitecki, *Aksjologiczne…*, op.cit., p. 34.
[36] Ibidem, p. 34.
[37] Ibidem, p. 39.
[38] K. Denek, *Kształci i wychowuje*, „Forum Akademickie", 6/2009, p. 29.
[39] D. Luber, op.cit., p. 155.
[40] J. Kostkiewicz, *Nauka i wolność- wartości fundujące uniwersytet*, [w:] J. Kostkiewicz (red.), *Uniwersytet* i *wartości*, Impuls, Kraków 2007, p. 19.
[41] J. Gnitecki, *Aksjologiczne…*, op.cit., p . 33.
[42] J. Winnicka-Gburek, *Krytycyzm wobec prawdy i piękna jako nieprzemijających wartości edukacji uniwersyteckiej*, [in:] J. Kostkiewicz (red.), *Uniwersytet* … op.cit., p. 160.

In educational teleology one can already notice changes characterised by an increased significance attributed to the subjective part of personality and axiological issues. It is analysed, among others, by A. Krajewska who makes an observation that we are witnessing a reorientation of educational goals "and the new perception includes the following system: personality development, shaping of attitudes, the world of values, view-point, the preparation for self-development – equipping with skills and knowledge"[43]. It is imperative to implement cognitive and supracognitive goals – affective and psychomotoric ones in an integral fashion. It shall enable a multi-faceted personality development of the studying youth – "discovering, developing and displaying all the potential of individuals, their shaping in three complementing areas – *to be, to act and to know*"[44].

Numerous scientists postulate that the education of the 21st century should in its humanistic dimension focus on values. Those values should encompass and inform the entire process of teaching and educating. Among the fundamental goals of the modern education in an academic facility should be educating specialists characterised by high professional qualifications, improving and retraining of the previous qualifictions – but also and perhaps above all – providing motivation for the young people to consciously develop their own identity based on the universal system of values as well as creating conditions which are conducive to fulfilling the developmental needs of individuals. Values play an essential role in the process of personality formation. Both exceeding and having an awareness of one's identity – "which conditions the sense of one's identification" [45]. „The discovery of one's identity is a process of constant struggle for life in accordance with it – and as long as a human being is able to do that - he or she can retain this identity; if, however, this human being is too weak and immature to correctly solve practical issues which require certain moral resolution and decisions, if he or she is unable to "focus" – then they are lost in meaningless details of everyday life and illusory pursuit of virtual values"[46] – concludes W. Wołoszyn. S. Głaz, on the other hand, emphasises that a human being can only retain their identity if he or she knows who they are. Such knowledge is necessary in order to make important life choices in accordance with one's system of values – which is why this system of values needs to be accepted and agreed with

---

[43] A. Krajewska, op.cit., p. 285.
[44] Ibidem., p. 285.
[45] K. Chałas, *Wychowanie ku wartościom. Elementy teorii i praktyki*, Jednoś́ć, Lublin-Kielce 2003, p. 58.
[46] W. Wołoszyn, *Istota odpowiedzialności*, [in:] A. Tchorzewski (ed.), *Odpowiedzialność jako wartość i problem edukacyjny*, WERS, Bydgoszcz 1998, p. 16.

since a developed identity forces a human being to make decisions in accordance with his or her internal beliefs and adopted system of values[47].

Young people should be taught ethical values on which the entire process of education if based. A. Śniegulska claims that "such an education can be perceived more and more as a means of releasing developmental potential of respective individuals, a tool to overcome threats of the modern world and spread peace - as well as the way of shaping a person who is able to conduct dialogue, interact and cooperate with other people"[48]. Humanistic pedagogy might be a good example of that – it strives to find internal balance and harmony, to inspire respect for universal values and efficiently cooperate within communities[49]. The basic goal of humanistic pedagogy is comprehensive and individual development of individuals as well as shaping within a given person a skill of critical and creative thinking[50]; among other ones are: subjective treatment, preparation for self-development, self-realisation and activity – and, above all, inspiring within a student a high level of moral awareness.

W. Cichoń is another one to notice the necessity of philosophical justification of educating goals and aspirations taking into consideration the current state of the Polish education system. It is mostly related to the need of preparing the range of issues in the sphere of axiology and education encompassing problems connected with the role of values in the process of education, formulation of the goals of education as well as analysing the knowledge on values. All of it has an impact on an educator's orientation in the world of values as well as helps in the process of choosing appropriate educating methods and specific contents[51]. Properties of a person – an individual – are acquired by the man in the process of implementing ethical values which give personal character to various aspects of human life. Such an individual is able to decide for themselves and experience personal responsibility[52].

It is virtually impossible to discuss pedagogical axiology without mentioning an immense authority in this sphere – John Paul II whose philosophy of education is based on personalism. In Christian personalism, an attribute of man's subjectivity is constituted by his values understood as a gift and good. Cardinal Wojtyła perceives three of them as the fundamental ones: freedom, responsibility and love. Freedom as a gift but also obligation is "the

[47] S. Głaz, *Rola kościoła w integralnym rozwoju młodzieży*, WAM, Kraków 2010, p. 58.
[48] A. Śniegulska, *Wychowanie a miłość*, [in:] J. Łach (ed.), *Człowiek a wychowanie. Europejskie możliwości i zagrożenia*, WUR, Rzeszów 2007, p.95.
[49] K. Denek, *W kręgu edukacji, krajoznawstwa i turystyki w szkole*, Eruditus, Poznań 2000, p. 52.
[50] A. Śniegulska, *Humanistyczne relacje między nauczycielem a uczniem jako podstawa współczesnych oddziaływań edukacyjnych,* [in:] J. Szempruch (ed.), *Eduakcja wobec wyzwań i zadań współczesności i przyszłości. Teoria i praktyka pedagogiczna,* WUR, Rzeszów 2006, p. 362.
[51] W. Cichoń, op.cit., p.7.
[52] S. Olejnik, *Eudajmonizm. Studium nad podstawami etyki*, TNKUL, Lublin 1958, p. 181.

freedom for values, a potential for the man to choose specific good"[53]. According to John Paul II, freedom is essential for the existence of man and mankind as it activates him as "a subjective entity in the spheres of action and valuation owing to which a human being becomes more able to accept values and implement them"[54]. A human being has a right to make important life decisions, decide about his or her existence and goals – this is how human freedom is manifested. He or she is an individual entity, autonomous in decisions concerning their existence. By making important decisions a human being obviously experiences their consequences – as freedom always presupposes responsibility[55]. Developing a free and responsible person should be the main pedagogical challenge for all European countries - and possibly – the whole world. "The new man should realise in life strong and inseparable connections between freedom, morality and responsibility"[56]. All participants of the educating relations are free, autonomous people endowed with dignity and having the right to respect, ethicality and tolerance. Personalistic education presupposes and implements the subjective nature of participation in educating processes on the way of dialogue which is to lead to transformation, renewal and is to help in a conscious participation and mutual opening in educating relations.

Only a responsible man can be sensitive to the world of values which is to put his entire world in order. In the process of "being the man", a responsible, subjective being – the thing which forms the core is the moral attentiveness and the ability to make decisions and assessments. This concerns the world of values – and only a human being is capable of that. "The sense of responsibility will always be dependent on the degree of awareness with which the man perceives the relation between a given situation with a value or its lack, the degree with which he or she will notice requirements put forth by values. The formation within a man of the sense of responsibility will always be conditioned by the ability to discover what is good and better, by seeing oneself in relation to a discovered good or bad, awareness of one's strength and ability to take action and a choice of means and their implementation"[57]. One of the principal goals of enlightened education and a foundation for meaningful life should be the responsibility understood as being decided and ready to always follow the path of values, regardless of external conditions and personal situation[58]. Karol Wojtyła believed that life is

---

[53] K. Wojtyła, *Osoba i czyn*, PTT, Kraków 1985, p.147.
[54] D. Luber, op.cit., p. 154.
[55] Z. Matulka, *Prawda i wolność jako naczelne wartości kultury i wychowania*, [in:] Z. Matulka, M. Wójcik (ed.), *Wybrane problemy współczesnej pedagogiki społecznej,* WPS, Mysłowice 2008, p. 10.
[56] S. Kawula, *Wychowanie „Nowego Człowieka" w świetle III Forum Pedagogiki Europy*, [in:] A. Tchorzewski (ed.), *Z problematyki metodologicznej teorii wychowania*, WSP, Bydgoszcz 1993, p. 122.
[57] D. Hildebrand, J. von Kłoczkowski, A. Paściak, J. Tischner, *Wobec wartości. W drodze*, Poznań 1984, p. 32-33.
[58] Ibidem, p. 32-33.

strictly connected to responsibility and is a link in the relation of the person and value; he also observed that love makes one more sensitive to values – it makes one more open to them.[59]

The pope reminds us that ”symptoms of various crises that plague current communities and societies – usually the richest ones - crises which mostly affect young generations (including university students) are a vivid proof that the act of education is not conducted by institutions (using even the best material measures) but a human being (and their moral authority) is the most important factor – resulting from the truth of rules and actions based on them (…) a human being spiritually mature, fully educated – able to educate oneself and others”[60]. This goes to show the necessity of realising the huge responsibility and a role of an academic teacher as – according to J. Partyka – this responsibility "precedes their freedom"[61]. This responsibility for another person inspires one to do good, to conduct dialogue. When two people meet ”there arises a bond of obligation, relation of mutuality, expanse of sense which is an area full of potential for discovery and betterment in one's humanity"[62].

Educating adults is a complicated, complex and long-lasting process as it encompasses a period of reeducation. Previous experiences need to be replaced with new, more desirable and valuable patterns of action, information, cognitive formulas, motives and methods of action. L. Turos emphasises that ”modifying, unteaching, eliminating old convictions and habits is always more difficult than shaping new ones as it entails overcoming fixed stereotypes and modes of acting"[63], and so teaching and educating in a higher education institution requires the teacher to be an educator and transmitter of knowledge, but also a searcher, discoverer, creator, commentator, translator and narrator of reality. The most convincing and effective way to build attitudes of caring for basic values – not only in case of youth – is demonstrating them with one's own life, showing their significance in one's activity, standing by them regardless of circumstances – and being happy because of that[64].

A. Węgrzecki believes that ”academic quality might be understood as a certain form of maturity. An academic teacher should place challenges in front of the youth – ones that this youth is able to undertake without sacrificing freedom. In academic education, autonomy is as

[59] K. Wrońska, *Osoba i wychowanie, wokół personalistycznej filozofii wychowania Karola Wojtyły – Jana Pawła II*, WUJ, Kraków 2000, p.49.
[60] Jan Paweł II, *Wiara i kultura. Dokumenty, przemówienia, homilie*, Rzym 1986, p. 71-72.
[61] J. Partyka, op.cit., p. 190.
[62] Ibidem, p. 190.
[63] L. Turos, *Andragogika ogólna*, Żak, Warszawa 1999, p. 29.
[64] K. Wrońska, *Edukacja aksjologiczna pedagogów a problem przekazu wartości w wychowaniu*, [in:] J. Kostkiewicz (red.), *Aksjologia* … op.cit., p. 148.

important as creating conditions for development"[65]. Academic education should implement classical academic ideals, lead towards wisdom and understanding of the modern world. An ability to understand and interpret phenomena takes place on the way of dialogue which entails admitting various beliefs, opinions – values diversity which is an inherent trait of our times. Dialogue is a remedy to isolation and loneliness, intolerance and confusion in the world; it should prevent an excessive superiority of a teacher or educator. It entails communicating facts and provokes the confrontation of expectations – enables a discussion about values[66]. "Educating dialogue (...) requires mutual openness, honesty, patience and trust in relation to another person as well as a systematic correction of oneself in view of arguments of discussion's partner"[67], for it to exist a personal meeting is necessary – in order to exchange beliefs, needs and aspirations. Interpersonal contact of teacher and student is a basic condition of social and emotional development. Only in case of meeting someone as a person can we refer to it as real meeting, only if there is a "You" and "I" type of contact can we talk about any real mutuality. An additional value is the fact that after meeting "You" we also discover "I" – oneself[68]. Effective functioning of school is always dependent on "to what extent is the relation between a teacher and a student really educating"[69]. Meanwhile J. Bińczycka makes an observation that "the modern academic facility is usually associated with an anonymous crowd where people meet only in formal situations (classes, exams, meetings) in order to pass on certain information, where there is no time nor place for the master-student type of relation, where all interpersonal contacts are impersonal in nature"[70]. Relation between a teacher and a student is not (and cannot be) equal – and its character is described by J. Tarnowski, who states that "a teacher is in a way superior to students, but should be available to them – like a servant"[71].

Every man is constantly looking for values which are to give meaning to his or her life. Education in an academic facility can be described as looking for values or aspiring for values which entail educating goals[72]. In the process of constant becoming a subject and searching for meaning – an adult needs to independently raise one's qualifications – not only professional ones – as "it is assumed that an adult in the process of education is an autono-

---

[65] A. Węgrzecki, *O etosie nauczyciela akademickiego*, [in:] J. Filek (ed.), *O etosie nauczyciela akademickiego*, WAE, Kraków 1998, p. 24.
[66] M. Partyka, op.cit., p. 186.
[67] Ibidem, p. 188.
[68] Ibidem., p. 189.
[69] Speech of John Paul II in Castel Gandolfo, [in:] Kard. S. Dziwisz, P. Ptasznik, S. Hasiorowski (ed.), *Anioł Pański z Papieżem Janem Pawłem II,* Watykan 2006, p. 12.
[70] J. Bińczycka, *Studenckie spotkania z wartościami pedagogicznymi*, „Ruch Pedagogiczny" 1985, no 5, p. 16.
[71] J. Tarnowski, *Pedagogika egzystencjalna*, [in:] Z. Kwieciński (ed.), Pedagogika, WN PWN, Warszawa 2003, p. 73.
[72] J. Gnitecki, *Aksjologiczne* op.cit., p. 41.

mous product of their development and in the process of studying they need to receive assistance in the scope of recognizing and directing their needs, interests and aspirations as well as overcoming problems connected with their implementation." – as is pointed out by J. Krupa, A. Murawska [73].

Conclusion

Humanistic sensitivity is an immensly important guarantee of preserving human values in a dehumanised world; one could mention here sensitivity to human experience – especially where human matters are concerned – and where empathy and mutual understanding is required[74]. Education is a huge responsibility – not only for educators – but also, especially at the level of academic institutions – of the educated ones. "A human being is an entity open to values he or she is responsible for and because himself or herself is also a value – he or she is also responsible for their own value"[75] and development. From the educational point of view, the most important goal is developing a certain axiological condition of the whole society ruled by common respect, justice and goodness [76]. Looking for objective values and meanings in one's life is in harmony with human nature. A human being is not self-sufficient – and so looks for complementation since he or she is imperfect. The world of objective values inspires the process of discovering the meaning of one's existence. Because of values a human being has an opportunity for realisation – for "becoming". Values are a quality for human existence, allow for reaching the full growth; they inspire individual's whole potential and make it possible to surpass limitations and social barriers – to go beyond "oneself"[77]. K. Chałas observes that "man's obligation connects him with the world of values, opens himself to it, constitutes the need to implement those values – and in the process they become personality traits, deepening humanity"[78].

Those values have a particular significance in the process of a correct development of academic youth. The obligation to educate in values in academic education is dictated by the role and function of values in human life. As K. Denek argues "values decide about man's existence, meaning and quality of life, interpersonal relations, ability to solve problems, atti-

---

[73] J. Krupa, A. Murawska, *Obraz studentów studiów zaocznych i jego implikacje pedagogiczne*, „Edukacja Ustawiczna Dorosłych", 3/2000, p. 33.
[74] I. Wojnar, *Humanistyczne intencje edukacji*, Żak, Warszawa 2000, p. 28.
[75] D. Luber, op.cit., p. 154.
[76] W.W. Szczęsny, op.cit., p.113.
[77] S. Głaz, *Rola kościoła w integralnym rozwoju młodzieży*, WAM, Kraków 2010, p.55.
[78] K. Chałas, *Wychowanie ku wartościom. Elementy teorii i praktyki,* Jednośc, Lublin-Kielce 2003, p. 176.

tude to oneself, groups, communities in which he lives and functions"[79]. Education for values in an academic institution should aim to develop human character which is an internal system of values. Hence, education in a higher education institution aspires to develop systems of values of academic youth in the process of achieving educating goals through the implementation of classical academic ideas and understanding the modern world.

Bibliography

Bińczycka J., *Studenckie spotkania z wartościami pedagogicznymi*, Ruch Pedagogiczny 1985, nr 5.

Chałas K., *Wychowanie ku wartościom. Elementy teorii i praktyki*, t.1, Jedność, Lublin-Kielce 2003.

Cichoń W., *Wartości, człowiek, wychowanie*, WUJ, Kraków 1996.

Denek K., *Aksjologiczne aspekty edukacji szkolnej*, Adam Marszałek, Toruń 2000.

Denek K., *W kręgu edukacji, krajoznawstwa i turystyki w szkole*, Eruditus, Poznań 2000.

Głaz S., *Rola kościoła w integralnym rozwoju młodzieży*, WAM, Kraków 2010.

Hildebrand D., von Kłoczkowski J., Paściak A., Tischner J., *Wobec wartości. W drodze*, Poznań 1984.

Jan Paweł II, *Wiara i kultura. Dokumenty, przemówienia, homilie,* Rzym 1986.

Jaskot K. (red.), *Wprowadzenie do pedagogiki szkoły wyższej*, In Plus Oficyna, Szczecin 2006.

Jedynak S. (red.), *Mały słownik etyczny*, Branta, Bydgoszcz 1999.

Kloska G., *Pojęcia, teorie i badania wartości w naukach społecznych*, PWN, Warszawa 1982.

Kostkiewicz J. (red.), *Uniwersytet i wartości,* Impuls, Kraków 2007.

Kostkiewicz J., *Nauka i wolność- wartości fundujące uniwersytet,* [w:] J. Kostkiewicz (red.), *Uniwersytet i wartości*, Impuls, Kraków 2007.

Kostkiewicz J. (red.), *Aksjologia w kształceniu pedagogów*, Impuls, Kraków 2008.

Kubiak-Szymborska K. (red.), *Podmiotowość młodzieży akademickiej*, WAB, Bydgoszcz 2003.

Łach J. (red.), *Człowiek a wychowanie. Europejskie możliwości i zagrożenia*, WUR, Rzeszów 2007.

Matulka Z., Wójcik M.(red.), *Wybrane problemy współczesnej pedagogiki społecznej*, WPS, Mysłowice 2008.

Modrzewski J., *Środowisko społeczne młodzieży studiującej*, Poznań 1989.

Olejnik S., *Eudajmonizm. Studium nad podstawami etyki*, TNKUL, Lublin 1958.

Szczepański J., *Elementarne pojęcia socjologii*, PWN, Warszawa 1972.

Szczęsny W.W., *Edukacja moralna*, Żak, Warszawa 2001.

[79] K.Denek, *Wartości i cele edukacji szkolnej*, Poznań-Toruń 1994, p.4.

Taraszkiewicz M., *Wartości i cele osobiste młodzieży*, „Psychologia Wychowawcza", 4/1985.

Tarnowski J., *Pedagogika egzystencjalna*, [w:] Z. Kwieciński (red.), *Pedagogika*, WN PWN, Warszawa 2003.

Tchorzewski A. (red.), *Odpowiedzialność jako wartość i problem edukacyjny*, WERS, Bydgoszcz 1998.

Tchorzewski A. (red.), *Z problematyki metodologicznej teorii wychowania*, WSP, Bydgoszcz 1993.

Turos L., *Andragogika ogólna*, Żak, Warszawa 1999.

Tyszkowa M., Żurawkowski B. (red.), *Wartości w świecie dziecka i sztuki dla dziecka*, PWN, Warszawa – Poznań 1984.

Wojnar I., *Humanistyczne intencje edukacji*, Żak, Warszawa 2000.

Wojtyła K., *Osoba i czyn*, PTT, Kraków 1985.

Wrońska K., *Osoba i wychowanie, wokół personalistycznej filozofii wychowania Karola Wojtyły – Jana Pawła II,* WUJ, Kraków 2000.

Kazbek Gaysanov

Pomeranian University in Słupsk, Poland

THE ROLE OF ETHNIC VALUES IN DEVELOPING «LIFEWORLD» OF STUDENTS

Summary

This article presents the role of ethnic values in developing "lifeworld" of students belonging to ethnic minorities. It was indicated that every ethnic group has its own ethno-cultural («life») world. It was shown that ethnic values are particularly important in student communities. They reflect in a certain way a manner in which various ethnic groups present their "lifeworld". In the process of analysing the system of relations among various ethnic student groups it was concluded that their basis is formed by ethnic values specifying distinction and characteristics of "the lifeworld".

Introduction

Dynamics of political and socio-economic processes related to the process of globalization significantly influences an expansion of multicultural expanse. The functioning of various ethnic groups in a multicultural community determines the process of adapting of respective members of different ethnic communities to the current socio-cultural situation. In this process an important role is played by values and motivation which – to a large extent – modifies the awareness of intentional actions on the part of ethnic group members. An ethnic group is based on a network of social interactions – and one of the crucial factors of internal cohesiveness and organisation of an ethnic group is a sense of its distinctiveness (expressed in various ways), specific valuation in comparison with other cultural groups.

Culture has a significant impact on the process of individuals' adaptation to new conditions. As A. Kłoskowska argues – national culture is a system consisting of immensely diversified elements[1], including language, religion, customs, art and organisation. It is this last aspect that in the process of ethnic groups' adaptation fulfills an integrating role. The proof can be found in the fact of establishing in one social expanse a valuating and normative system owing to which an understanding can be reached in the matters of mutual regulations (of actions and permanence of these actions) concerning "lifeworlds" of ethnic minorities. It contributes to the development of open-minded attitudes towards multiculturalism.

---

[1] A.Kłoskowska, *Kultury narodowe u korzeni*, PWN, Warszawa 1996, p.110.

The essence and characteristics of "lifeworld"

The term of "lifeworld" – Lebenswelt - was introduced into the theory of communicative action by J. Habermas and it signifies «the world of action, common for ourselves and other people» and forms the basis for life experience of an individual[2]. According to J. Habermas, a community of lifeworld consists of previously acquired knowledge collected in culture and, particularly, in language.

The theory of communicative action describes the development of «lifeworld» in the course of evolution consisting in the development of human cognitive skills. J. Habermas compares the mythological and modern way of perceiving the world and argues that the difference between them consists in the difference between conceptual systems in which an individual interprets the world on their own. Existing systems of world-views have two varietes – mythological («close») and modern («open»)[3]. Apart from that – according to J. Habermas – it is the modern understanding of the world which is based upon analytical division of the modern world into objective, subjective and social life which makes it more rational.

Habermas argues that lifeworld is rational – but not originally as it has numerous irrational characteristics. It also has «internal potential of rationalization» which is then expressed in the social development. According to Habermas, rationalization of «lifeworld» offers the opportunity to see social changes and pathologies like distorted communication as well as coordinate social actions of people – and diversification of its structure is aimed at the recreation of the culture of society and personality.

However, in a practical sense, an evaluative organisation of ethnic group's «lifeworld» is crucial. *«Lifeworld» of an ethnic group encompasses evaluative senses based upon ethnic culture as well as social experience of a given ethnos*[4].

«Evaluative senses» manifest themselves in various elements of culture: language, mutual relations between people, traditions, base norms etc., which are shared by representatives of national minorities and which is specified by a relation of «us-them». They form the basis for social interactions.

The essence of «lifeworld» is formed in everyday life which is accompanied by the acquiring of social experience which changes according to a character of a given historical period of society's development. From the initial phase such a formation takes place in evaluative and

[2] Por.: J.Habermas, *The Theory of Communicative Action*, London: Heinemann, 1984; J.Habermas, *Teoria działania komunikacyjnego*, PWN, Warszawa 1999.

[3] И.А.Громов, А.Ю.Мацкевич, В.А. Семенов, *Западная теоретическая социология,* Изд-во «Ольга», Санкт-Петербург 1996, p.242.

[4] И.А. Сурина, *Ценности, ценностные ориентации, ценностное пространство,* Социум, Москва 1999, p. 54.

orientational spheres in the process of original socialization. It is only afterwards that – along with an expansion of social environment, acquiring and diversification of social experience, changes in the intensity of social interactions, an increase in the mobility of various evaluative and orientational spheres - «lifeworld» changes its configuration, auto-organises itself – changing accordingly in space, time and the evaluative and orientational dimension.

It is believed that language is a fundamental ethnic value which acts as a crucial ethno-diversifying trait. It is on the level of language that the classification of people by representatives of various ethnoses transpires – into «our own and alien»[5]. In the modern socio-cultural situation, language acts not only as a sign of ethnic identification, but also a symbol of an evaluative expanse of an ethnic community. According to Ju.V. Arutyunyan, L.M Drobizhev, A.A. Susokolov, «every phenomenon in culture may acquire a meaning of an ethnic element»[6].

Understanding of the world by an ethnic group is formed both on the basis of both mythical and modern concepts (this trait, indeed, distinguishes such an understanding of the world from conceptual rules formulated by J. Habermas). It is only ethnos that makes it possible to enable existence and acceptance of mythological beliefs which coexist and combine with modern views of the world – in the process retaining continuity of history from generation to generation. It is here that rationality manifests itself – combining «close» and «open» (according to J. Habermas) view of the social reality. By that, «lifeworld» of ethnic group is semi-open, which is conditioned by a relatively high stability of national culture elements – including everyday tradition. In this sense, formation of a viewpoint by an ethnic group can be considered a rational phenomenon. Such formation supports explication (development) of national awareness and formation of national self-identification.

"Lifeworld" of academic youth

It is the youth that attracts largest scientific interest. Student community is a multicultural one. Lifeworld of youth reflects the perception of the world which we see as a cohesive concept of the global reflection of the world – which lies at the basis of an individual (or group) viewpoint – representing crucial properties and traits of the world in their understanding – and being a result of mostly their social activity. The perception of the world is dualistic in its essence. It exists as a nonmaterial element of awareness and life activity of the man

[5] И.А.Сурина, К.Р. Гайсанов, *Этнические ценности студенчества: сущность, структура и методы исследования*, Социум, Москва 1998, p.76-80.
[6] Ю.В.Арутюнян, Л.М.Дробижева, А.А.Сусоколов, *Этносоциология*, Москва 1999, p.153.

– as well as in the type of material signs which appeared as a result of life activity of the man. ”Imprints” of the world's reflection can appear in a language, gestures, fashion, methods of economic administration, socio-cultural stereotypes of human behaviour – and, most importantly – in the system of values of the given social subject.

«Lifeworld» of youth is characterised by ”its” specific – cultural – shape. L.G.Ionin argues that the life form is a manner of satisfying needs; institutions regulating common life and norms of behaviour in relation to those of other people[7]. «Life forms - are not universal moral norms, but historically changeable and specified regulations concerning perception, judgment and behaviour»[8].

«Lifeworld» of the youth of national minorities and ethnic groups is understandable only for the representatives of «one's own» (separately understood) community since it is based upon accepted systems of concepts (especially of «one's own» subculture) including the language which results in the fact that it is understandable and recognizable.

«Lifeworld» of an ethnic group is changeable as a result of changeability of the accepted viewpoint. It is conditioned by the influence of «external senses». In other words – according to J. Habermas - «lifeworld» is divided into subjective, objective and social worlds.

The subjective world of the youth is understood as the world of the young built upon the understanding by the community of itself – upon «their» own beliefs, the perception of the world, culture – which signifies that it is a self-organizing and self-realising quality – and – in essence - «a world in itself». On the other hand, the objective world of youth is a «world», which exists «outside» a community of the young (outside its boundaries) but also a given «world» of the young places next to itself, evaluates and compares with - «the world exceeding its boundaries»[9].

Evolutional processes of youth create the possibility for the subjective and objective world to combine within the coherent social expanse. Subjective world is more focused in the socio-psychological sense. However, like the objective one – it is changeable. The changeability of the subjective world is based on the communicative action and leads to the understanding on the part of youth of «themselves» in the social expanse as well as the change of viewpoint as a whole. Communicative action in this case signifies simultaneous strategic, normative and dramaturgic action (explanation according to J. Habermas).

---

[7] Л.Г. Ионин, *Социология культуры*, Логос, Москва 1998, p.172.
[8] Ibidem, p. 173.
[9] И.А.Сурина, Ценности… op.cit., p.57.

Subjective and objective world mutually condition and influence each other. This interaction of given worlds takes place on the basis of communicative influence which specifies the fluctuating nature of the social change of youth. Therefore, in case of a strong influence of the subjective world of youth on elements of the objective world – it is those «alien» groups which are led to the utmost unbalanced state, in other words – to a specific kind of socio-cultural chaotic state. There is an obligation – after passing the point of bifurcation – to find such parameters of socio-cultural control and use them – especially in an objective expanse in order to form a relative stability and ”cultural (life) balance” ensuring the possibly safest social functioning of youth (and conversely). However, communicative action both within one of the worlds and between them might be distorted. This gives birth to social pathologies both in the society as a whole and specifically in youth groups.

Partial closing of an ethnic community creates a possibility for the subjective and objective world to combine within one social expanse. The subjective world is more focused in the ethnosocial sense. However, like the objective one – it is changeable. The changeability of the subjective world is based on the communicative action and leads to the understanding on the part of youth of «themselves» (as an ethnic group) in the social expanse as well as the change of viewpoint. Communicative action signifies here simultaneous strategic, normative and dramaturgic action (explanation by J. Habermas).

«Lifeworld» of youth as a social community is still in the process of searching for the relatively stable state (in agreements concerning the influence of social development changes on it) to enable the implementation of social needs of young people. Transformations taking place in all spheres of social life lead to a gradual change in the perception of the surrounding reality on the part of youth. The structure of lifeworld is conditioned by objective and subjective diversification of concepts concerning reality and perceptions of life events both on the level of personality and a social collective.

Organisation of «lifeworld» is the controlling mechanism and identifies itself as a reaction (to events) as a result of which happen reconstruction processes and changes of «lifeworld» due to the effect of social transformations on the way of regulation, coordination and arrangement of its elements. The system of values' orientation plays a crucial role here.

Significance of values in developing ”lifeworld” of academic youth

According to K. Valaskakisa as quoted by M. Ejsmant, B. Kosmalska – the system of values “(...) includes beliefs, ideals and preferences. Beliefs encompass what an individual believes is the true viewpoint and explain the nature of the moral order of the world assumed by this individual. Ideals enable to establish criteria of what one aspires to – what is moral, beautiful and appropriate. Finally, preferences are manifested in the acceptance or sympathy for certain phenomena, situations, subjects or states of things"[10].

In the case of youth one may notice that the values it chooses and appreciates condition its relation towards the surrounding world and constitute a factor of a cognitive development. In view of that one could conclude that "the values which exist in the objective reality have the potential of attraction. They are the reality which orients a person >>towards<< somebody or something"[11]. Youth choosing and believing in certain values discovers, learns and experiences reality. Therefore, the values chosen and believed in are a factor inspiring their life activity and helping individuals in the participation of social life. "Values play an important role in the creation of one's identity – understood as a qualification to act and solve problems. They allow an individual to experience the sense and meaning of one's subjective and personal existence"[12].

In a multicultural community, social actions of an ethnic group are regulated by values and norms it accepted – they acquire a more rational charakter. Such actions are «controlled» not only by «one's own», but also «alien» evaluative and normative system, and so they mutually have impact on one another and are taken into consideration in «life strategies» of ethnic groups within one social expanse. In such a case - rationality may appear as a justification of action expected from «alien groups»[13].

While analysing "lifeworld" of various ethnic student groups one can conclude that the basic trait characterising its existence – is constituted by values. For such groups they condition having a family, citizenship, relation to family, origins etc. – in other words: everything which enables establishing social placement of ethnic student groups.

Orientation of values appear as a controlling parameter of the organisation of social life and lifeworld of youth. This is explained by the fact that value orientation occupying a higher level of the hierarchy of dispositions – regulate social interaction. Value orientations –

---

[10] M. Ejsmant, B. Kosmalska, *Media, wartości, wychowani,* . Oficyna Wydawnicza „Impuls", Kraków 2005, p. 79.

[11] K. Chałas, *Wychowanie ku wartościom. Elementy teorii i praktyki*, Wydawnictwo JEDNOŚĆ, Lublin- Kielce 2003, p. 30.

[12] Ibidem, p. 31.

[13] Cf.: I.Surina, K.Gajsanow, *Międzykulturowe wzajemne oddziaływanie jako sposób poznania obrazu świata,* [in:] J.Chaciński (ed.), *Pokój jako przedmiot międzykulturowej edukacji artystycznej*, Akademia Pomorska, Słupsk 2007, p.267-275.

as controlling parameters – enable the preservation of «boundaries» of lifeworld and its internal saturation[14].

Value orientations condition not only behaviour but also shape – on the basis of cognitive and emotive components – the perception of social reality beyond the lifeworld – that is during interaction with other ethnic groups. Value orientations may be variously directed in comparison with generally accepted direction. In this case – if the vector of orientation agrees with the generally accepted one – then in specific social conditions and under the influence of social influences there might transpire changes in the social life of youth. In the opposite case, in the presence of «specific orientations and values», it acts against changes of social life and might block them[15].

In the social world there are not only systems of values – variously directed according to their qualitative characterizations and orientation - but also specified by them normative foundations of the social world. The clash of variously directed orientations of the systems of values within the scope of sector of social expanse may lead to social contradicions or even conflicts. The common ground for such contradiction is a failure to accept values. Conformity and consensus within the systems of values may finally lead to a convergence or combination of evaluative foundations of the organisation of social life of various ethnic groups. Most accurately such a convergence can be observed in the social life of a young person in a polycultural (and especially different) cultural environment.

Student community can to the same extent reflect the fluctuation of the relations of "us" and "them" on the border of different evaluative systems and clearly show them. It is especially apparent in "break-through" periods of social development.

Ethnic values and "lifeworld" of students

Research concerning students' ethnic values in conditions of a multicultural community was rather thoroughly conducted in recent times – and it possesses its own specifics which was formed by changes in the system of multicultural relations as well as situation of ethnic student groups - especially in such conditions. This fact inspires the analysis of diverse aspects of the formation of national awareness, ethnic identity of specific student groups as well as the impact of ethnic values – firstly, on the adaptation process in multicultural environment, and secondly – on the degree of ethnic interaction.

[14] Cf.: I.Surina, K.Gajsanow, *Wartościująca organizacja „życiowego świata" wspólnoty etnicznej*, [in:] A.Klim-Klimaszewska, T.Zacharuk (ed.), *Konflikt pokoleń czy różnic cywilizacyjnych?* Część 3, Akademia Podlaska, Siedlce 2006, p. 127-134.

[15] И.А.Сурина, Ценности…op.cit., p.111.

Ethnic values are particularly important in a student community where they reflect in a certain way the presentation of "lifeworld". It is among students that "national" aspect in the course of contacts and mutual influence of individuals of different national and ethnic origins – in an ethnically alien environment assumes a form of a specific ethnic influence. Such a type of relations in the process of ethnic identification is most frequently reflected in the form of division into "us" and "them". In such an opposition the role of the system of values is especially important – along with the acceptance by an ethnic group of values and patterns of a local society. In a number of scientific studies it was observed that mutual ethnic interactions in an ethnically alien student environment are formed especially on the basis of specific stereotypes of thinking and behaving.

Ethnic values serve as an element of the national awareness integration, specify an individual's relation to the past, the present and the future of their nation, influence the formation of other values and are one of the factors specifying a method, manners and direction of behaviour. Apart from that ethnic values serve as a specific indicator of mutual interaction of various groups in a multicultural student environment.

Students of different ethnic groups in interpersonal relations assume attitudes of the so-called mutual ethnic influence. It consists in the construction of relations in the ethnic identification of the "us" – "them" type. In the process of socio-cultural adaptation, members of respective groups mutually accept new forms of action – but with an orientation towards the values of society in which they live. Relations constructed in such a fashion are conducive to forming mutual interest in the style of life and social norms – which, in turn, leads to a change of the "us" – "them" relation at a later stage.

It is also characteristic that within a student environment there are several hierarchally *embedded* systems of values. It is dependent on national traditions and on an awareness of one's own group's locality in an alien ethnic environment[16].

In an ethnic group's system of values one can observe a tendency not towards the change of values but rather their updating in the evaluative and orientational system. The content of the system of values will be different which indicates a subcultural distinctness and tightness of an ethnic group. One may refer to it as "lifeworld" of such a group. It is relatively stable and understandable only for "us" as it operates within conceptual systems specific to the given culture.

[16] Por.: И.А.Сурина, К.Р. Гайсанов, op.cit.

It is interesting to note that a viewpoint of an ethnic community functioning in "its own" cultural environment and living on "its own" territory is considerably narrow. Such a viewpoint expands significantly if an ethnic collective is situated in a multicultural environment. This is caused by intensive processes of cultural convergence – as the perception of the world in the first case is narrowed down to the boundaries of "one's own ethno-world", and, in the second – expanded by "experiencing one's own and alien cultural traditions". It is conducive to achieving success in the process of adaptation to a different socio-cultural situation.

Constructing similar worlds of social life of various national and ethnic groups possible on the basis of parallel living agreements as well as focal reflection of values and orientations towards them which are transmitted and passed over from generation to generation – for instance, in a family. Parents not only educate their children according to specific values but also transmit to them an image, style and normative foundations of life. On the basis of that requirements and demands for children are formed – so that they would act in accordance with accepted norms and proper family values. «Parental world» in a family forms within children not only stereotypes of behaviour but also images of thinking and the act of understanding the surrounding reality. It also establishes the evaluative and superior senses of real events specifying the boundaries of lifeworld and the pace of children's world. Those senses are transmitted by children in their own lifeworld and pace of the world in a given period of biography.

However, there cannot be identical lifeworlds. They can be similar in the respect of identical «core» of values and identically directed orientations towards them. Change in the organisation of lifeworld within the scope of a social expanse is possible on the basis of diffusion processes as a result of which a mutual exchange takes place as well as a distribution and introduction of («alien») values and orientations towards them, a change evaluative and superior senses of events in a given social reality. Diffusion processes may also take place between various lifeworlds as a result of their interaction and clashes.

One of important traits influencing the formation of the system of ethnic values is the mutual permeating of cultures of different generations within the scope of one family. On the basis of studies conducted among Polish students[17], the families of whom are multicultural it was observed that there are 24,5% of international marriages (father and mother are of different nationalities – it concerns both the second and third generations), in the case of 6,5 % of students one of parents is not Polish, in the case of 81,3 % of the polled students one parent

[17] Sociological research conducted in April-May of 2009 in Szczecin by a Polish-Russian research team.

was born in a former USSR state bordering with Poland (mostly Ukraine, Belarus and Lithuania) – and in the case of 18,7 % - a parent comes from the USA, Germany or China.

In the case of 18 % of the polled students – in the third generation the families are international. One of grandparents comes from the former USSR (77,3 % - Ukraine, Russia, Belarus and Lithuania), and in the case of the remaining 22,7 % - a grandmother or a grandparent comes from Germany, the USA, France, Bulgaria, Sweden and Austria.

The average age of students whose parents are an international marriage is 31 years – and whose grandparents are an international marriage – 28 years.

On the basis of the study results presented above, one could conclude that students whose families in different generations were or are multicultural have a more "enriched" (with elements of various cultures) system of values than other ones. They tend to be more tolerant and are better at adapting to the surrounding social environment – finding there their meaningful place. Students who come from multicultural families (as the second generation) and were born in Poland – completely identify with Poland and the Poles – also assuming their values. It might be caused also by a generation gap, a new face of their parent culture – but also, to an extent, by a willingness to open to socio-cultural changes.

Conclusion

Within the framework of the social system of values of the modern student community situated in a multi-cultural environment - there is a slightly different (in terms of hierarchy) system of values – including the ethnic ones. A given system lies at the foundation of ethnic interaction and is a sign of ethnic diversification of "us – them" as well as specifies to a large extent a direction of international value relations in a student environment.

Probably in such a way a conclusion is justified that ethnic groups of modern students situated in a multicultural environment and a different time sphere than their parents – form their own subculture which – to a large extent – specifies the generation gap of parents and children and also considerably transforms the image of "parent culture" and "lifeworld". On the other hand, multicultural mutual interactions in student communities create "lifeworld" and youth subculture which act as media of innovatory potential which is conducive to renewing traditional culture in the conditions of multi-style cultural system of the modern world.

Bibliography

Chałas K., *Wychowanie ku wartościom. Elementy teorii i praktyki*, Wydawnictwo JEDNOŚĆ, Lublin – Kielce 2003.

Ejsmant M., Kosmalska B., *Media, wartości, wychowanie.* Oficyna Wydawnicza „Impuls", Kraków 2005.

Habermas J., *Teoria działania komunikacyjnego*, PWN, Warszawa 1999.

Habermas J., *The Theory of Communicative Action*, Heinemann, London 1984.

Kłoskowska A., *Kultury narodowe u korzeni*, PWN, Warszawa 1996.

Surina I., Gajsanow K., *Międzykulturowe wzajemne oddziaływanie jako sposób poznania obrazu świata,* [w:] J.Chaciński (red.), *Pokój jako przedmiot międzykulturowej edukacji artystycznej*, Akademia Pomorska, Słupsk 2007.

Surina I., Gajsanow K., *Wartościująca organizacja „życiowego świata" wspólnoty etnicznej*, [w:] A.Klim-Klimaszewska, T.Zacharuk (red.), *Konflikt pokoleń czy różnic cywilizacyjnych?* Część 3, Akademia Podlaska, Siedlce 2006.

Арутюнян Ю.В., Дробижева Л.М., Сусоколов А.А., *Этносоциология*, Москва 1999.

Громов И.А., Мацкевич А.Ю., Семенов В.А., *Западная теоретическая социология*, Изд-во «Ольга», Санкт-Петербург 1996.

Ионин Л.Г., *Социология культуры*, Логос, Москва 1998.

Сурина И.А., Гайсанов К.Р., *Этнические ценности студенчества: сущность, структура и методы исследования,* Социум, Москва 1998.

Сурина И.А., *Ценности, ценностные ориентации, ценностное пространство*, Социум Москва 1999.

Henryk Porożyński
Pomeranian University in Słupsk, Poland

MULTICULTURALISM IN EDUCATION

Summary

The phenomenon of multiculturalism implies two kinds of objectives that education has been confronted with. The first has consisted of a set of tasks for the specific area of national minorities, while the second has been aimed at the implementation of tasks in society as a whole. The tasks of multicultural education, therefore, have arisen from the need to adapt education to the phenomenon of multiculturalism whereas intercultural education tasks has been concerned with upbringing towards multiculturalism, to meet its expectations. The opportunity to view the complexity of educational issues more broadly, including problems of schools and multicultural education, seems to be comparative studies, referring to psychological, sociological theories in addition to diverse political, social, cultural and economic contexts.

Introduction

Multiculturalism as a social phenomenon is a result of the same processes that lie at the roots of globalisation. The relation between multiculturalism and the Polish reality inspires discussions concerning not only the very essence of multiculturalism, but also consequences and challenges it gives birth to in diverse spheres of our life.

In Poland, one should currently take note of a significant activity of minority communities and their organisations as subjects of this policy. Activity on the part of those organisations, to a large extent, focuses on developing and preserving their own culture – but also their participation in the social and political life of the country. The state's contribution, on the other hand, primarily consists in the creation of convenient legal norms which enable activities of this type. Another significant aspect is making audiovisual media accessible to minorities – especially at the regional level. The domain of the state's activity is also education as most schools for ethnic minorities are public.

From the perspective of legal and ideological principles, there exists a certain vision of multiculturalism – relating to the Polish society as a whole. Both political practice and cultural diversification itself has – to a large extent – a regional character; in other words, in Poland, there are regions "less multicultural" or "more multicultural", and the latter type mostly concerns our ethnic and national borderlands. It is worthwhile to emphasize – after J.

Nikitorowicz – that intercultural education in Poland can only develop within the framework of regional education and that is should be regionally diversified[1].

In my study, I would like to outline principal problems the modern Polish education needs to face in the context of multiculturalism which is becoming a more and more significant factor in our society.

Multicultural education and intercultural education

Education is not only a subject of multicultural policy, but also an important element in the process of constructing its ideas. Intercultural or multicultural pedagogy, also practised in Poland, constitutes an element of multicultural ideology and contains directions for educational practice. One needs to remember, however, that education as an element of multicultural policy formulates its goals and tasks under the influence of multiculturalism as a social phenomenon.

The phenomenon of multiculturalism indicates two types of goals that are set forth in front of education. The first one specifies the scope of tasks for respective national minorities, namely, guaranteeing equal opportunities for members of society by their preparation for life in this society and teaching them the language and the culture of one's own ethnic group. The second goal involves the implementation of tasks in a society as a whole – enabling the contact between members of various ethnic groups, learning (especially on the part of the dominant group) about different cultures – and, by that – educating in the spirit of social tolerance and respect between national groups. Those tasks can be executed jointly or separately[2].

Various goals that multiculturalism assigns to education might prompt one to classify some of them as a part of multicultural education and the others – as a part of intercultural education. This distinction – although unclear and inseparable– partially refers to the same usage of those terms that pedagogy employs; intercultural education, however, is understood in a much wider sense than the multicultural one. This similarity of terminology can also be found in the fact that tasks of multicultural education result from the need to adapt the educational system to requirements of multiculturalism, and tasks of intercultural education consist in the education towards multiculturalism, learning to welcome it. A fundamental difference of the presented distinction in relation to the concept of education in educational activity lies in the fact that recognition of educational purposes is developed here from

[1] J. Nikitorowicz, *Pogranicze, tożsamość, edukacja międzykulturowa*, Białystok1995, p. 57.
[2] T. Lewowicki, E. Grodzka-Mazur, A. Szczurek-Boruta (ed.), *Edukacja międzykulturowa w Polsce i na świecie*, Katowice 2000, p. 18

sociological theories of multicultural society and only serves the sociological analysis of the issue of education in the context of multiculturalism[3].

The phenomenon of multiculturalism in educational practice on the example of ethnically varied areas of borderland

The above-mentioned functions and tasks of the educational system specify the scope of challenges faced by schools in the context of the phenomenon of multiculturalism. All these problems translated into school practice can be studied in a closer fashion while analysing the functioning of educational system in ethnically diversified areas of borderland.

The subject of educational policy regarding the functioning of an Ukrainian minority on an area near border is, above all, the state. An Ukrainian school (joined with a secondary school) which operates in Przemyśl, as well as eight other institutions in which, on an optional basis, Ukrainian language was introduced – has a status of a public institution. The second subject of this policy is The Association of Ukrainians in Poland. It runs two points teaching Ukrainian language; in addition, local circles of this association actively cooperate with certain public schools.

Educational system for national minorities primarily fulfills functions connected with multicultural education. The first of those functions might be described as integration-related as its goal is to prepare an individual for the life in society – in the process guaranteeing equality for all members of a minority group in a predominant community. The very concept of those facilities' operation enables the implementation of this goal. All schools with an optional Ukrainian language have the same syllabus as other primary or secondary schools and – what is crucial – all subjects are taught in Polish. Learning the native language and culture constitutes additional teaching content and so it does not happen at the cost of integration. Ukrainian communities in the south-east of Poland have already solved the dilemma facing the Poles in Ukraine. Certain Polish local communities in Ukraine are still discussing whether to create Polish schools with Polish as its teaching language or still have their teaching conducted in Ukrainian while further expanding their syllabus with elements of Polish culture, history and language[4].

The second goal for this type of schools is transmitting the native culture and language of one's national group. An ethnic function resulting from that is fulfilled by a school through

[3] T. Lewowicki (ed.), *Poczucie tożsamości narodowej młodzieży. Studium z pogranicza polsko- czeskiego*, Cieszyn 1994, p. 8.

[4] J. Nikitorowicz, *Młodzież pogranicza kulturowego Białorusi, Polski, Ukrainy wobec integracji europejskiej*, Białystok 2000, p. 77

conducting the teaching process in an ethnic language or merely providing language and ethnic culture lessons, nurturing ethnic traditions, observing national anniversaries and holidays. A degree of this goal's implementation is varied and dependent on numerous factors which are external to schools.

J. Nikitorowicz argues that this example of Polish-Ukrainian borderland indicates that multiculturalism poses really diverse challenges for educational system which deals with them with varied degrees of success – depending on a level of difficulty and a type of environment in which schools operates. However, the most difficult challenge posed by multiculturalism is education in the spirit of tolerance and transmitting knowledge concerning a culture of minority to a dominant group[5].

Another example of the operation of educational system on an ethnically varied area of borderland is Podbeskidzie – which covers the area of the southern Poland which lies on the border of two great regions: Silesia and Małopolska. Here, intercultural education does not constitute a separate subject at school but is one of rules and forms of activity in certain schools. Noble principles underlying this kind of education are implemented mainly in two dimensions: international and, above all, local.

In the first case, the most important form of educational activity comes down to exchange and cooperation of youth from various countries which fulfills the function of getting acquainted and understood on a mutual basis. In the second case, the subject of educational activity are occasional meetings, contacts of representatives of various cultures, religions – but with the preservation of one's "distinctiveness".

Intercultural communication as the foundation of crossing boundaries of one's culture

Such actions – in accordance with the theory of intercultural pedagogy – perceived in Germany as "the pedagogy of meeting cultures" come down to the fact that owing to the elimination of various barriers, but – a crucial matter – with the preservation of "distinction", there will transpire a cultural exchange between representatives of respective cultures which will lead to enriching both individuals' personality and entire cultures – while preserving their original identity.

---

[5] J. Nikitorowicz, *Edukacja regionalna, wielokulturowa i międzykulturowa*, [in:] *Demokracja a oświata, kształcenie i wychowanie.* Materiały z II Ogólnopolskiego Zjazdu Pedagogicznego, Toruń 1996, p. 35

M. Śliwiński argues that there are three categories of matters the knowledge of which is essential in all intercultural interactions: human emotions, knowledge concerning cultural differences and foundations of those differences[6].

According to M. Sobecki, when people from different cultures meet – they shall experience various emotions. They tend to feel anxiety, irritation caused by the fact that they will surprise one another with their actions. A cultural shock is a normal – though unpleasant -reaction in such circumstances. A danger lies in the fact that after perceiving a situation as unpleasant, people might become even more entrenched in their prejudice and misguided reactions. This is where an awareness of roots of cultural differences might prove useful – those basic causes behind manifested cultural differences. Humna personal development requires a benevolent attitude to people belonging to other cultures, their better understanding and realization concerning existing prejudices[7].

Intercultural communication is the basis of crossing the boundaries of one's own culture in order to become internally enriched and notice the need of cultural pluralism in the world. In such a fashion, education nurtures regional traditions, highlights them and enables treating one's culture as a part of the global culture – and, in the process, enriching it with elements that are related to it.

It should be indicated that in Podbeskidzie a strategy is being developed of intercultural education with a tendency to treat various minority groups in an equal fashion. Schools and other educational institutions do not merely limit themselves to developing in youth a sense of relation with their regional community – but also teach an open-minded approach regarding various cultures through the formation of a habit of constant dialogue and negotiation.

Significance of intercultural education in teaching youth

Introducing by schools elements of intercultural education increased in intensity at the beginning of the 90s of 20th century due to integration processes between Poland and the EU. Considerations regarding necessary changes in Polish schools resulting from processes of development and adaptation of Poland in Europe can be found in numerous pedagogical, sociological and psychological publications as well as in policy papers of the Ministry of National Education and the government. UNESCO and Club of Rome reports might also prove useful for this purpose. In those papers, an issue is raised of the Polish educational system's opening to exchange and international cooperation – as well as placing a larger emphasis on

---

[6] M. Śliwiński, *Świadomość narodowa, świadomość pogranicza*, „Kultura i Społeczeństwo" 1992, no 2, p. 44
[7] M. Sobecki, *Funkcja etniczno-kulturowa szkół mniejszości narodowych*, Białystok 1997, p.56

the preparation of pupils and students for further education and self-education, participation in activities in conditions of a highly developed technical civilization, confrontation of cultures and lifestyles, humanization of school as a social system[8].

Within an ideal of European education, there are, among others, the following ideals: educating in the spirit of religious, social, racial and political tolerance, open-minded attitude to others, exchange of information, friendship, dialogue, supporting others, learning foreign languages (as a condition to implement other slogans/values) as well as culture.

The modern youth has needs of a new variety. They arise as a result of a growing number of computers in Poland, an increase in the popularity of foreign languages, revolutionary opening of communication and exchange with the Western world (multi-channel television, internet, tourism). Nobody and nothing can stop the inflow of diverse patterns. Family, school, Church rapidly lose their influence to peer groups and mass media (the so-called socialization shift).

In the context of constant inflow of numerous offers, schools ought to develop qualifications enabling making wise and responsible axiological choices. Every human being is a separate subject functioning in a complex social reality – he is a citizen of a country, a member of numerous social groups (sometimes minorities), a neighbour, friend, consumer, manufacturer, creator and simultaneously a recipient of culture and intercultural relations. Schools – according to Z. Kwieciński – are institutions created for professionally conducted long-term training which teaches numerous skills, norms and conscious rules of proper coexistence in a society[9].

It would be naive to expect that intercultural education conducted in schools will eliminate inequalities of social, cultural, ethnic (etc) character. Such an assumption could be countered with at least three arguments. Firstly, this question should constitute a subject of concern for every citizen on whom lies a responsibility of work for the public good – and so education is a part of obligation for all of us. Secondly, our society started to believe in the power of education. Education enables achieving a success in life: economic, political and cultural ones. This argument relates to a conviction that an educated person would not suffer poverty and shall be a rightful member of our social and political system. This amply demonstrates that rational and pragmatic reasons are predominant in human behaviour. Thirdly, we live in a multicultural world and our educational system should take this aspect of reality into consideration. An environmental, ethnic and linguistic diversity of students – just like their

---

[8] S. Bednarek (red.), *Edukacja europejska w zreformowanej szkole*, Wrocław 2000, p. 74.
[9] Z. Kwieciński, *Edukacja wobec nadziei i zagrożeń współczesności*. III Polish Nation-wide Meeting of Educators, Poznań 1998, p. 8

differences in the skill level – is huge. In order to satisfy their educational needs, a teacher needs to consider intercultural education.

An analysis of forms of implementing intercultural education in schools of the borderland cannot be limited to learning the folklore of other nations, organizing shows of "fraternization" or presenting idealized images of various countries. This will not suffice in order to acquire skills of intercultural communication, accepting in everyday life cultural pluralism and inspiring motivation for enriching one's own personality through learning about various cultures. A participation in general culture requires one to experience one's own identity and enrich it through a direct contact with other people and a training which develops skills enabling cooperation with others[10].

In addition, one needs to realize that future societies shall be multicultural communities. Life and coexistence in such societies might be made possible by intercultural education which is characterized by striving to make diverse cultures permeate one another – simultaneously enriching the identity of one's own. Difficult local and global problems should help our society realize the necessity of surpassing the boundaries of one's own culture, taking up the goals of open education.

Conclusion

Polish experiences in the scope of intercultural education appear relatively insignificant. Therefore, it is advisable to take advantage of achievements made by societies which have implemented different types of this education for numerous years. In the context of our country, predominant issues are those existing in the borderland regions: Polish-Czech, Polish-Belarussian and Polish-Ukrainian. The issues studied in a majority of papers mostly refer to matters of multicultural identity, intercultural dialogue and its importance in regional education as an element of intercultural education, attitudes of youth regarding national, religious, cultural diversity, activity of schools and various organisations (concerning the issue of multiculturalism). A considerable interest was shown in problems that European education brings with it as well as the significance and role of the Churches in the process of shaping dialogue-type attitudes – open-minded towards diversity[11].

---

[10] D. Markowska, *Teoretyczne podstawy edukacji międzykulturowej*, „Kwartalnik Pedagogiczny" 1990, no 4, p. 66

[11] Cf.: H. Porożyński, *Polityka oświatowa Unii Europejskiej. Wyzwania edukacyjne dla Polski*, [in:] J. Kwapiszewski, H. Porożyński (ed.), *Wyzwania edukacyjne na progu wejścia Polski do Unii Europejskiej*, Słupsk 2004, p.33-35; the same: *Europejski model edukacji*, [in:] M. Żurawska, A. Łukasik (ed.), *Szkoła w nurcie koncepcji badań i doświadczeń*, Toruń 2008, p. 11-12; J. Hauziński, H. Porożyński, *Założenia współczesnej reformy szkolnej w Polsce*, [in:] J. Prokop (ed.), *Kotazkam srovnavaci pedagogiky*, Praha 2003, p. 161

An opportunity for a wider perspective concerning complex educational issues – including problems of school and multicultural (intercultural) education – appears to be offered by comparative studies drawing from psychological, sociological (etc) theories as well as considerably varied political, social, cultural and economic contexts. Such an approach might be found, among others, in studies by T. Lewowicki, Z. Kwieciński, J. Nikitorowicz and H. Porożyński[12].

The above-mentioned considerations are, obviously, not exhaustive in their analysis of problems related to multiculturalism as a challenge for Polish education – nor do they present an exact image of the state of research and its perspective of this complex problem. To conclude, however, one should indicate (after Z. Kwieciński) that in a discussion regarding the model of Polish education, it is very important to find balance between wise integration with the culture of the West and endeavours to preserve the Polish identity and prevent us from neocolonization. It is still uncertain to what extent a contact with diverse foreign influences and distinctiveness (cultural or linguistic) is dangerous to national or cultural identity – and to what extent it leads to close cultural relations[13]. What type of education should be conducted then, what majors/directions need to be promoted? A question remains relevant whether in the context of a struggle between two tendencies – one which aims to blur differences and is favourable to creating global community, and the other based on values specific to local and national societies, it is possible to form a new model of school combining advantages of both tendencies. It is probably safe to assume, however, that the implementation of the idea of intercultural education is – and will be – dependent on initiatives undertaken in schools, local communities, as well as activities on the part of various associations and persons understanding an underlying sense of such education.

Bibliography

Bednarek S. (red.), *Edukacja europejska w zreformowanej szkole*, Wrocław 2000.

Hauziński J., Porożyński H., *Założenia współczesnej reformy szkolnej w Polsce,* [w:] J. Prokop (red.), *K otazkam srovnavaci pedagogiky,* Praha 2003.

Kwieciński Z., *Edukacja wobec nadziei i zagrożeń współczesności. III Ogólnopolski Zjazd Pedagogów,* Poznań 1998.

[12] H. Porożyński, *Polykulturalität im Polen der Zwischenkriegszeit und Heute – eine pädagogische Herausforderung,* „Humanisierung der Bildung“ Jahrbuch 2001 der Internationalen Akademie zur Humanisierung der Bildung, Herausgegeben von Reinhard Golz und Rudolf W. Keck, Frankfurt am Main 2001, p. 187.

[13] Z. Kwieciński, *Edukacja wobec nadziei* … op.cit., p. 8

Lewowicki T. (red.), *Poczucie tożsamości narodowej młodzieży. Studium z pogranicza polsko- czeskiego,* Cieszyn 1994.

Lewowicki T., Grodzka-Mazur E., Szczurek-Boruta A. (red.), *Edukacja międzykulturowa w Polsce i na świecie,* Katowice 2000.

Markowska D., *Teoretyczne podstawy edukacji międzykulturowej,* „Kwartalnik Pedagogiczny" 1990, nr 4.

Nikitorowicz J., *Edukacja regionalna, wielokulturowa i międzykulturowa,* [w:] *Demokracja a oświata, kształcenie i wychowanie. Materiały z II Ogólnopolskiego Zjazdu Pedagogicznego,* Toruń 1996.

Nikitorowicz J., *Młodzież pogranicza kulturowego Białorusi, Polski, Ukrainy wobec integracji europejskiej,* Białystok 2000.

Nikitorowicz J., *Pogranicze, tożsamość, edukacja międzykulturowa,* Białystok 1995.

Porożyński H., *Europejski model edukacji,* [w:] M. Żurawska, A. Łukasik (red.), *Szkoła w nurcie koncepcji badań i doświadczeń,* Toruń 2008.

Porożyński H., *Polityka oświatowa Unii Europejskiej. Wyzwania edukacyjne dla Polski,* [w:] J. Kwapiszewski, H. Porożyński (red.), *Wyzwania edukacyjne na progu wejścia Polski do Unii Europejskiej,* Słupsk 2004.

Porożyński H., *Polykulturalität im Polen der Zwischenkriegszeit und Heute – eine pädagogische Herausforderung, „Humanisierung der Bildung" Jahrbuch 2001 der Internationalen Akademie zur Humanisierung der Bildung,* Herausgegeben von Reinhard Golz und Rudolf W. Keck, Frankfurt am Main 2001.

Sobecki M., *Funkcja etniczno-kulturowa szkół mniejszości narodowych,* Białystok 1997.

Śliwiński M., *Świadomość narodowa, świadomość pogranicza,* „Kultura i Społeczeństwo" 1992, nr 2.

SECTION II

TEACHER AND STUDENT IN THE EXPANSE OF THE MODERN SCHOOL

Ewa Murawska
Pomeranian University in Słupsk, Poland

IN BETWEEN THE TRAP OF STEREOTYPES AND THE ATTEMPT OF BREAKING THEM. CONSIDERATIONS FOCUSED ON EDUCATIONAL STEREOTYPES

Summary

Stereotypes describe reality in a simplified and overly shortened manner. They do not have to – and, indeed, rarely happen to be – accurate, fair and justified. In the field of science they are consolidated by numerous publications and, through the educational process, passed on to the next generations. The information provided for individuals is filtered by the stereotypes existing in the expanse of their linguistic code and consciousness. The power of stereotypes does not only rely on the fact that they are "immune" to changes, but – above all – on the fact that they influence man's decision-making processes. They fulfill the role of satisfying human need for safety, facilitate the process of developing the individual identity and are conducive to the development of the group identity.

Stereotype – exemplification of the concept

On the basis of emotions and experiences, simplified and generalizing convictions are created due to which we develop a specific attitude towards people and social groups. Stereotype (gr. *stereotype; stereos* - hard, *typos* - pattern, imprint), then, is a simplified generalization concerning a certain group of people – ascribing to them identical traits in accordance with a given prejudice on the part of a given person[1]. To refer to its definition – "stereotype is a simplified, schematic view of people, groups and social relations created on the basis of incomplete or false knowledge about the world perpetuated by tradition and difficult to change"[2].

Stereotype usually has a verbal character and constitutes a certain generalization regarding a group in the scope of which identical characterizations are ascribed to all its members, regardless of real life differences between them. The essence of stereotype is its permanence. It is a pattern – or its component – a cognitive structure resistant to any changes. Stereotypes are mutually compatible – which means that they have a tendency to combine

[1] E. Aronson, *Człowiek istota społeczna.* PWN, Warszawa 2004, p. 454.
[2] B. Petrozolin – Skowrońska (red.), *Encyklopedia powszechna*, PWN, Warszawa 1996, p. 811.

within wider contexts, for example, emphasizing certain characteristic traits – out of which each is a specific stereotype – leads to stereotypification[3].

Another view of stereotype is that it is "a thought construct, usually typical among members of a given social group and based on a schematic and simplified perception of reality (social or cultural phenomena or a certain category of people) with a certain evaluative angle, frequently based on prejudice and incomplete knowledge"[4]. Stereotypes are both individual (they express personal beliefs concerning traits and properties of a certain subject) and collective in character – they can be formed by sets of beliefs and information related to convictions and expectations towards specific groups of people shared by members of a given society. Stereotypes rooted in a certain culture are transmitted from generation to generation in the process of socialization. They form areas of "common knowledge" which exerts a specific influence on behaviour and attitudes of community members towards stereotypified persons. Although social sterotypes usually concern racial, ethnic, sexual and professional groups – they may also encompass all categories of people – for example, classified on the basis of their place of residence, external appearance, age etc.[5]

The term of a stereotype, used in 1798 by a French printer named Didot, originally referred to a description of a manner of printing using ready, fixed plates – instead of single, movable types. At the end of 19th century this term began to be used by psychiatrists in reference to unchanging, compulsively repeated manners of patients' expression. Also I. P. Pavlov, a Russian physiologist, stressed the compulsiveness of behaviour related to stereotype which – in his view – documented fluidity of boundaries between a normal state and pathology[6]. Those definitions probably became the basis for the eventual formulation (in 1922 by W. Lippmann) of the definition of stereotype to describe human tendency to describe people or objects as similar/having similar attributes on the basis of their common traits. According to Lippmann, all of us have "mental images" of the external world. They resemble templates owing to which we are able to simplify frequently ambiguous information reaching us from our surroundings. The genesis of the stereotypization process – argues Lippmann – consists in our acceptance of what had previously been defined by culture. Stereotypes tell us what portion of social information we encounter needs to be noticed and which should be ignored. This process further establishes (usually) already existing stereotypes through focusing on

---

[3] Cf.: K. Serwin-Jakubowska, *Podstawy psychologii społecznej.* Oficyna Wydawnicza Politechniki Warszawskiej, Warszawa 2006, p. 29-30.

[4] D. Pankowska, *Wychowanie a role płciowe,* Gdańskie Wydawnictwo Psychologiczne, Gdańsk 2005, p.19.

[5] Ibidem.

[6] Quoted after: H. Pietrzak, *Następstwa i efekty stereotypowego postrzegania człowieka i świata społecznego.* Wydawnictwo Wyższej Szkoły Pedagogicznej, Rzeszów 2000, p. 13.

information which is compatible with stereotypes and rejecting all impulses that do not agree with them[7].

A stereotype is automatically transmitted in the course of the socialization process and most frequently has no common points with experience of a given person. It is perpetuated through the process of social learning[8].

Stereotypes are determined by numerous factors. They are formed as a result of combined influences of many different mechanisms and, therefore, they can reflect mutually connected impacts of diverse processes. While researching the nature of those mechanisms and their functioning – the usual focus were specific, isolated processes. A particular role in stereotype formation is played by cognitive, affective, socio-motivational and cultural processes. Cognitive mechanisms which are involved in the formation of stereotypes are: categorization, failure of correspondence, apparent correlation as well as diversifying perception of groups[9].

- Categorization

Categorization is an inseparable aspect of human cognitive processes. In every second in our immediate surrounding there are hundreds and maybe even thousands of impulses. If we were to analyse each of them in a detailed fashion – in order to grasp the nature and function of a given impulse – we would end up achieving nothing at all. Instead, we gradually study various impulses, which are then combined in groups on the basis of their common traits, attributes or functions. In a short period of time we learn the skill of categorization to such an extent that the process itself becomes automatic, relieving our attention capabilities and, at the same time, allowing us to focus on new impulses appearing in our surroundings or on tasks we are accomplishing at a given moment. Categorization helps to reduce the complexity of impulses which flow from the social environment[10].

A basic manner in which we categorize others is a division into people that resemble us and those who are different. Although we can categorize others on the basis of any real or perceived trait – usually we resort to the fastest and easiest available ways of categorization. We employ categories such as race, gender or age. Stereotypes we use in relation to a given person or those distorting the influence of this initial categorization are frequently determined by accidental factors – and our way of categorizing others (for example, on the basis of social

[7] Cf.: T. D. Nelson, *Psychologia uprzedzeń*. Gdańskie Wydawnictwo Psychologiczne, Gdańsk 2003, p. 25.
[8] K. Serwin-Jakubowska, *Podstawy psychologii ... op.cit.*, p. 31.
[9] C. N. Macrae, Ch. Stangor, M. Hewstone, *Stereotypy i uprzedzenia. Najnowsze ujęcie*. Gdańskie Wydawnictwo Psychologiczne, Gdańsk 1999, p. 41.
[10] T. D. Nelson, *Psychologia uprzedzeń... op.cit.*, p. 42-43.

role, gender, race or profession) is determined by matching the categories we chose to the knowledge that is currently available in our memory. Another important factor influencing a perception of another person is the relations he or she has with the observer in a given social context. Categorization facilitates formulating stereotypes concerning other people. If we consider a group of people as a part of a certain category on the basis of their certain properties (for example, because they are all women), then we begin to make assumptions or guesses: since all of them share one trait - that probably means they are similar in many other respects as well[11].

- Failure of correspondence

One of the reasons behind appearing distortions of social perception is a tendency to see behaviour of an actor as remaining in accordance with his inner nature – even if one can easily observe limitations placed by social roles or requirements. It might, therefore, be concluded that observers tend to make assumptions on the basis of such behaviour. A failure of correspondence is a particularly significant mechanism in the process of stereotype acquisition since it is connected to a spontaneous process of making assumptions about dispositional traits, and stereotypes are related to perceiving groups through a prism of such attributes[12].

- Apparent correlation and diversifying perception of groups.

People strongly respond to impulses which are distinctive in their environment – we tend to notice strange and unusual things; however, this phenomenon does not stop there. Such responsiveness also encompasses sensitivity to certain impulses simply because they occur relatively seldom. Very frequently we notice and pay attention to events just because they do not happen on a regular basis. An apparent correlation is a belief on the part of a given observer that there is a connection between two variables in a situation where information which this belief is based on does not provide sufficient reasons to prove such a connection. Usually, an observer notices a relation which was not included in the piece of information he was presented with - an apparent correlation – and such an association might appear as a result of an arbitrary focus on distinctive impulses. Regardless what kind of mechanism lies at the foundation of the phenomenon of correlation, as a result of this process – despite the pieces of information concerning two groups being potentially tantamount – the studied persons saw those groups in different fashions. Differences in evaluative perception of both groups are not based on any real properties of the obtained information, but constitute a consequence of a common trait of our information processing mechanisms. A failure of an apparent

[11] Ibidem, p. 43-44.
[12] C.N. Macrae, Ch. Stangor, M. Hewstone, *Stereotypy i uprzedzenia... op.cit.,* p. 45-46.

correlation might be the first independent foundation element for the development of a stereotype since the process of stereotypization requires the initial diversifying perception of groups[13].

Affective mechanisms which are involved in the formation of stereotypes

Despite the fact that the perceptions of a stereotype tend to be of purely cognitive character – it is obvious that people frequently experience strong feelings and emotions (especially when they are the focus of attention). Affective reactions appear to be particularly important in one's early views of social groups.

In accordance with the traditional perception of stereotypes within the framework of social psychology, they are cognitive structures, in other words – systems of beliefs concerning properties of groups and their members. If a given group or an individual is able to inspire emotional reactions in an observer, it happens mainly because those affective reactions were combined with beliefs regarding a given group. Affect is so inseparably connected with perceiving groups that it constitutes an integral part of the process of stereotype formation[14].

Affect is frequently controlled by a number of various mechanisms which might participate in the creation of stereotypes. One of such mechanisms is the process of classical conditioning of stereotypical emotions. This conditioning takes place when a person or object which is frequently associated with a specific emotion – eventually begins to inspire this emotion. As a result of this process, repeated experiencing of this emotion in a situation of group activization might be transferred onto this group. As a consequence of classical conditioning, seeing members of this group, information heard about it – or even a mere thought about it - is able to inspire anxiety, fear or anger which were initially activated by an emotional experience. At first, only experiences related to a given group are negative – at the end it is the group itself that appears negative. The second affective mechanism is the phenomenon of exposition. Certain studies prove that a frequent and natural exposition to an impulse enhances positive attitudes towards this impulse. Such a mechanism contributes to the formation of positive stereotypes – especially regarding members of one's own group whom we frequently meet[15].

Socio-motivational mechanisms and their impact on the creation of stereotypes

Negative stereotypes regarding other social groups are frequently created as a result of an individual's need or striving to deal with a certain internal conflict, dissatisfaction or a

[13] Ibidem, p. 47-49.
[14] Ibidem, p. 49-50.
[15] Ibidem, p. 50-51.

sense of threat. According to modern theoretical theories regarding functions – and, at the same time, stereotype formation – a thesis is promoted that opinions of a given person regarding other groups are partly determined by his or her needs and aspirations (motivational mechanisms). Stereotypes regarding groups result from the perceived relative status of a given group in relation to other groups as well as its reactions to this status. The way in which one's own group is perceived in relation to other important groups is considered as one of crucial motivational factors in the process of stereotype formation[16].

Researching intergroup relations is hugely influenced by the theory of social identity according to which people's group classification influences their self-evaluation and this is why individuals demonstrate motivation to achieve and preserve positive social identity, which has its roots in the groups they belong to. In view of this theory, even the fact of belonging to a temporary group might ensure for an individual a positive social identity – if such a group can be considered a superior one to remaining alternatives. Regarding stereotype formation, mechanisms related to social identity constitute a source of motivation to ascribe positive traits to one's own group and negative ones – to an alien one. It could reflect a motivation to positively perceive groups which a given person is connected with (or a positive distinction of one's own group among other groups)[17].

Participation of cultural mechanisms in stereotype formation

Participation in a given culture involves learning and accepting beliefs of a given culture regarding its own and other groups. Stereotypical perceptions regarding groups are frequently socially transmitted and acquired in their final form.

The first and the most powerful source of information regarding other social groups are parents. A huge role is also played by peers and other members of the social environment. Those influential figures do not need to transmit those stereotypes in a direct fashion, although it frequently happens in this manner. A child also learns stereotypes through observation and imitation – listening to offensive labels ascribed to various groups or degrading jokes that result in bursts of laughter, conforming to rules observed in one's family which forbid playing with those "other" kids, growing up with a conviction that discriminated groups deserve their fate.

Another – after parents and peers – crucial transmitter of cultural stereotypes is mass media. Expression of group norms in art, literature, drama and film both reflects and transmits

---

[16] Ibidem, p. 53.
[17] Ibidem.

stereotypes deeply-rooted in a given culture. Media images might exert an even stronger influence on beliefs regarding other groups than our own. Research proves that people spending considerable amount of time in front of their TV sets most frequently see the content of television programmes as a true depiction of the real state of things[18].

The socially transmitted stereotypes usually constitute a reflection of social norms – universally accepted ways of thinking, feeling and acting which people belonging to a given group unanimously consider proper and just. From this point of view, acquisition of stereotypes could be perceived as conformity in relation to social norms[19]. It frequently happens that external appearance is the basis for stereotype formation and most of stereotypified groups could be distinguished precisely on the basis of their external appearance[20].

A very important aspect of stereotypization is the specific content of group stereotypes. We will be unable to understand group stereotypes if we fail to learn who is classified within a given category and the reason behind it, as well as what attributes are involved - and why they are associated with different categories. In classifying someone as a part of a given category, a considerable role is played by the external appearance of a given classified individual. The most important categorization determinants are physical indications of age and gender – as well as noticeable impulse properties which are a source of socially useful information. Specific content of group stereotypes might originate partly from tendencies for overgeneralizations of real information regarding mental traits which can be provided by external appearance[21].

Based on the ecological approach to visual perception created by Gibson, the ecological attitude to stereotypization results from this fundamental assumption that noticeable impulse properties in the manner of walking, tone of voice and facial expression of a given person provide socially useful information. Impulse properties that provide this information are usually configurational and dynamic, owing to which they constitute a far richer source of information than verbal category labels employed in most traditional studies regarding stereotypization. Those noticeable properties reveal behavioral potential created by a given person. As a result of noticeable traits common for members of a given group, there might appear char-

---

[18] Ibidem, p. 58-60.
[19] Ibidem, p. 60-61.
[20] Ethnic and racial groups differ on the basis of appearance – just like men and women – or elderly and young people. Stereotypes of certain groups are based exclusively on their appearance – attractive, obese, short, redhaired. Even professional and social groups may differ on the basis of appearance – frequently by their own choice; Cf. the same source, ibidem, p. 66.
[21] Ibidem, p. 67-68.

acteristic behavioral possibilities in respective social groups – in other words, group stereotypes. Therefore, it would seem that appearance by itself might determine stereotype content[22].

In accordance with the ecological approach, intergroup differences (classified according to stereotype content) reflect group differences between noticeable differences and, very frequently, are accurate. This results from this theory's assumption that social perception fulfills adaptational function – either for the preservation of the species or for achieving personal goals. Explaining incorrect observations (like certain stereotypes), the evolutional theory makes the assumption that errors might be ascribed to overgeneralization of observations that are usually accurate and adaptational. Social attributes accurately indicated by functionally crucial external features – such as signs of age, emotional state, health, species and individual identity – due to overgeneralization might be ascribed to those whose external appearance resembles a specific age bracket, emotional and health state, species classification or a given individual. In the process of characterization, external features are usually referred to in the first order. A tendency to begin a description with external appearance takes place even when people are asked to describe someone – in order to help in imagining emotions provoked by remaining in the company of a given person. Such a prevalence of external appearance in descriptions of other people appears very early – and little children base their view of a given person almost solely on the properties of appearance. External appearance is a distinctive aspect of social perception and people are very competent at recognizing human faces. There is a connection between facial features and assumptions made regarding an individual's personality. Physically similar people are also perceived as ones who have similar personalities, while those who are physically different – are believed to be different in terms of character as well. Human faces influence the perception of their motives and personality traits. This influence reflects not only racial, sexual or age stereotypes. Appearance might have an impact on assumptions made in the sphere of personality traits – without exerting any influence on categorization. Distinctive external features have a particularly strong influence: assumptions regarding people possessing such features are more extreme and susceptible to apparent correlation which might contribute to the formation of negative and extreme stereotypes (for example, regarding minority groups), but also influence the content of group stereotypes[23].

[22] I refer to: ibidem, p. 68.
[23] Ibidem, p. 71-74.

Types, functions and applications of stereotypes

A stereotype resembles an attitude – in other words, a general assessment of a given object. Traditionally, there are three components of an attitude: behavioral, affective and cognitive. Hence, stereotypes are defined as intergroup attitudes which consist of three components. Stereotypes are equivalent to the cognitive component of intergroup attitudes. The two remaining components of these attitudes – affect and behaviour - respectively refer to prejudice and discrimination. Prejudice is a biased assessment of a given group based on real or imagined properties of its members. Discrimination, on the other hand, is a negative behaviour towards a certain individual based on a group classification[24]. Stereotypes are strongly related to prejudice and discrimination. Focusing one's thoughts on a specific group automatically brings out this group's cognitive pattern including stereotypes, affect and behavioral inclinations towards members of this group. It is related to a thesis that intergroup attitude consists of convictions, evaluations and behaviours regarding a given group[25]. The traditional concept of stereotypes, prejudice and discrimination suggests a relatively simple relation between those phenomena. If stereotypes relate to the cognitive aspect of prejudice, one could expect that a stronger stereotypization will be connected with an increase of prejudice. Stereotypes constitute attributes of negative traits as prejudice is defined as a negative phenomenon. Therefore, on the basis of prejudice it is possible to directly anticipate negative discrimination[26].

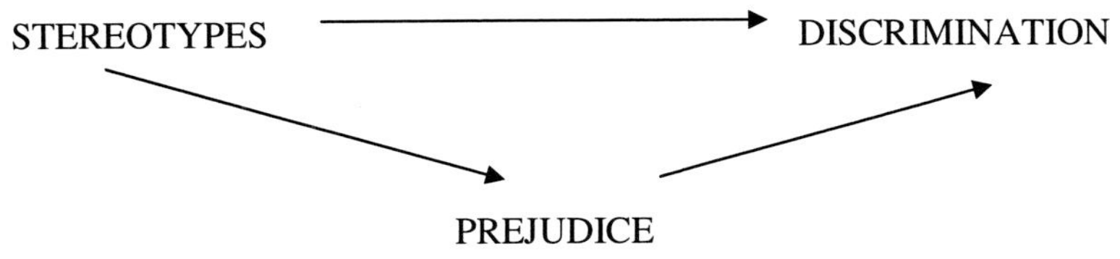

Chart 1. Possible relations between stereotypes, prejudice and discrimination
Source: Macrae C. N., Stangor Ch., Hewstone M., *Stereotypy i uprzedzenia. Najnowsze ujęcie.* Gdańskie Wydawnictwo Psychologiczne, Gdańsk 1995, p. 232.

Every stereotype consists of two layers. They are:

- the content layer – it is a cognitive component (beliefs, opinions, observations);
- the emotional layer – this component is evaluative and emotional (associations resulting from feelings)[27].

[24] T. D. Nelson, *Psychologia uprzedzeń... op.cit.,* p. 28.
[25] Ibidem, p. 34.
[26] Ibidem, p. 232.
[27] K. Serwin-Jakubowska, *Podstawy psychologii społecznej*, Oficyna Wydawnicza Politechniki Warszawskiej, Warszawa 2006, p. 31.

For most of people, a stereotype signifies negative properties associated with a given group of people (for example, a group characterized by undesirable traits such as laziness); in addition, most of us know more negative than positive stereotypes concerning various groups[28].

Two kinds of stereotypes are distinguished:

- the adaptive kind – when we create a certain stereotype intending to use an already existing network of stereotypes;
- the non-adaptive kind – when we create new stereotypes, different from the already existing ones in the society we live in and this is why it is difficult for us to adapt[29].

The main functions of stereotypes according to K. Serwin-Jakubowskiej are:

- economisation of reality – when reality becomes more accessible, it is easier to form judgements regarding the world and other people;
- providing a sense of security – we know in advance how to approach a given person; we are able to say how our stereotype will look regarding a specific issue/this person;
- fulfilling a communicative function – in other words, by employing a certain stereotype we communicate with the world, other people;
- channeling aggression – for instance, subcultural slogans of specific groups (discharging negative emotions in solidarity);
- helping to manipulate people[30].

Therefore, we can talk about two approaches towards stereotypes, namely:

- the individual approach
- the collective approach.

The individual approach towards a stereotypical representation is formulated on a microanalytical level and specifies cognitive systems which enable an individual to effectively store and use stereotypes. The main principle of the individual approach is that, in the course of time, people tend to develop beliefs regarding features of important social groups in their environment – and this knowledge influences their reactions regarding representatives of those groups. Stereotypes, as a type of knowledge regarding social world, are created during a process in which a given person is collecting knowledge concerning his or her environment. Such collected information regarding social groups is interpreted, encoded in memory and later brought out and used in controlling reactions. As mental representations of the world –

---

[28] Cf. T. D. Nelson, *Psychologia uprzedzeń... op.cit.*

[29] K. Serwin-Jakubowska, *Podstawy psychologii... op.cit.*, p. 30.

[30] Ibidem, p. 29-31.

stereotypes influence what type of information concerning members of different social groups is sought by a given person and also – what type of information he or she notices and memorizes. They also exert influence on his or her social behaviour. In the individual approach, it is assumed that the process of learning and a potential change of stereotypes are, above all, a result of acquisition by an individual of information through a direct contact with members of other social groups. In each stereotype, there is "a grain of truth" - but it might be subject to exaggeration as a result of the process of information transformation[31].

The collective approach to stereotypes is wider than the individual one in terms of scope. In this approach, the society constitutes the foundation of stored knowledge and stereotypes are considered as collections of information (spread among members of a given culture) regarding social groups. In this perception, stereotypes – although they exist in the minds of recipients belonging to a given community – constitute a part of the very structure of the society. Stereotypes common for a given society constitute one aspect of the collective knowledge of its members – encompassing customs, myths, ideas, religious systems and scientific knowledge. The individual approach focuses on stereotype acquisition through direct interactions with others and the collective approach takes into consideration the methods of stereotype learning as well as its transmitting and changing by intermediary sources – for example, information obtained from parents, teachers, political and religious leaders, as well as this acquired from mass media[32].

Stereotypes might fulfill numerous functions – out of which the most important are[33]:

- adaptation (providing a sense of cognitive control over social situations);
- defence and fear reduction (improvement of self-esteem, especially if we subject a positive stereotype of ourselves to a confrontation with a negative stereotype of Others);
- indicating differences between dominant and minority groups;
- defending the values of one's own group to prevent the acquisition of "foreign" values (one's own group consists of people closest to an individual or individuals in the presence of whom they feel safe and comfortable; the foreign group, on the other hand, consists of people excluded from the circle of one's own group, people that are not to be trusted, but avoided);
- channeling aggression and justifying violence against others;

[31] C. N. Macrae, Ch. Stangor, M. Hewstone, *Stereotypy i uprzedzenia... op.cit.,* p. 15-16.
[32] Ibidem, p. 20.
[33] J. Ambrosewicz-Jacobs, *Tolerancja. Jak uczyć siebie i innych.* Wyd. Stowarzyszenie Willa Decjusza, Kraków 2004, p. 33.

- making sure we are able to anticipate human behaviour;
- communication;
- manipulation;
- politics and propaganda.

While analysing functions of stereotypes, we can also discuss epistemological functions as well as stereotype functions related to self-esteem.

- Epistemological functions of stereotypes

One of the fundamental human motives is striving for learning, understanding and making predictions regarding others; the most crucial function of stereotypes is providing useful information about others. At the individual level, stereotypes are a useful tool – helpful in making evaluations, both inductive and deductive in nature. People constantly meet new persons they know very little about – save for their membership of a given social category. Therefore, they use this particular knowledge for making assumptions regarding dispositional traits of a newly met person. In other cases, people notice behaviour of others using this knowledge in connection with their stereotypes in order to establish affiliation of the observed individuals with specific categories. Also at the collective level stereotypes serve as the basis for obtaining a more accurate perception of social events. These explanations provide information and structure where before there was only ignorance and chaos. Stereotypes at the individual level frequently organize cognitive representations of the world and at the social level they simplify communication – enabling people to limit the number of words they use during conversations concerning others and with others.

Collectives frequently use stereotypes in situations of crisis – such as a war, economic recession or natural disasters, in order to reduce potential ambiguities, suppress resistance or establish a clear collection of behavioral norms. Very frequently, stereotypes also serve the function of rationalization or justification of current economic and political conditions. Just as individuals justify suffering of others by denying the value of suffering people – so collectives justify, through stereotypes, actions regarding other groups that in a different context would be unjust or reprehensible. Stereotypes allow societies to justify not only collective actions - but also failing to implement them. Privileged groups which feel that the system unjustly provides them with special rights and awards might justify their privileged status through attributing failures of others to their innate weaknesses of character. If enslaved, persecuted and oppressed populations are perceived through the prism of negative stereotypes, such beliefs might justify collective indifference of those responsible for this oppression and persecution[34].

- Stereotype functions related to self-esteem

In order to function effectively, a human being needs positive thinking both regarding themselves and the group he or she belongs to. Stereotypes could be perceived from the point of view of their connection with the need to maintain a positive self-assessment or self-esteem. Temporary threats to one's own value inspire stronger stereotypical reactions and prejudice within an individual. One could make a hypothesis that stereotypes are developed to a larger extent if they satisfy basic functions of increasing one's self-esteem. While analysing the relation between one's own self-esteem and the functioning of stereotypes at the level of groups and collectives, an assumption was made that if an individual underestimates the value of other groups or favours one's own – as a result, his or her own's relative status is increased, which, in turn, increases his or her own opinion of themselves. Through underestimating the value of other groups or favouring one's own – a given person can also maintain standards observed in a respective culture which is believed to be one of the fundamental sources of a high self-esteem. What results from both of those assumptions is the fact that feelings of individuals regarding themselves are dependent on their group or collective self-evaluation or on other collective values. Such collective self-esteem is connected to aspects of group identity shared by members of a given group – which have the function of increasing individual self-esteem. It appears to exert a considerable influence on favouring one's own group. Obtaining the acceptance of people with authority is also an important means of obtaining a positive self-esteem. This need of social acceptance is a crucial motivational factor which lies at the roots of both individual and collective activities. Having and expressing previously culturally accepted stereotypes of other groups, people are able to more easily obtain the acceptance of the remaining members of the group. Every person who fails to understand stereotypes and emotions can be considered as foreign to a given culture. On the other hand, by behaving towards members of other groups in a stereotypical manner – an individual expresses his or her own group identity and, because of that, they have a larger likelihood of being awarded in the form of acceptance by one's own group[35].

Very frequently, stereotypes influence the way we perceive other people – and lead to the phenomenon of stereotypization (expressed by observations and judgements regarding

[34] Ibidem, p. 30-32.
[35] Ibidem, p. 32-34.

specific individuals). Based on the way we perceive specific individuals or groups of people, we can distinguish diverse kinds of stereotypes[36]:

- racial;
- ethnic (national);
- sexual (sexism, depreciation of one of the sexes);
- religious;
- professional;
- social (for example, the homeless, homosexuals, drug addicts etc.)

Teacher "surrounded with stereotypes"

We cannot discuss stereotypes in separation from social reality. Educational stereotypes are simplified generalizations functioning in a society which concern the process of teaching, educating, school, students and teachers – everything which, directly or indirectly, is related to schools and education[37].

Among educational stereotypes, one can distinguish general and detailed ones. General educational stereotypes lie at the roots of both pedagogy and the world in which it operates. General stereotypes are perceived in a philosophical fashion as ones that were formed at the basis of the world's structure. It is on the level of those stereotypes that we can analyse the issue of stereotypicality in pedagogy. Detailed stereotypes are, above all, about the dominance – most frequent occurrence – of the emotional factor in thinking, acting and every specific situation. They mostly concern specific educational situations perceived in a schematic fashion[38].

Stereotype formation in thinking about the educational process is a result of at least three factors[39]. **The first factor** is the ideologization of pedagogy itself. The knowledge concerning teaching and educating young generations has always – to a lesser or larger extent – been subordinated to the interest of authorities which tried to exert a maximum influence on education in order to ensure the maximum control of society. Conditions were created for stereotype formation, both among those who constructed the theory and those who used it in practice. **The second factor** which facilitates the creation of stereotypes was – and remains to be – the scientific dimension of pedagogy, in other words, the requirement of using a consistent, uniform method during studies concerning the educating process. The acceptance of

[36] K. Serwin-Jakubowska, *Podstawy psychologii ... op.cit.*, p. 31.
[37] Cf.: P. Śmidoda, A. Tońska, C. Tyborska, *Stereotypy pedagogiczne. Próba przezwyciężenia negatywnego myślenia o stereotypach.* [in:] Wydawnictwo Uczelniane Wyższej Szkoły Pedagogicznej, Bydgoszcz 1996, p. 69.
[38] Ibidem, p. 70
[39] Based on: H. Pietrzak, *Następstwa i efekty... op.cit.*, p. 16-17.

knowledge acquired through a scientific method as the only acceptable and unquestionable truth concerning the world led to rejecting the knowledge obtained in a different fashion – thus, limiting the scope of perception and understanding of phenomena – both on the part of scientists and those who benefit from science. Granting science an exclusive right to truth led to the creation and consolidation of schematic thinking, which transformed into stereotypes that became deeply-rooted in our consciousness. **The third source** of stereotype formation is the social reality itself. To a large extent, it is the society which accepted the thesis that the state is entitled to enforce a model of education and became resigned to the fact that school is the only institution competent enough to properly develop a young person and a dominant teacher who, as a state official, is the right person to conduct educational tasks.

The work of a teacher is constant manoeuvring on a terrain resembling a mine field on which there are numerous psychological "traps". One of such "traps" is the evaluation system since teachers frequently formulate their assessments under the influence of cognitive patterns. Stereotypes and cognitive patterns very often influence teachers' functioning in a society. There is a common assumption inherent in stereotypes that all members of a given social group are exactly the same[40].

Stereotypes are a side effect of a normal manner of human mind's functioning, namely, classifying others according to categories. Because of that, individuals are able to function in their surrounding reality while saving cognitive resources; they do not have to "learn" every new person from the beginning. In order to form an assessment, they can use any previously acquired knowledge concerning human types. Stereotypes and cognitive patterns enable the possibility that even if information acquired about a certain person is incomplete, one may still form their assessment. In such a situation, it is possible to complement any missing information using elements resulting from a stereotypical perception of a given person[41]. However, by seeing individuals in this fashion we risk an error (referred to as a stereotype error). This kind of error consists in classifying a person as a part of a specific group, for example, on the basis of their appearance – and forming conclusions about such a person's (or the whole group's) mental traits based on those specific external features[42].

Frequently, school assessments are rooted in factors which make them subjective. Teachers, while grading, tend to let the information they have regarding their students influence their judgement. For example, "talented" students are perceived as nicer than inept ones

---

[40] In accordance with the essence of a stereotype – as a generalized representation of a group of people distinguished on the basis of a noticable trait specifying a social identity of members of a given group.

[41] Cf.: B. M. Radtke, *Nauczycielu – nie musisz być sam. W pułapce stereotypów*. „Przegląd Oświatowy" 2008, no 3.

[42] Cf.: K. Serwin-Jakubowska, *Podstawy psychologii... op.cit.,* p. 24.

- and so, an assessment of achievements of the former tend to be more favourable than in the case of the latter; a teacher responds to both categories of students in completely different ways. The mechanism of stereotype functioning, its influence on any assessments we might formulate – on the one hand, facilitates our life (saving time and resources), but on the other – causes that those formulated assessments are much more simplified and, what follows, on certain occasions – significantly inaccurate[43].

T. Hejnicka-Bezwińska and R. Leppert[44] enumerate diverse stereotypes regarding school, education, students and teachers. Among others, they are:

- *A good school is one that is liked by a student*;
- *Labelling students by teachers is a very common phenomenon in Polish schools.* For example, if a student received C grades for the first two years of a secondary school, then he should not receive a B in the third year. This is very harmful to such a student who starts to believe that he does not deserve a B grade due to his insufficient knowledge;
- *Teachers as the main responsible people for school failures of a student*;
- *Polish teachers mostly complain about low salaries, material conditions, shortage of basic teaching materials, low status in school in society*;
- *Teachers see students as anonymous people – merely an element of a larger picture – the view of a student is very general and schematic;*
- *Teachers believe that a child's intellectual development is determined by his or her IQ level;*
- *Social origins discriminate a student if he or she comes from the so-called low-life surroundings. A teacher believes that such a student will not achieve much – or, at least, will achieve very little. Due to the lack of talent in such a student, a teacher does not focus on their development as much as on that of other children. And obviously, it is the first kind of student that should be paid more attention to in order to compensate for any holes and negligences of development. Such students need to be offered help.*

Other kinds of stereotypes regarding teachers and schools are presented by M. Wilgat. Those stereotypes result from the attitude of parents towards teachers. A considerable number

[43] Cf.: B. M. Radtke, *Nauczycielu – nie musisz być sam... op.cit.*
[44] T. Hejnicka-Bezwińska, R. Leppert (ed.), *Przełamywanie stereotypów (pedagogicznych i edukacyjnych).* Wydawnictwo Uczelniane Wyższej Szkoły Pedagogicznej, Bydgoszcz 1996.

of parents believe that the modern school has a corrupting influence on their children. They think that[45]:

- *Nobody can win against teachers or schools.*
- *Teachers are people who tend to vent their frustration at the expense of students. They are people who failed at other careers and so they chose to work at school.*
- *One cannot expect much of students if schools are mediocre.*
- *School is a seat of evil (drugs,violence, alcohol, cigarettes, sex).*

Parents also have numerous other objections towards teachers[46]:

- *Teachers favour those mothers and fathers who maintain systematic contact with school, have secondary (or higher) education and good material situation and avoid those whose sons or daughters come from a poverty-ridden, uneducated families.*
- *Teachers have no time for parents, any conversations are inspired by students' failures and never successes.*
- *There is no cooperation among teachers – instead, we have their increasing competition for better grades, posts, their headmaster's recognition.*
- *Teachers are always in a hurry.*
- *Teachers can only admonish, advise and rule.*
- *Teacher constantly have claims.*
- *Teachers can only evaluate and criticize; they fail to see their own mistakes.*
- *Teachers do not really care about cooperation with parents.*
- *Teachers have plenty of free time – and yet, all they do is complain.*

However, parents ascribe not only negative traits to teachers. Out of positive traits, we need to enumerate the following:

- *Teachers want children to like school.*
- *Teachers strive to educate a wise generation.*
- *Teachers aspire to real cooperation and partnership for the sake of children.*
- *Teachers protect children from threats.*

Among educational stereotypes, it is worthwhile to analyse the approach focused on a person (humanistic education of PCA – *Person Centered Approach*) originating in

[45] M. Wielgat, *Między szkołą a domem.* [in:] A. Balejko, M. Zińczuk (ed.), *Terapia pedagogiczna w teorii i praktyce.* Wyd. „Logopeda radzi", Białystok 2006, p. 155.
[46] Ibidem, p. 155-158.

humanistic pedagogy of C. Rogers. What follows are the most essential assumptions of this approach[47]:

- The fundamental condition of the PCA model is teachers' trust towards themselves and their students, as well as a conviction that students – like their teachers – can think about themselves and learn for themselves.
- Teachers are jointly responsible for the process of learning – along with students, their parents and school authorities.
- Teachers provide teaching materials – in the process using their knowledge, experience, literature and social experience.
- Students build and develop their own program of learning – on their own or with assistance of others. They consciously choose a direction of their own learning – realizing their own responsibility and consequences of their choice.
- In a student group, an atmosphere is gradually formed, initially created by a teacher – and, in the course of time, students themselves create it. Mutual learning becomes an important factor. As a result, external discipline is replaced by self-discipline. Students themselves conduct evaluation of their studies – taking advantage of their teacher's assistance and that of other members of their group.
- The process of learning tends to deepen, accelerate and increasingly combine with students' life and behaviour. Direction of studies is their own choice and learning – their own initiative; a student is involved in the process of studying on every level.

Social perception of the teaching profession

Currently, the profession of a teacher is perceived as a difficult one – associated with constant time pressure, unpredictability of everyday situations, constantly changing rules, new concepts on how to reform Polish educational system which are introduced without any contact with the school reality, in which a young teacher earns several times less than a physical worker, constant training and improvement of professional qualifications. Overcoming difficulties which are faced by today's teachers require from them new methods of work, original and creative solutions, resourcefulness combined with flexibility. Currently, a good teacher is an effective one. It is a specialist able to deal with didactic and educational responsibilities, a professional who can control students and convey knowledge and new skills in an attractive way and - most importantly – taking into consideration their needs and possibilities[48].

---

[47] P. Śmidoda, A. Tońska, C. Tyborska, *Stereotypy pedagogiczne... op.cit.*, p. 74.
[48] B. M. Radtke, *Nauczycielu – nie musisz być sam... op.cit.*, p. 26.

H. Kwiatkowska formulated a thesis stating how the teacher's professional ethos has undergone crucial and disturbing changes in the social opinion. Those changes are described as a process of constant deterioration of the quality of teachers' work and reducing the value (including the economic one) of its social function (which signifies a specific depreciation of this function)[49].

M. Wajs-Kacprowska made an attempt to compare the social opinion on teachers with their own observations. The purpose of her research was to specify the degree of compatibility between professional self-definition of a teacher and views of the teacher's profession by people of other professions – society in general. The teacher's professional self-definition was described as a collection of assumptions specifying how a teacher defines himself in terms of his professional function, how he perceives and interprets his occupation and professional environment. The author assumed that teachers as a professional group have a sense of their profession's significance – a profession which, in essence, constitutes the foundation for the modern society's development. M. Wajs-Kacprowska researched two groups – teachers and representatives of other professions – doctors and IT specialists. The author posed a number of questions to representatives of both groups and what follows are the most important conclusions from the research[50]:

- Teachers' opinions concerning the social significance of their profession indicate a decrease in teachers' social position.
- Teachers do not feel they receive a sufficient level of respect and recognition from their social environment.
- Modern educators do not feel they are a chosen group – important among other professional groups.
- A general assessment of the profession of a teacher is extremely low according to the social opinion. Higher social position is ascribed to people with higher salaries and the profession of a teacher is not one of them.
- The profession of a teacher is considered attractive neither by the society nor by teachers themselves.
- Modern candidates choosing the pedagogical studies base their decision on the economic aspect and the organisation of a teacher's life, fewer working hours, acquiring specialty – and, due to this: a higher salary. The profession of a teacher is

[49] Quoted after: M. Wajs-Kacprowska, *Samookreślenie zawodowe nauczycieli a określenie zawodu nauczycielskiego przez ludzi innej profesji.* [in:] A. A. Kotusiewicz (ed.), *Myśl pedeutologiczna i działanie nauczyciela.* Published by Trans Humana, Białystok 2000, p. 176.

[50] Ibidem, p. 175-189.

perceived from the career point of view – not as a vocation.

- According to both researched groups, the most effective factors in inspiring teachers to work are those which result from the specifics of this profession – freedom to decide how to perform one's work, good cooperation of teachers and a creative atmosphere in a teaching collective as well as stability of employment. Economic factors are the least stimulating.
- Motives behind choosing the teaching profession of modern teachers are most frequently the following ones: vocation, willingness to work with children, love for this profession.
- Teachers and the society have different views regarding the aspect of creativity in teaching. According to IT specialists and doctors, modern teachers have a critical attitude towards any novelty in teaching due to a certain routine nature of their work; teachers, on the other hand, believe their activity is creative. Teachers aware of their creative function claim that they fulfill their creative inspirations not only in the scope of methods and forms of teaching, syllabus content, but – particularly – if it comes to work with children and in the evaluation of students' work.
- Research has proved that over a half of teachers is satisfied with effects of their work while a prevailing social conclusion is that in no way can they be satisfied with them.
- Teachers satisfied with their work owing to good relations with students, organisation of circles of interests as well as their students' accomplishments at olympiads of higher levels.
- The society believes that teachers are most satisfied with a large number of free days and effects of good work.
- Both according to teachers and the society – teachers conduct the educational process through the future-oriented categories of thinking. All participants of the research are aware of responsibilities faced by educators. It is them who are to prepare youth for life in the world of progress, scientific and technical development.

In conclusion of her research, M. Wajs-Kacprowska[51] argued that the profession of a teacher is performed by inadequate people, most often choosing it by a way of accident – and basing this choice upon the factor of fewer working hours, a large number of free days or an excuse for not being drafted to the army. It leads to crucial and alarming transformations in

[51] Ibidem, p. 189.

the intellectual and moral spheres of modern teachers. This changes their attitude to students and tasks the school poses in front of them – it acquires an official character. Teachers distance themselves from difficult issues, withdraw from participation in the social life of the country. Currently, the economic status indicates intellectual and social position – this might be the reason why there is such a low social opinion of teachers and a decrease in the prestige of the teaching profession.

Meanwhile, teachers are required to possess a high level of professionalism, wide methodical qualifications (including moral ones), courage, interpersonal skills, diligence, reliability, active attitude towards all spheres of professional activity, high self-esteem, ambition, a tendency to maintain a continuous development and broaden their knowledge. Apart from that, a teacher should be interesting, genuine, open to changes, down-to-earth, practical, full of dignity, competitive, assertive, interested in culture and modern[52]. If a stereotypical image of the modern teacher will become close to such a characterization – then such stereotypes will serve the process of building prestige of this professional group and such social perception of this occupation needs to be considered a positive/desirable stereotype.

Teachers on stereotypical opinions regarding their profession

I asked a hundred teachers from schools in Słupsk (including those who are extramural students at Pomeranian University in Słupsk) about their observations regarding stereotypes related to their profession[53]. Respondents whom I asked about attitudes concerning positive stereotypes relating to their profession stated the following[54]:

- *Teachers aspire to educate wise generations*– (92% of teachers)
- *Teachers try to make children like school* – (82% of teachers)
- *Teachers protect children from threats* – (80% of teachers).

Among negative stereotypes regarding the profession of teacher – with which the polled people agree – are the following:

- *Teachers in Poland constantly complain about low salaries, material conditions,*

[52] B. Karolczak-Biernacka, *Kondycja nauczyciela.* „Edukacja i Dialog" 1996, no 1, p. 25-27.

[53] Teachers I asked about stereotypical perceptions of their profession work at various levels of education. Primary school teachers constitute 32% of the total number of the polled and pre-school teachers – 26%. Almost 1/5 of the polled work in upper secondary schools (19%), and 5% work in junior high school. Out of the polled teachers, 17% confirmed they work both in primary and junior high schools. A considerable majority of the polled are women (84%). Men constitute merely 16% of respondents and they are workers of primary and upper secondary schools. None of the polled men is a worker of a pre-school. Almost every second teacher is at the initial stage of his career – with a job seniority between one and ten years (48% of the polled). Teachers with a job seniority between 11 and 20 years constitute 27% of the polled, and teachers with the largest job seniority (more than 21 years) constitute 23% of the respondents.

[54] Original phrasing of replies was retained.

shortage of basic teaching materials, their low status is the society and schools (such an answer was given by as many as 85% of teachers).

- *Teachers' remuneration is not proportionate to the work input – which might result in the sense of inferiority and inadequacy (opinion of 42 teachers).*
- *There is no cooperation among teachers – instead, we have their increasing competition for better grades, posts, headmaster's recognition - (this stereotype is confirmed by every second polled person - 52%).*

Out of negative stereotypes regarding the teaching profession, the respondents do not agree with the following:

- *Teachers are people who tend to vent their frustration at the expense of students.* (this stereotype is rejected by 94% of teachers).
- *Teachers do not care about a cooperation with parents* – (according to 80% of teachers, this stereotype is false).
- *One cannot expect too much from students since schools are mediocre and teachers have a small amount of knowledge* – (this stereotype is rejected by almost all teachers – 96%).
- *Teachers are the main responsible people for students' failures* (72% of teachers do not agree with this stereotype).
- *Teachers favour those mothers and fathers who maintain systematic contact with schools, have secondary (or higher) education, a good material situation and avoid those whose sons or daughters come from a poverty-ridden, uneducated families* - (88% of teachers believe this stereotype is false).
- *Teachers have no time for parents, any conversations are inspired by students' failures and never successes* – (68% of teachers do not agree with this stereotype).

Analysing all replies of the polled teachers – the conclusion is that they agree with all stereotypes which positively shape the image of teacher and his profession. They also agree with two of the listed negative stereotypes regarding their professional group. They are: *Teachers in Poland complain about low salaries, material conditions, shortage of basic teaching materials, low status in society and school* and - *There is no cooperation among teachers – instead, we have their increasing competition for better grades, posts and their headmaster's recognition.*

When asked what stereotypes function in the social awareness concerning teachers and their profession – most respondents were unable to specify even a single example. Only 24 out of 100 teachers indicated stereotypes they are familiar with and provided their examples. What follows is a list of those stereotypes:

- *teachers used to have authority which they no longer possess* (2 cases)
- *teachers have exceedingly high educational requirements* (2 cases)
- *teachers work only 18 hours a week* (2 cases)
- *teachers fail to educate children properly*
- *teachers have their favourite students and only work with them*
- *in preschool education, there are no proper teachers, only nursery school teachers who fail to teach anything specific*
- *teachers at school – work, teachers at preschool level only play with children*
- *all female teachers are stupid*
- *teachers' work is difficult, mentally exhausting and numerous teachers are not competent enough*
- *if you cannot think of a better thing to do with your life – go and teach at school*
- *teaching is an easy profession*
- *teachers practise for numerous years the same system of teaching, evaluating, working methods, conducting classes and educating – failing to introduce any novelties*
- *teachers do not enjoy their work*
- *teachers only work in their profession for long periods of vacations*
- *teachers work few hours and earn a lot.*

Most of the stereotypes mentioned by the polled teachers do not project a favourable image of the teacher. Teachers, according to social reception, are negatively perceived, criticized and frequently ridiculed in mass media – and what is more, they tend to identify with this image. It does not influence their work in a positive fashion; the same applies to their level of identification with profession and motivation for didactic and educational work.

The teaching profession is considered as one of a low prestige and unattractive. It is caused, among others, by a low remuneration received by teachers as well as treating this profession as an unrewarding, stressful and dangerous. The profession of a teacher is perceived as a difficult, mentally exhausting one. It is mostly caused by teachers' considerable responsibility for students' security, teaching results, a high risk of professional burnout as well as hardly proportional remuneration for the amount of their work – leading to their sense of inferiority and low self-esteem.

In general, we might formulate a conclusion that teachers' knowledge concerning stereotypes related to their profession is hardly impressive. In teachers' view, from social opinions and stereotypes concerning their profession, results an unfavourable image of their profession. It is worthwhile, however, to be aware of the fact that stereotypical thinking is a consequence of the cultural and socializing conditioning; it results from a natural human need to simplify social perception. Harmful and detrimental stereotypes need to be overcome and contradicted; it is necessary to demonstrate their groundlessness. However, it is also important to reject the notion of a "negative stereotype" - signifying that all stereotypes are harmful and we need to combat them. Creating and preserving stereotypes is a natural phenomenon and, as such, one needs to accept them. In order to understand the surrounding world, people need to simplify, put in order and facilitate the perception of (increasingly) complex phenomena. Therefore: "Certain educational patterns should not be rejected, but studied – so that one might see the truth on their basis; so that one might search for the truth by using them"[55]. An analysis of current beliefs regarding the character of stereotypes constitutes a valid step in this direction.

Bibliography

Ambrosewicz-Jacobs J., *Tolerancja. Jak uczyć siebie i innych.* Wyd. Stowarzyszenie Willa Decjusza, Kraków 2004.

Aronson E., *Człowiek istota społeczna.* PWN, Warszawa 2004.

Hejnicka-Bezwińska T., Leppert R. (red.), *Przełamywanie stereotypów (pedagogicznych i edukacyjnych).* Wydawnictwo Uczelniane Wyższej Szkoły Pedagogicznej, Bydgoszcz 1996.

Karolczak-Biernacka B., *Kondycja nauczyciela.* „Edukacja i Dialog" 1996, nr 1.

Kotusiewicz A. A. (red.), *Myśl pedeutologiczna i działanie nauczyciela.* Wyd. Trans Humana, Białystok 2000.

Macrae C. N., Stangor Ch., Hewstone M., *Stereotypy i uprzedzenia. Najnowsze ujęcie.* Gdańskie Wydawnictwo Psychologiczne, Gdańsk 1995.

Nelson T. D., *Psychologia uprzedzeń.* Gdańskie Wydawnictwo Psychologiczne, Gdańsk 2003.

Pankowska D., *Wychowanie a role płciowe.* Gdańskie Wydawnictwo Psychologiczne, Gdańsk 2005.

Petrozolin-Skowrońska B. (red.), *Encyklopedia powszechna.* PWN, Warszawa 1996.

Pietrzak H., *Następstwa i efekty stereotypowego postrzegania człowieka i świata społecznego.*

[55] P. Śmidoda, A. Tońska, C. Tyborska, *Stereotypy pedagogiczne ...* , p. 71

Wydawnictwo Wyższej Szkoły Pedagogicznej, Rzeszów 2000.

Radtke B. M., *Nauczycielu – nie musisz być sam. W pułapce stereotypów.* „Przegląd Oświatowy" 2008, nr 3.

Śmidoda P., Tońska A., Tyborska C., *Stereotypy pedagogiczne. Próba przezwyciężenia negatywnego myślenia o stereotypach.* [w:] Hejnicka-Bezwińska T., Leppert R. (red.), *Przełamywanie stereotypów (pedagogicznych i edukacyjnych).* Wydawnictwo Uczelniane Wyższej Szkoły Peda-goggicznej, Bydgoszcz 1996.

Wajs-Kacprowska M., *Samookreślenie zawodowe nauczycieli a określenie zawodu nauczycielskiego przez ludzi innej profesji.* [w:] A.A. Kotusiewicz (red.), *Myśl pedeutologiczna i działanie nauczyciela.* Wyd. Trans Humana, Białystok 2000.

Wielgat M., *Między szkołą a domem.* [w:] A. Balejko, M. Zińczuk (red.), *Terapia pedagogiczna w teorii i praktyce.* Wyd. „Logopeda radzi", Białystok 2006.

Julitta Nowak
Pedagogical University of Warsaw, Poland

DYNAMICS OF THE CHANGE IN THE IMAGE OF A TEACHER-LECTURER IN THE CHANGING EDUCATIONAL REALITY

Summary

The contemporary societies largo sense extort from teacher's profession, performing the functions and duties, going beyond the traditionally petrified stereotype. The changes in the social, economical, cultural, political relations and many other factors of the public processes impose on the lecturers an obligation of extended teaching, well–adapted to the real school programme needs as implication of the labour market demands as well as students preparation for participation in the multi–faceted compound social life. It is also dictated by limited range of educational family function, offloading the burden of upbringing and responsibility onto the school institutions as well as teachers' involvement in it. The institutional segmentation of the educational process in the contemporary society unclearly defines the responsibility areas for education and upbringing of the youth who, in coming generation is assuming the participation in creating the social life in the scopes of the country and the sovereign structures in the global categories. Professional creations of the modern teacher realizing an own mission, by nature, are the essential conditions of the contemporary society quality parameters, the identity and the cultural continuity, as well as the national consciousness in the world aiming at the omnipresent standardization and unification.

Introduction

The modern society forces a teacher to fulfill functions and obligations which exceed the traditional scope of didactic and educational responsibilities. Changes in socio-economic, cultural and political relations, as well as numerous other factors, require teachers to fulfill responsibilities of *extended* teaching, suited to real needs of school syllabuses as an implication of the labour market demands as well as a preparation of students for the participation in a multi-faceted social life. It is also caused by a decreasing scope of family's educational functions, transferring the responsibility for education to educational institutions and teachers. An institutional segmentation of the educational process in the modern society leads to an unclear specification of responsibilities for education and teaching of young generations which shall take over a participation in the future development of social life within a state and in sovereign structures perceived according to global categories.

Requirements set before teachers are considerable and their execution has a crucial impact on this profession's perception by the society[1]. Every teacher's behaviour is dependent on two factors – a role specifying a general framework of a teacher's conduct and a given teacher's personality traits. To quote J. Szczepański: a social role is a collection of regulations which specify how a person on a given position should or should not behave. Szczepański argues that "a social role is a relatively permanent and internally consistent system of behavioral patterns which form reactions to other people's behaviour which follow more or less clearly an established formula"[2]. Therefore, teachers' social roles are answers to social expectation – especially those of pupils and/or students in relation to teachers.

Professional role of teachers

The act of fulfilling a role is an expression of a given person's awareness of his or her actions. A teacher's primary concern is a didactic process, influencing by information with a conscious objective to implement an educational goal. Results of educational elements of the educational process are manifested in students' social conduct which constitutes a test of educational effectiveness of teachers. "A manner in which a didactic awareness is perceived can assume a similar form to the one of social awareness on the basis of the sociology of knowledge. Its initial perception is as follows: a didactic awareness is a branch of knowledge concerning similar behavioral patterns of people dealing with teaching on a professional basis. Even knowledge concerning a social position (in a grading sense) of the teaching profession leads to its *didactic* (διδακτικός) classification"[3].

In view of the new reality – formed every single day – "(...) what also changes is the role of teachers and students in the process of teaching and learning. Teachers gradually lose the main role in the sphere of transferring knowledge – they becomes more of analysts, specialists in the scope of teaching materials, consultants, so that, as a result of fulfilling those roles, they might have an increasing influence on implementing changes in students as a consequence of creating a new learning environment which is based on the rules of cooperation. Teachers need to take into consideration the fact that students should be given sufficient time

---

[1] cf.: *Być nauczycielem – opiekunem – wychowawcą. Między teorią a praktyką.* Redakcja: Grażyna Durka i Ewa Murawska, Wydawnictwo Adam Marszałek, Toruń 2012.

[2] J. Szczepański, *Elementarne pojęcia socjologii*, PWN, Warszawa 1970, p.308.

[3] B. Gębski, *Świadomość dydaktyczna nauczycieli akademickich - refleksje o socjologicznych seminariach licencjackich i magisterskich,* [in:] *Paradygmaty współczesnej dydaktyki*, ed. L. Hurło, D. Klus-Stańska i M. Łojko, Wyd. Impuls, Kraków 2009, p. 411.

to deal with problems, test various strategies, discuss, experiment with research, as well as make necessary assessments. In this respect, the role of teachers is similar to that of a coach or an expert. Teachers should influence attitudes. They constitute an example to follow – they solve model problems and conduct diverse researches"[4].

R. B. Woźniak[5] presents roles fulfilled by a teacher-educator:

1. a teacher as a guide – suggesting to students methods of individual knowledge acquisition,
2. a teacher as a controller – suggesting works and supervising their completion,
3. a teacher in the role related to offering *backup assistance* – providing advice when necessary,
4. a teacher as an initiator – placing students in situations which inspire to study and work.

In scientific literature dealing with this subject, we can also find other attitudes regarding the issue. There is a certain concern among those who research the phenomenon of teaching that this profession is somehow socially relevant and important. T. Gołaszewski[6] offers the following *scope* of teachers' social roles:

1. The professional role – it can be divided into a few more detailed ones which overlap (the ones who conduct classes, educate, fulfill functions in school administration or guardians of student groups),
2. the family role (particularly, parental, marriage-related, a family representative),
3. the social role (regarding colleagues, acquaintances outside the circle of teachers, friends),
4. the role of a citizen of one's country (manifested, for example, by following economy and politics-related events).

Among factors contributing to fulfilling the professional role of teachers are the following: his or her knowledge, experience, school conditions, self-education and professional training, participation in cultural events, relations outside schools as well as their personality.

If we discuss the social role – an issue that cannot be ignored is *social position.* Social position is a place one occupies in a stratification structure of a given society, specified by a prominence of this place[7]. In every society, there is an official hierarchy which structures its classes and layers into a stratification system which indicates superiority or inferiority of those classes or layers. Social position of a given class/layer is specified by an official defini-

[4] L. Kacprzak, *Możliwe i niemożliwe propozycje w pracy nauczyciela oraz w życiu szkoły i środowiska,* [in:] *Możliwe – niemożliwe. Jakościowy wymiar pedagogiki aktualnej,* red. E. Gaweł-Luty, M. Szczepańska, Słupsk 2003, p. 221.

[5] R. B. Woźniak, *Zarys socjologii edukacji i zachowań społecznych*, Koszalin 1997, p. 393.

[6] T. Gołaszewski, *Szkoła jako system społeczny*, Warszawa 1977, p. 125.

[7] P.M. Blau, *Wymiana i władza w życiu społeczny,* Zakład Wydawniczy NOMOS, Kraków 2009.

tion of superiority or inferiority accepted in the official nomenclature of a given society[8]. The said position is indicated by the following factors:

1. a profession and post in a given position,
2. an income received as financial remuneration for work and in the form of various privileges,
3. participation in cultural life,
4. participation in structures of authority and offices as well as the scope of one's power in public matters,
5. external symbols of social status – i.e., lifestyle, manner of clothing and furnishing, etc.,
6. social awareness, an acceptance of a prevalent ideology and a political identification with a new system[9].

A large number of cognitive attitudes presented by various authors indicates a significant complexity of roles, functions (etc) of teachers in creating a social reality. I shall refer to a viewpoint of L. Sołoma, who – based on her research – indicates the following factors of teachers' social position – specified axiologically. Indicators of social position listed below are highly debatable; for instance, item 1 is archaic in nature since teachers are generally *externally controlled*[10], items 9 and 11 stress the elements about ignoring the teaching profession:

1. compatibility of behaviour with one's own beliefs,
2. education and knowledge,
3. participation in the social work for the sake of one's environment,
4. sympathy and recognition shown by one's environment,
5. personality traits-based.
6. respect shown because of the fact of the teacher's profession,
7. living conditions,
8. clothes, caring for one's appearance,
9. local authorities taking into consideration teachers' opinions,
10. number of people willing to maintain social contacts,
11. salary level[11].

The teaching profession from the standpoint of pedeutological research

There have been so many studies regarding the teaching profession (formerly referred to as *pedeutology*[12]) with variously emphasized indicators specifying their position within social

[8] Cf.: J. Woskowski, *O pozycji społecznej nauczyciela*, Warszawa – Łódź 1964, p.33-34.
[9] K. Duraj-Nowakowa, *Nauczyciel: kultura - osoba - zawód*, MEDIATOR, Kielce 2000, p. 69-70.
[10] D. Riesman, *Samotny tłum*, Seria *Spectrum*, Warszawskie Wydawnictwo Literackie MUZA, Warszawa 1996, p. 225.
[11] L. Sołoma, *Nauczyciele o swojej pracy i pozycji społecznej*, Wyd. WSP, Olsztyn 1994.

structure that one might think of it as a special profession. This aspect of being special has a statistic nature. In various post-war periods, in Poland, over 600 thousand teachers worked in primary and secondary schools; during the last decade approximately 100 thousands teachers worked in academic institutions. In the process of a further review of opinions regarding conditions behind this profession, I shall present certain research results.

Studies conducted by T. Pilch indicate that most factors indicating the teacher's position have an objective character. A recognition for the teacher's profession is related to "improving the significance of education, professionality and attributing a huge meaning to issues regarding problems of younger generations. This profession enjoys a high significance due to the strength of tradition and certain habits influencing the fact that a teacher is perceived as a role model"[13].

Certain polls conducted by CBOS indicate that among all listed professions, an academic professor has enjoyed the highest prestige for numerous years (since 1996 it has been listed as the first). A teacher in 1996 occupied the fourth place, in 1999 – the third. The polls conducted by CBOS in 2004 named "The social opinion regarding professions of public trust" show that a teacher is ranked fifth in the hierarchy – surpassed by a doctor, judge, policeman and a politician[14].

The latest proposition of functions and tasks for a teacher of adults is presented by C. Banach, who distinguishes the following:

1. teaching (didactic) – understood in a developmental manner,
2. educating,
3. tutorial,
4. environmental,
5. innovatory,
6. research-related,
7. orientational (life orientation) and socialization-related[15].

To functions formulated in this way, the author matched a corresponding scope of professional qualifications of a teacher of adults:

1. teaching, supporting development,
2. education and self-education of students,

---

[12] Cf.: pioneering empirical research concerning the teaching profession by Bolesław Sadaj, who has been nearly forgotten in the scientific literature on the subject.
[13] T. Pilch, *Szkoła i nauczyciel w procesie przemian środowiska wiejskiego*, PWN, Warszawa 1977, p. 93.
[14] www.cbos.pl (retrieved on 29.12.2004),
[15] Quoted after: G. Orzechowska, *Nauczyciel dorosłych w teorii i praktyce oświaty dorosłych*, [in:] *Z problematyki zawodu nauczyciela*, red. L. Hurło, wyd. WSP TWP w Warszawie, Warszawa 1998, p. 95.

3. tutelage, equalizing educational conditions,
4. analysing,
5. resocialization,
6. reforming and innovatory activity,
7. cooperation with the working and living environments,
8. organisation of one's own and collective work[16].

According to A. Nowicki, a teacher should be a person who:

1. represents a high intellectual level (including a proper education, research curiosity and a personal culture),
2. cooperates with a student in the process of a scientific perception and transformation of reality,
3. has and transfers his own beliefs grounded in personal experience,
4. emphasizes a subjective treatment of a student based upon a mutual respect and tolerance as well as an attitude of a mutual openness,
5. is active and creative,
6. continuously develops intellectually and spiritually (perceives spirituality only in a contact with culture and art)[17].

A research conducted at the Pomeranian Pedagogical Academy in the academic year of 2004/2005 yielded the following results:

1. students claimed that a woman is more competent in the profession of a teacher (47% of the polled students) than a man (35%); 18% of the polled students argued that gender bears no significance in this respect. Such data might be caused by the fact that women outnumber men in this profession – also at the Academy. The polled students are also mostly women,
2. among attributed personality traits – fairness is ranked as the first, later follow: patience, leniency, a sense of humour, self-control, kindness and responsibility,
3. missing personality traits of teachers-lecturers are,
4. fairness and a sense of humour are ranked first, next follow: punctuality, kindness and honesty, later – patience, considerateness, diligence, accuracy, goodness and truthfulness, at the fourth position – levelheadedness, selflessness, orderliness, responsibility, and finally – ambition, perseverance and courage.

---

[16] Ibidem.
[17] A. Nowicki, *Spotkania w rzeczach*, PWN, Warszawa 1991, p. 201-205.

5. students unanimously advocated teacher's/lecturer's open-mindedness (100% of them); in addition, they favoured a demanding teacher (77%), rather than an undemanding one (23%). An attitude of an inaccessible teacher was significantly frowned upon,

6. 63% of students claimed that lecturers have adequate skills and employ modern didactic equipment during classes – although this equipment frequently belongs to a lecturer and not their academic institution. 27% of teachers were considered incapable to use such equipment,

7. students notice the obligation of continuous training of teachers (92%), which results from rapid changes taking place in all spheres of our life,

8. 72% of the polled students claimed that they feel comfortable during lectures while the rest argued that their well-being depends on the form of conducted classes – they enjoy classes where audio-visual measures are used,

9. if it comes to a level of conducted classes - 16% claimed it is high, 70% saw it as average and 14 % as low. The reasons behind average and low level of conducted classes were seen in the failure to transfer knowledge, shortage of up-to-date, new content, obsolete methods, insufficient usage of audio-visual equipment, predominance of academic book content (definitions etc) and shortage of real life examples,

10. the polled students like teachers/lecturers who are unhesitating, do not change their opinions easily, cannot be manipulated by students and know how to maintain discipline (87%); on the other hand, students do not like teachers who fail to maintain discipline during classes and often hesitate,

11. 68% of the polled students claimed that they respect their lecturer for his knowledge, skills, conduct, a manner of being and an attitude towards people. Students (future teachers) want to identify with them, follow their example. 23% of the polled students do not respect their teachers,

12. the reason behind choosing pedagogical studies by the polled was, among others: willingness to work with children and youth (25%), interests (19%), vocation (14%), dreams (12%), shortage of good educators (10%); the remaining part claimed that their reason is purely accidental (an escape from military service, a failed exam at another academic institution, no financial means to study at a private academic institution, free studies at a state institution etc.)

The poll conducted by D. Bubnowski[18] suggests that a majority of the polled teachers (55%) claimed that a teacher does not occupy a high social position. 35 % of the polled teachers stated that they are losing their position in view of the society.

[18] D. Bubnowski, *Tworzenie się autostereotypu współczesnego nauczyciela. Praca magisterska napisana pod kierunkiem dr Julitty Nowak*, PAP, Słupsk 2005.

In the academic year of 2006/2007, I conducted a research among students of the first year regarding their opinion concerning upper-secondary schools. The polled students[19] expressed their opinion that teachers unjustly evaluated students with a low social background and a low educational level of parents (approximately 68%). Those students stated the following:

1. teachers offended such children more often,
2. they made official negative comments more often,
3. teachers were frequently strict and unpleasant to me,
4. they made fun and ridiculed students,
5. they called me names,
6. they frequently disciplined such students,
7. they frequently shouted at me and then I did not succeed in anything,
8. they often drove me from my class to a cloakroom – while they never had the courage to do it to children from rich families.

Approximately 38% of students observed that teachers fairly treat students at upper-secondary level while an unfair treatment was noticed by over 60% of students, most frequently, they indicated an unjust evaluation of knowledge, a rash evaluation of youth's behaviour, a privileged treatment of the so-called well-born (youth coming from upper social layers), their favourites, social activists and sportsmen.

Full-time students indicated an unfair evaluation on the part of academic teachers – based on those students' social origins, education level of their parents and social position (23%). Extramural students stated that academic teachers unfairly assess students – taking into consideration social origins, parents' level of education (only 7% of the polled). They claimed that academic teachers have a limited contact with their students or knowledge of them – mostly because of few hours, rare meetings and, most frequently – written exams.

In the academic year of 2011/2012, I asked the second year students[20] why during classes at the first year they did not want to contribute spontaneously, while – whenever asked directly – answered in a sufficient and intelligent fashion. The polled students claimed that during their classes at the first year:

---

[19] The research focused on students from Pomeranian University in and Higher teacher education school TWP in Warsaw, branch faculty in Szczecin in the academic year of 2006/2007. Altogether, 366 students were polled.

[20] The research was conducted in Higher teacher education school TWP in Warsaw, branch faculty in Szczecin. Altogether, 115 students were polled.

1. nightmarish memories are still fresh of secondary school questioning – when it is best not to contribute unasked since one can obtain a negative grade for a wrong answer – 67% of respondents,

2. we did not know one another at the first year, there was no integration – 43%,

3. we feared of being ridiculed – 65%,

4. lack of courage to express one's observations – 38%

5. the polled students stated that during the second year of studies:

6. most of them (over 60%) willingly contribute because their lecturers allow them to voice their opinions, do not interrupt them or criticize,

7. for being active, especially during exercises – one can obtain a better grade at an exam – or even be released from the obligation to take exam – 45%,

8. group presentations are prepared for classes – which need to be presented in the public – 30%.

M. Kostera and A. Rosiak[21] argue that one of advantages of exercises is the fact that they provide students with an opportunity to prepare presentations (ideas, studies, projects) as well as to conduct a presentation of papers. In a group of 30-40 people, it is possible to discuss their colleagues' presentations and openly evaluate them. Students have an opportunity to prepare their presentations in such a manner so as to interest their colleagues – while simultaneously demonstrate their skills. Paper presentations undoubtedly teach one how to behave before an audience. Number of students in an exercise group is so low that novice lecturers do not feel stressed to the extent they would be before a wider audience. Students receive feedback about their performance, are able to polish their skills, bridge any deficiencies. In addition, the polled students stated that:

(a) high professional qualifications are the basis for one's correct functioning in the profession of a teacher (approximately 58 % of the polled students believe this), about 17% claim that high qualifications do not guarantee a correct fulfillment of the role of a teacher , the rest of the students were hesitant,

(b) the polled students – apart from their specific field knowledge – notice a significance of numerous other factors influencing a correct functioning of teachers in their profession, i.e., an ability to transfer knowledge, experience, proper attitude towards youth and a true calling.

[21] Cf. M. Kostera, A. Rosiak, *Nauczyciel akademicki*, Gdańskie Wydawnictwo Psychologiczne, Gdańsk 2008, p. 113.

It turned out that students' expectations towards their teachers have been slightly transformed. Currently, teachers are mostly respected for their:

1. qualifications and knowledge,
2. ability to listen and respect opinions and beliefs of other people,
3. kindness and patience,
4. ability to form contacts,
5. organisational skills,
6. ability to inspire activity,
7. professional and life counseling.

Conclusion

Education is a crucial component of life in every human community. To quote F. Znaniecki: "education is a social activity the subject of which is a person who is a candidate to be a member of a social group and the goal of which – conditioning its intentions and methods – is preparing this individual to become a full member"[22].

The rapidly changing world causes that youth need to be taught and educated in such a manner that it could face various changes and create new values in a new fashion. To further quote F. Znaniecki - "to inspire, develop and consolidate in each individual this core of creative predispositions natural to them and, simultaneously, teach every individual to express their creative aspirations in a solidary cooperation with other people in order to implement common ideals – this is (...) a great task before modern upbringing (...). A student is to cooperate with their educator in the process of developing their own person, actively influence their own development so as to help this educator in achieving such goal*"*[23].

To approach reflections concerning the profession of teachers in a holistic fashion, I postulate submitting a research project to conduct a detailed study of a modern conditioning behind the role of teachers, a determination of behaviour, an awareness of their position and a professional mission as well as their social role and cultural output related to this profession. *The obligation aspect* – emphasized so frequently in properties of teachers' professional activity – should not be excessively exposed. Far more important are social determinants of conducting this profession, especially in view of the fact that "new, dynamically developing information technology aspects require developing new skills – both on the part of teachers as students. So far – in the process of educating students – passive qualifications were empha-

[22] F. Znaniecki, *Socjologia wychowania*, Warszawa 1973, p. 12.
[23] Ibidem, v.1, p. 420.

sized, those related to reading comprehension or interpreting (for example, a movie). We should develop active qualifications connected with employing media – as tools for communication. Students need to be taught how to create and look for information – in the world where information overflow is a problem"[24]. As a form of conclusion – I shall emphasize that problems related to teachers' social functioning result from those teachers' insufficient professional consolidation, a low awareness of their role and consistency of social actions.

Bibliography

Blau P.M., *Wymiana i władza w życiu społeczny,* Zakład Wydawniczy NOMOS, Kraków 2009.

Bubnowski D., *Tworzenie się autostereotypu współczesnego nauczyciela. Praca magisterska napisana pod kierunkiem dr Julitty Nowak*, PAP, Słupsk 2005.

Burakowski K, *Kompetencje komunikacyjne współczesnego nauczyciela*, [w:] Kompetencje współczesnego nauczyciela, red. K. Żegnałek, WSP TWP Warszawa 2008.

Duraj-Nowakowa K., *Nauczyciel: kultura - osoba - zawód*, Mediator, Kielce 2000.

Durka G., Murawska E. (red.), *Być nauczycielem – opiekunem – wychowawcą. Między teorią a praktyką*, Wydawnictwo Adam Marszałek, Toruń 2012.

Gębski B., *Świadomość dydaktyczna nauczycieli akademickich - refleksje o socjologicznych seminariach licencjackich i magisterskich,* [w:] *Paradygmaty współczesnej dydaktyki*, red. L. Hurło, D. Klus-Stańska, M. Łojko, Wyd. Impuls, Kraków 2009.

Gołaszewski T., *Szkoła jako system społeczny*, PWN, Warszawa 1977.

Kacprzak L., *Możliwe i niemożliwe propozycje w pracy nauczyciela oraz w życiu szkoły i środowiska*, (w:) Możliwe – niemożliwe. Jakościowy wymiar pedagogiki aktualnej, red. E. Gaweł-Luty, M. Szczepańska, Wydawnictwo WSP, Słupsk 2003.

Kostera M., Rosiak A., *Nauczyciel akademicki*, Gdańskie Wydawnictwo Psychologiczne, Gdańsk 2008.

Nowicki A., *Spotkania w rzeczach*, PWN, Warszawa 1991.

Orzechowska G., *Nauczyciel dorosłych w teorii i praktyce oświaty dorosłych*, [w:] Z problematyki zawodu nauczyciela, red. L. Hurło, Wyd. WSP TWP w Warszawie, Warszawa 1998.

Pilch T., *Szkoła i nauczyciel w procesie przemian środowiska wiejskiego*, PWN, Warszawa 1977.

Riesman D., *Samotny tłum*, Seria *Spectrum*, Wyd. Literackie MUZA, Warszawa 1996.

[24] K. Burakowski, *Kompetencje komunikacyjne współczesnego nauczyciela*, [in:] Kompetencje współczesnego nauczyciela, ed. K. Żegnałek, WSP TWP Warszawa 2008, p. 231.

Sołoma L., *Nauczyciele o swojej pracy i pozycji społecznej*, Wyd. WSP, Olsztyn 1994.

Woskowski J., *O pozycji społecznej nauczyciela*, PWN, Warszawa – Łódź 1964.

Woźniak R.B., *Zarys socjologii edukacji i zachowań społecznych*, Wyd. BWSE, Koszalin 1997.

Znaniecki F., *Socjologia wychowania*, PWN, Warszawa 1973.

Roma Kwiecińska, Jolanta Rybska-Klapa
Pedagogical University im. KEN in Cracow, Poland

SPECIAL NEEDS STUDENT IN THE EDUCATIONAL EXPANSE OF PUBLIC SCHOOL

Summary

The study contains an analysis of the elements of school education in meeting the needs of students requiring psychological – pedagogical help. The authors are pointing to the strengths and weaknesses of the school (primary, middle school and high school) as the institution responsible for securing the correct course of education in this group of students. Examinations conducted by the author are showing, that possibilities guaranteed in the formal space don`t have the proper reference and are not fully implemented in other areas - in physical, educational and social space.

Dimensions of the educational expanse of school

Schools, their multi-layered structure and expanse can be perceived in numerous ways. Aleksander Nalaskowski emphasizes that "entire depth and reality of this institution lies in its multi-faceted nature of half-transparent layers [...] which form a multidimensional and spacious image of an educational facility".[1] Each subject of a school community – students, teachers and parents – has their own specific image of this place and its function. Educational expanse is constituted by both above-mentioned subject, material assets (school architecture, didactic equipment) and an organisational structure, a school culture including a student and teacher atmosphere as well as peer influence.[2]

As D. Klus-Stańska states: "students attending a school are << natural >> inhabitants of this ambiguous and difficult to grasp reality".[3] However, are the needs of all those inhabitants recognized and satisfied? A research conducted by Zbigniew Kwieciński indicates that schools have a considerable power of selections which eliminate what "forms out of public uniform school – a medium creating << an inferior class >> of people without opportunities for work, entering culture and citizen activity. On the other hand, status and profession-related orientations of youth indicate they are lost. Perhaps a considerable part of youth which is best

[1] A. Nalaskowski, *Przestrzenie i miejsca szkoły,* Wyd. Impuls, Kraków 2002, p.9.
[2] Cf.: Z. Kwieciński, B. Śliwerski (ed.), *Pedagogika,* Wyd. Nauk. PWM, Warszawa 2003, p.240-244 and J. B. A. E. Mc Whirter, *Zagrożona młodzież*, Wyd. Ed. PARPA, Warszawa 2005, p. 115.
[3] D.Klus-Stańska, *Dokąd zmierza polska szkoła?,* Wyd. Akad. „Żak", Warszawa 2008, p. 10.

prepared to achieve academic and professional successes will cross << blind streets >> of education, following fashion and media advice – and not their recognition of their own real needs and offers of the labour market" [4] (our own emphasis: R.K; J.R-K).

Since schools are supposed to ensure possibilities for individual development of a person which leads to "educating wise, independently thinking individuals who are open to other people and goodness of the world [...], people able to think critically, in a sovereign fashion, bravely facing their life and responsible for creating a decent society",[5] then their expanse needs to be organized so that it provides opportunities and be open to diverse needs of all students – including those with special educational needs.

The significance of expanse and place for the quality of education as well as recognition of individual needs is emphasized by A. Nalaskowski: "didactic practice focuses on methods and means of teaching, on the structure of content and knowledge assessment (unfortunately, this knowledge is all too frequently understood by teachers as a collection of information and academic knowledge – note: R.K. and J. R-K.), on teaching materials and textbooks. It almost never touches upon the teacher's dress code, lesson's staginess, not to mention teaching locations. It is (for the didactic practice) virtually unnoticed, without meaning – it exists, because it has to in some form or other".[6] For the school to be able to teach independent acquisition of knowledge, approaching it, showing how others did it, exploration of it – it requires to eliminate barriers between students and teachers, to redefine knowledge[7] as well as create proper expanse for those processes and students' needs. Aleksander Nalaskowski draws attention to the fact that "by looking for the most refined methods of teaching, surrounding ourselves with expensive media-based technologies and using costly equipment – we attempt to effectively eliminate all obstacles appearing between students and knowledge transferred to them by teachers. We appear to have forgotten, however, about one of them – the place where the process of education transpires. It can be as uncomfortable as too tight shoes or too dark sunglasses".[8]

The significance of educational expanse was emphasized by H. Kwiatkowska. She classifies it – next to time and place - as one of "neglected educational categories".[9] Accord-

---

[4] Z. Kwieciński, *Wykluczanie,* Wyd. UMK, Toruń 2002, p. 149.
[5] Z. Kwieciński, *Wystąpienie na otwarcie VII Ogólnopolskiego Zjazdu Pedagogicznego w Toruniu,* [in:] M.M. Urlińska, A. Uniewska, J. Horowski *„Po życie sięgać nowe". Teoria a praktyka edukacyjna,* Wyd. Adam Marszałek, Toruń 2012, p. 28.
[6] A. Nalaskowski, *Przestrzenie... op.cit.,* p.52.
[7] D. Klus-Stańska, *Dokąd zmierza polska szkoła?,* Wyd. Akad. „Żak", Warszawa 2008, p. 14 and subsequent ones
[8] A. Nalaskowski, *Przestrzenie...op.cit.,* p.54.
[9] H. Kwiatkowska, *Czas, miejsce, przestrzeni - zaniedbane kategorie pedagogiczne.* [in:] A Nalaskowski, K. Rubacha (ed.), *Pedagogika w progu trzeciego tysiąclecia,* Wyd. UMK, Toruń 2001.

ing to the author – "education of expanse inspires unlimited reflection, opening to diverse thinking options, tolerance of differences and information-related contradictions. This type of pedagogy aims to achieve a version of identity which does not limit movement, which could – and even has to - be exchanged for other ones".[10] M. Mendel understands this category in a similar fashion – referring to a representative of humanistic geography, Yi-Fu Tuan: "expanse is open and associated with freedom, a place – on the other hand – is a form of its closing; it is a proper space, our world, marked by our presence, a house we love".[11] Therefore, an expanse can be considered "a certain composition of places and distances between them – or places out of which some constitute distances between them".[12] School is also an expanse with a certain composition.

Various definitional perceptions of expanse (for example, encyclopedic ones by Yi-Fu Tuan, M. Mendel and socialization- and philosophy-related) lead one to conclude that it is an ambiguous concept – which, on the one hand, constitutes an impediment and, on the other – allows for a multi-faceted analysis.[13]

From a pedagogical viewpoint, a concept of expanse formulated by E.T.Hall appears to be useful.[14] The author indicates its hidden nature and influence that we mostly do not realize (expanse as "mute language"). This hidden character is also emphasized by R. Meighan. This author sees both its influence on teachers and students' behaviour and specification of a certain kind of relation between them – as well as influencing possibilities and manners and styles of teaching.[15]

E.T. Hall distinguishes three types of expanse:

1. Permanent expanse like buildings. It influences and indicates a large part of our actions ("we shape our buildings and they, in turn, shape us").

2. Semi-permanent expanse – management of permanent expanse using portable objects such as furniture. It can assume a pro-social character – favouring interactions/ communication or non-prosocial one – limiting and inhabiting those processes.

3. Informal expanse - social distances maintained by people: intimate, individual, social and public. In each of them there are two phases: closer and further.[16]

---

[10] Ibidem, p. 64-65

[11] M. Mendel, *Wstęp,* [in:] M. Mendel *Pedagogika miejsca.,* Wyd.Nauk. DSWE TWP, Wrocław 2006, p.10.

[12] Ibidem, p. 15.

[13] Cf.: M. Dagiel, *Znaczenie i przestrzeń – próba interpretacji wieloprzestrzenności szkoły.* W: M. Nowicka (ed), *Nauczyciel i uczeń w przestrzeniach szkoły,* Wyd. Uniwersytetu Warmińsko-Mazurskiego, Olsztyn 2002.

[14] E.T.Hall, *Ukryty wymiar, Wyd. Muza S.A., Warszawa 1997, p. 138 .*

[15] R. Meighan, *Socjologia edukacji, Wyd. UMK., Toruń 1993.*

[16] E.T.Hall, *Ukryty...op.cit..*

A. Nalaskowski refers to this concept by E.T. Hall. While describing school expanse, he specifies three incarnations: public, private and intimate.[17]

Public expanse. Actions within its scope are subordinated to fulfilled roles and result from the awareness of life in society. Its essence is masking private and intimate expanses. Within its scope, we can distinguish three dimensions:

- ritual, referring to common values functioning within a given collective, forcing the usage of a specific language or objects (because a given group decided so);

- formal - which defines forms of expense in order to achieve a certain expected action. Such formalization enforces order on all participants;

- service-related – derived from the formal type of expanse, but as opposed to that – actions are expected which are based on official legal regulations .[18]

Private expanse. It is defined as a collection of places and types of behaviour related to them – which are limited by individuals: their personal culture, hierarchy of values and needs. Spatial identification is predominant here, as well as the possibility to undertake one's own tasks, and a high indicator of safety. In architectural projects, it has a recreational character.[19]

Intimate expanse. It is a part of private expanse. It can only be approached by those who are allowed to do so by an individual. It is encrypted for outsiders and an act of entering it infringes social – and even legal – standards (for instance, in the case of correspondence).[20]

Therefore, school is a public expanse in all of its three dimensions (ritual, formal and service-related). Students are most frequently devoid of their private expanse within its scope: "as it was characterized by one pupil <<in school, there is nowhere to hide – except for the toilet >>".[21] Everything is controlled (sometimes using surveillance systems) as teaching staff believes that with a thorough control most cases of infringement of school discipline are eliminated. Hence, a pupil in unable to protect his secrets and virtually all his actions take place before a school audience.

A question can be posed here: can elements of expanse condition effectiveness of school's functioning? Usually, effectiveness is measured by school test results. Such an approach, however, appears to be too narrow and does not take into consideration criteria such as an ability of making decisions, critical thinking or elements of school expanse. As Roland

[17] A. Nalaskowski, *Przestrzenie...op.cit.*, p.33 and further
[18] Ibidem, p.33-34.
[19] Ibidem, p.57-58.
[20] Ibidem, p. 62-63.
[21] Ibidem, p. 60.

Meighan[22] emphasizes – they can (and usually do) have an influence on students' individual successes – also ones with special educational needs. This thesis is confirmed by the results of studies conducted by the Mc Whirters.[23] They indicate that the results of education are also dependent on such elements of school expanse as: school culture, organizational structure of school and class, as well as peer influence.

It seems that all schools are, on some level, identical – and different on others. What makes schools specific is probably their culture which is understood by the Mc Whirters' as a collection of behavioral guidelines, common values, beliefs, rituals and ceremonies which may lead to improvement of students (for instance, students proud of the culture in their school work more efficiently).[24] Authors divide it into two categories: student atmosphere and teacher-staff atmosphere. David Touhy, as well, emphasizes a significance of school culture for educational results as well as development and change. He perceives it – in the vein of E.H. Schein – as a pattern of basic guidelines created, discovered and developed by a studying group. It could be recognized by products (rituals, roles and norms), guidelines (referring to the network of ideas and convictions regarding school, its organization and tasks) and values (maintained by an organization such as school). [25]

The quality of school atmosphere (which could also be specified as a psycho-social atmosphere) also has an influence on creating a concept of oneself and student's self-evaluation. In addition, it can have an impact on the ability to learn to make choices out of available options, making decisions, independent problem-solving and self-evaluation.[26] Therefore, a good atmosphere leads to a better school environment for students.

Another important (for student development) element of school expanse is its mission (philosophy) and organizational structure resulting from it – division into classes. The structure of a class might be conducive to creating a sense of subjectivity, provide a possibility to contribute to one's group's activity as well as encourage acceptance and acknowledgement of differences (it is particularly important in cases of students with special educational needs).

School expanse also involves peer contacts which teach proper ways to communicate with other people, an ability to control one's own social actions, to share successes, defeats and problems. For youth, this aspect of school life appears to be one of the most important

---

[22] R. Meighan, *Socjologia...op.cit..*
[23] J.J.; B.T.; A.M.; E.H.Mc Whirter *Zagrożona... op.cit..*
[24] Ibidem, p.120-121.
[25] D. Touhy *Dusza szkoły. O tym, co sprzyja zmianie i rozwojowi,* PWN, Warszawa 2002, p. 22-27.
[26] J.J.; B.T.; A.M.; E.H.Mc Whirter *Zagrożona młodzież,* Wyd. Edukacyjne PARPA, Warszawa 2005, p.121 and further.

owing to their stage of development, time in their life when comments of peers measure their self-esteem and value.

We employed all those various interpretations of school expanse and its elements as a basis to create our own description including dimensions crucial from the point of view of a student with special educational needs: physical, formal, didactic and social ones. For all of them, we specified its scope and content:

✓ **Physical expanse** is a school building with all its rooms and surrounding terrains;

✓ **Formal expanse -** formed by regulations of Ministry of National Education, headmaster and resolutions made by teachers' board which are consistent with them, as well as health-related recommendations, decisions and expectations of parents;

✓ **Didactic expanse** filled with organisational elements concerning didactic process, school and external systems of actions supporting education, teaching craft and didactic and educational counseling;

✓ **Social expanse** (public and private) constructed through diverse human relations – manifested by school traditions and culture as well as a consistent system of educating influences.

The essence of the implementation of special educational needs

A new model of psychological and pedagogical assistance – gradually introduced at schools since 1 September of 2011 – presupposes another quality of implementing special educational needs. The roots of school problems of a relatively large group of students are developmental and/or social dysfunctions - usually of a long-term character which - to a considerable extent - influence the course and results of education. As H. Stępniewska – Gębik and R. Kwiecińska argue – this category of students "is a resultant of potential and deficiencies of a child - as well as of potential and deficiencies of their environment. Special educational needs students are both children and youth who possess a certificate stating their need for special education, and those who have problems while realizing standard syllabus requirements – resulting from any specifics of their cognitive and perception-related functioning (IQ lower than average, dyslexia, disgraphia, dysortography, dyscalculia), health-related one (children with chronic illnesses and disabled ones), environmental limitations (children socially unadjusted or at a risk of maladjustment), those who are in a crisis and a traumatic situation, have adaptational difficulties related to cultural differences, environmentally neglected – but also talented students".[27]

[27] Cf.: H. Stępniewska – Gębik, R. Kwiecińska, *Kryzys ucznia. Co powinien wiedzieć i zrobić pedagog? Znaczenie kompetencji z zakresu interwencji kryzysowej w pracy pedagogicznej*, „Ruch Pedagogiczny" 2012, no 2.

In materials prepared and distributed at schools by the Ministry of National Education[28], we can find a description of fundamental rules the implementation of which is to ensure a proper quality of teaching this significantly varied group of students. Among those are:

- rule of individualization of work with a student – executed during mandatory and optional educational classes – taking into consideration his or her psychophysical potential,

- rule of assistance closer to a student – the essence of which is organisation of help at the school a given student attends,

- rule of assistance closer to parents, taking into consideration advice, consulting, training and workshops conducted by teachers and specialists, the goal of which is to provide a widely understood support for solving educational and didactic problems,

- rule of assistance closer to teacher understood as substantial and organizational help resulting in the improvement of qualifications serving efficient helping process,

- rule of flexibility and adequacy - the aim of which is to eliminate formal barriers and organizational hindrances in the process of executing special needs,

- rule of institutional and personal partnership regarding various subjects in order to create a specific coalition for the sake of this group of students,

- rule of updating which introduces into classification and description of special educational needs current changes – possible in the course of improving medical, psychological and pedagogical knowledge,

- rule of trusting the professionalism of teachers and school as an institution of rapid response able to perform a quick and accurate diagnosis and efficiently provide help in forms that are proper for a child.

The essence of help lies in recognizing and satisfying needs. It is necessary to recognize not only the type and scope of dysfunctions, developmental and educational needs resulting from them, but also psychophysical potential of children – including their strengths. Actions referred to as the level of diagnosis are used for this purpose. Satisfying takes a form of preparing a concept of providing help (programming level – preparing a plan of supporting actions or an individual educational and therapeutic programme) and its execution by proper and competent people (practical level). A headmaster of a given institution is responsible for organization of help; he or she appoints programming and implementing teams.

[28]Cf.: M. Jas, M. Jarosińska, *Specjalne potrzeby edukacyjne dzieci i młodzieży*, Wyd. MEN, Warszawa 2010.

Methodological guidelines of the research

The purpose of this research conducted by the authors is an analysis of diverse scopes of public school's functioning as an institution in which an education is implemented for students with special needs.

The research problem is included in the following question: in what scope does an educational expanse of a public school take into consideration special educational needs of students?

Empirical data was obtained through an analysis of documentation conducted in psychological and pedagogical counselling centres – by school pedagogues, using polls and interviews.

The research was conducted in three schools and three psychological and pedagogical counselling centres. Participants included teachers (83 people), school pedagogues (3 people), psychologists and pedagogues from counselling centres (4 people). This choice of places was intentional – participants took part in the research on the basis of intentional and arbitrary choice.

Empirical material was collected in the school years of 2010/2011 and 2011/2012.

One also needs to emphasize that the research constitutes a part of a more extensive research project – and the presented results are of a fragmentary character.

Special needs pupils in the educational expanse of public school

All the schools participating in the research have pupils who require permanent, additional, individually profiled assistance.

And, specifically:

- In school A (primary), there is a group of pupils with specific learning difficulties, linguistic communication disorders, adaptational problems, coming from neglected environments, showing behavioral disorders, intellectually disabled and chronically ill. Altogether, they constitute 42,3% of the total number of students. A considerable majority of them were diagnosed by staff of psychological and pedagogical counselling centres.
- In school B (junior high school), special educational needs are demonstrated by pupils with specific difficulties in learning, with behavioral disorders, enviornmentally neglected, chronically ill, remarkably talented, with sensory defects. This groups constitutes 39,1% of the total number of students in this school. A considerable majority of them were diagnosed by staff of psychological and pedagogical counselling centres.
- In school C (secondary school), there is a group of pupils with specific learning difficulties, linguistic communication disorders, showing behavioral disorders, chronically ill

and remarkably talented. This groups constitutes 29,8% of the total number of students in this school. A half of them were diagnosed by staff of psychological and pedagogical counselling centres, a situation of the remaining students was recognized by teachers.

In all of the schools included in the research, dyslectics form a prevailing group (teachers estimate their number as approximately 25-26%), behavioral disorders concern about 7% students, the rest of those included in this category are rather individual cases. In all of those schools, there are also students who periodically need additional support – those are persons who experience a crisis or a traumatic situation.

Table 1. Elements of school expanse and implementation of special educational needs

The scope and elements of expanse	School A	School B	School C
Physical expanse			
Separate sectors (rooms, cloakrooms, corridor)	+	-	-
Office of school pedagogue	+	+	+
Offices where therapy is conducted	-	-	-
Place in classroom chosen to suit pupil's needs	+	-	-
Equipment and didactic measures suited to special needs of a pupil	+	-	-
Free access to teachers' room	+	-	-
Library (place, offer, time)	-	-	-
School clubroom (place, offer, time)	+	-	lack
School pitch and garden arrangement taking into consideration special needs	-	-	-
Formal expanse			
Knowledge of regulations by Ministry of National Education	+	+	+
Decisions on the part of principal and Teachers' Board made for the sake of special needs pupils (additional ones – not resulting from Ministry of National Education regulations)	+	+	+
Knowledge of psychological and pedagogical recommendations	+	+	+
Understanding and correct interpretation of psychological and pedagogical recommendations	+	+	-
Respecting health-related recommendations	+	+	+
Execution of formal applications reported by parents	+	+	+
Developing parental initiatives regarding diagnosing children's needs and their implementation	+	+	-
Didactic expanse			
Diversification of teaching content	+	-	-
Organisation of didactic process taking into consideration special needs	-	-	-
Adaptation of methodical craft of teachers.	+	-	-
Detailed and consistent execution of arrangements	+	-	-

included in internal school system of evaluation taking into consideration the potential of pupils with special needs			
Therapeutic and remedial classes	+	-	-
Systematically conducted didactic counselling	-	-	-
Possibility to take advantage of extracurricular system of supporting education	+	+	+
Respecting arrangements guaranteed in the system of external assessment	+	+	+
School's participation in professional counselling	-	+	-
School's participation in designing educational careers of pupils with special needs	-	-	-
Social expanse			
Private expanse of a special needs pupil	-	-	-
Individualized relations with teachers	+	-	-
Peer acceptance	+	+	+
Mutual support of teachers working with special needs pupils.	+	+	+
Support for teachers (including awards and other benefits) shown by school principal.	-	-	-
Parents as school allies	+	-	-
Consistency of educating activities	-	-	-

Source: own work

Based on the evaluation included in the table, one can conclude that only in the formal expanse there is a consideration for needs of pupils requiring special support in education. In physical, didactic and social expanses – only selective elements of the system of help for this group of students are realised. They are inconsistent and result rather from good will and preferences of teachers; they also have a temporary character – quite often interventional. Unfavourable situations are aggravated along with the growing age of children – the scope of help in primary schools is considerably reduced in junior high schools and at the upper secondary level of education.

Organization of the didactic process is consolidated and does not take into consideration any form of diversity. Methodological craft of teachers is not diversified to such an extent that they could flexibly adapt methods of work to specifics of children's problems, their learning conditions as well as to the currently taught knowledge. Schools only insignificantly implement didactic counselling which allows special needs pupils to learn proper, efficient learning techniques. In addition, schools neglect their obligation to design educational careers of their pupils. This task is taken over by parents, usually supported by psychologists.

Teachers, burdened by additional duties, do not receive any remuneration for the execution of those duties. This is why they treat work with special needs pupils as burdensome tasks or hours necessary to complete their obligatory teaching load. The basic criterion of giving teachers tasks connected with special needs is their weekly load and not substantial preparation and personality-related predispositions.

Final reflections

This narrow scope of research can hardly warrant any formulation of conclusions – but it offers some food for thought. In our opinion, this kind of reflection is essential. It concerns a significant number of students who should receive psychological and pedagogical help which would enable them to successfully continue their education; it also concerns all the teachers responsible for this process.

- Legal regulations prepared by Ministry of National Education - and currently in operation - provide the special needs pupils with a high standard of assistance in the scope of implementing education at subsequent levels. They also specify that the school is an institution where this assistance is concentrated – acting as an expert evaluating both the type and scope of dysfunctions inhibiting learning process and a scope of necessary help. Numerous schools have not yet prepared specific executive regulations regarding the number of such pupils, the characterization of their needs as well as the staff and facility-related capabilities of a given institution. Appointing tasks to teachers frequently takes place without any substantial justification.
- Diversity of educational problems related to special needs pupils requires from teachers a highly developed individualization of work. It is not possible in the traditional system of organising didactic process and lack of extracurricular therapeutic classes.
- Teachers are not interested in working with special needs pupils if it is perceived as an additional professional burden, the execution of which does not result in additional remuneration.
- Considerably (and alarmingly) decreases a number of children registered at psychological and pedagogical counselling centres by schools (teachers, school pedagogue, form-master). Any performed diagnosis results in a necessity to form teams preparing proper documents and executing tasks specified in them.

An excerpt from one teacher's opinion might be perceived as an illustration and a complementation of this reflection. We quote it also with a hope that the first years of functioning of the school system of assistance for special needs pupils in accordance with "the package" of 17 November, 2010 have provided a sufficient load of experiences to modify it.

"(...) each student who requires help needs to have his own card of individual needs, individual educational and therapeutic program and a plan of supporting actions. In practice, it boils down to copying diagnoses from psychological and pedagogical counselling centres. Tonnes of paper, heaps of folders and binders. For EVERY pupil (in my school there are over one hundred pupils with formal diagnoses) there needs to be formed a team consisting of teachers and specialists. Such a team is led by a coordinator and parents learn of the team's findings in a written form. That, of course, comes after they are informed about the forms of help which are offered to their child. A team prepares a plan of supporting actions for every child. Parents need to be invited to such meetings – in writing! (A worker of the Ministry of National Education– note: R.K, J.R.-K.), when asked about his view of writing plans, programs and cards for several dozen of pupils, reacted with a disarming surprise: "Really? I was sure that there are only five or six pupils with such diagnoses."[29]

Bibliography

Ainscow M., *Robić właściwe rzeczy. Potrzeby specjalne z perspektywy doskonalenia pracy szkoły,* [w:] Fairbairn G., Fairbairn S., (red.), Integracja dzieci o specjalnych potrzebach, Warszawa 2000.

Dagiel M., *Znaczenie i przestrzeń – próba interpretacji wieloprzestrzenności szkoły*, [w:] M. Nowicka (red.), *Nauczyciel i uczeń w przestrzeniach szkoły*, Olsztyn 2002.

Hall E.T., *Ukryty wymiar*, Warszawa 1997.

M. Jas, M. Jarosińska, *Specjalne potrzeby edukacyjne dzieci i młodzieży*, Warszawa 2010.

Klus-Stańska D., *Dokąd zamierza polska szkoła*, Warszawa 2008.

Kwiatkowska H., *Czas, miejsce, przestrzeń – zaniedbane kategorie pedagogiczne,* [w:] A. Nalaskowski, K. Rubacha (red.), *Pedagogika w progu trzeciego tysiąclecia,* Toruń 2001.

Kwieciński Z., *Wykluczanie*, Toruń 2002.

Kwieciński Z., *Wystąpienie na otwarcie VII Ogólnopolskiego Zjazdu Pedagogicznego w Toruniu,* w: M.H. Urlińska, A. Uniewska, J. Hornowski, *„Po życie sięgać nowe". Teoria a praktyka edukacyjna*, Toruń 2012.

Mc Whirter J.J.; Mc Whirter B.T.; Mc Whirter A.M.; Mc Whirter E.H., *Zagrożona młodzież,* Warszawa 2005.

Meighan R., *Socjologia edukacji,* Toruń 1993.

[29] Gabriela T., *Współczesna szkoła osiągnęła szczyt absurdu. Uczeń jest w niej najmniej ważny*, List tygodnia, "Wysokie Obcasy" 12 maja 2012, p. 4.

Mendel M., *Pedagogika miejska*, Wrocław 2006.

Nalaskowski A., *Przestrzenie i miejsca szkoły,* Kraków 2002.

Rybska-Klapa J., *Opieka nad dzieckiem o specjalnych potrzebach w warunkach szkoły ogólnodostępnej,* [w:] B. Muchacka (red.), *Szkoła w nauce i praktyce edukacyjnej.* Tom II. Kraków 2006.

Rybska-Klapa J., *Realizacja specjalnych potrzeb edukacyjnych w szkołach ogólnodostępnych – rzeczywistość i postulaty,* [w:] A. Karpińska (red.), *Edukacja w okresie przemian,* Białystok 2010.

Stępniewska- Gębik H., Kwiecińska R., *Kryzys ucznia. Co powinien wiedzieć i zrobić pedagog? Znaczenie kompetencji z zakresu interwencji kryzysowej w pracy pedagogicznej.* „Ruch Pedagogiczny" 2012,nr 2.

Touhy D., *Dusza szkoły. O tym co sprzyja zmianie i rozwojowi*, Warszawa 2002.

Maria Aleksandrovich
Pomeranian University in Slupsk, Poland

DIFFERENT SIDES OF GIFTEDNESS: WHAT MODERN TEACHERS HAVE TO KNOW?

Summary

In the paper the author presents different sides of giftedness, comparative characteristics of gifted students and twice exceptional students as well as teaching strategies for twice exceptional. The aim of the article is to discuss relevant characteristics of teachers for gifted children and some teaching tips for special competencies of teachers for gifted and talented students.

Introduction

Identifying and understanding of the gifted is not always easy. Unique potential does not always appear in everyday work in the classroom and in tests of academic achievement, and sometimes giftedness hides behind the learning disabilities or develops in the shadow of disability. The teachers should be conscious about individual differences as well as difficulties that may block the development of the abilities and giftedness. The understanding of needs and special features of gifted children we should start with clear modern definition of the terms "*giftedness*", "*gifted child*", "*gifted children with disabilities*" and "*twice exceptionality*" or "*exceptionally gifted*".

According to the Penguin Dictionary of Psychology "*gifted*" is a generic term used to refer to a person with a special talent, this talent may be a general intellectual one or a specific talent such as music or chess playing. And "*gifted child*" it is a child who displays special talents in any area of human behavior that society values. This meaning is based on the notion that giftedness may extend beyond those characteristics and talents assessed through standardized testing instruments[1]. APA Concise Dictionary of Psychology says that "*giftedness*" is the state of possessing a great amount of natural abilities, talent, or intelligence, which usually becomes evident at a very young age[2].

In 1997 following definition of gifted and talented was introduced: "Gifted/talented children are those children who possess an untrained and spontaneously expressed natural ability in at least one ability domain significantly beyond that typically seen in children of the

[1] A.S.Reber, *Penguin dictionary of psychology*. London: Penguin Books, 1995, p. 315.
[2] Ibidem, p.211.

same age. Giftedness comes in many forms and levels. It is found in students of all socio-economic groups, and of diverse personalities and backgrounds. It can be combined with other exceptionalities/special needs such as learning disabilities, socio-economic disadvantage, geographic isolation, aboriginality and having English as a second language"[3].

In 1997 Brody and Mills proposed the definition of gifted students with learning difficulties: "Gifted/LD students are students of superior intellectual ability who exhibit a significant discrepancy in their level of performance in a particular academic area such as reading, mathematics, spelling, or written expression. Their academic performance is substantially below what would be expected based on their general intellectual ability. As with other children exhibiting learning disabilities, this discrepancy is not due to the lack of educational opportunity in that academic area or other health impairment. Because academically gifted students with learning disabilities demonstrate such high academic potential, their academic achievement may not be as low as that of students with learning disabilities who demonstrate average academic potential. Consequently, these students may be less likely to be referred for special education testing"[4].

So, often gifted children may not be particularly high achievers in the classroom. They may have problems with attention (which may or may not be related to ADHD, autism spectrum disorders or other disability), have poor organizational skills and as a result have learning disabilities, have problems with adaptation the classroom being handicap or simply did not "find" the right teacher with appropriate teaching style.

"Exceptionally gifted" or "*twice-exceptional"* are children, who, on one side, are identified as gifted and talented in one or more areas of exceptionality (specific academics, general intellectual ability, creativity, leadership, visual, or performing arts) and, on the other side, are also identified with a disability: specific learning disability, significant identifiable emotional disability, physical disabilities, sensory disabilities, autism, or ADHD[5]. Research indicates that 2-5 % of the gifted population will have disabilities and 2-5 % of students with disabilities will be gifted[6].

These students are difficult to identify because in everyday life gifted characteristics may mask disabilities as well as disabilities may mask gifted potential. Either the strengths, the disabilities, or both may not be identified. To be considered twice-exceptional, the student

[3] D.Farmer, *Meeting the Needs of Gifted Students in the Regular Classroom*, 1997, http://austega.com/gifted/9-gifted/21-whatis.html date: 01/03/2013

[4] L.E.Brody & C.J.Mills, *Gifted children with learning disabilities: A review of the issues.* Journal of Learning Disabilities, 1997, 30 (3), p. 285, from http://www.ldonline.org/indepth/gifted date: 03/03/2013.

[5] J.Campanelli & C.Ericson, *Twice Exceptional Guide.* USA: Ohio Department of Education, 2007, p.3.

[6] J.R. Whitmore & C.J. Maker, (1985). *Intellectual giftedness in disabled persons.* Rockville, MD: Aspen, 1985.

must be identified for gifted education and special education services. Gifted students with disabilities are at-risk because their educational and social/emotional needs often go undetected. The resulting inconsistent academic performance can lead educators to believe twice-exceptional students are not putting forth adequate effort. Hidden disabilities may prevent students with advanced cognitive abilities from achieving their potential. Twice-exceptional students will continue to be at-risk until educators can learn about and understand the educational and social/emotional needs of twice-exceptional students[7].

Brody and Mills in 1997 underlined the importance of well-organized environment and flexible educational influence on such children, because many more students may be learning disabled and gifted than anyone realizes. And in spite of their high intellectual ability, such students remain unchallenged, suffer silently and do not achieve their potential because their educational needs are not recognized and addressed.

Gagne has developed the model, which allows to understand the role of the child's motivation and of factors in the child's environment (family, school, peers, etc) that may hinder the child's ability being realized into achievements[8] (Figure 1).

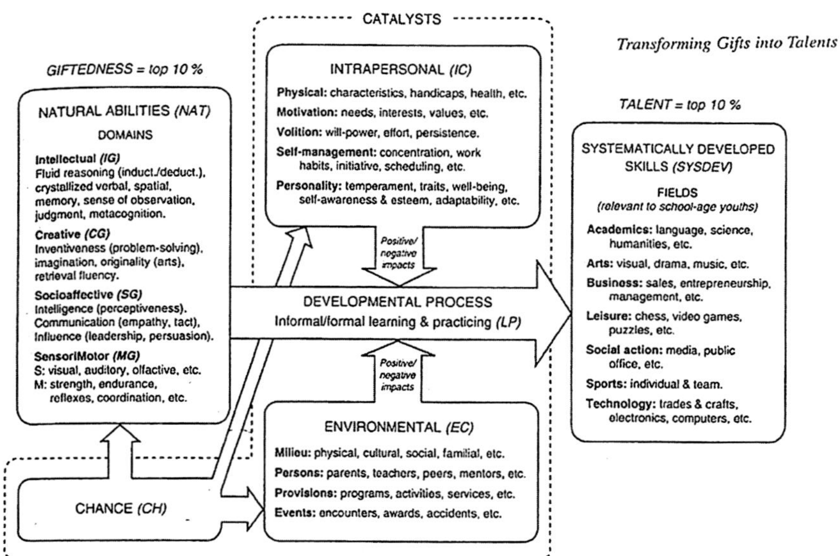

Figure 1. Françoys Gagné's Differentiated Model of Giftedness and Talent (2005)

[7] T.Anthony, L. Baldwin, M. Bianco, B. Bieber, B.Busby, J. Cornier, Ch. Franklin-Rohr, J. Medina, A.Miller, Sh. Muir, D.Pereles, K. Thurman, B.Trail, M.Worner, *Twice-Exceptional Students Gifted Students with Disabilities*. Denver, Colorado, 2009.

[8] F.Gagné, Transforming gifts into talents: the DMGT as a developmental theory. High ability studies, 2004, 15 (2), 119-147.

Gagné's (2005) distinguishes between interpersonal catalysts (motivation and personality) and ecopsychological catalysts (environment). All factors (catalysts), which are in particular (a) significant persons, (b) environment resources, (c) interventions, (d) meaningful events, and (e) coincidences, influence the improvement of the aptitudes to talents in a positive or negative way. Gagné's model is to understand more like a developmental theory, because learning and practice are the moderators that natural abilities are transformed into talents. "The 'gifts' are the genetic endowments while talents are the product of the synergistic interaction of genetic predispositions with home, school, and the physical and social environment surrounding a child"[9].

According to Gagné (2004, 2005) all talents are developed from natural abilities (genetically determined gifts) through learning (informal or formal) influenced (positively or negatively) by inner and outer catalysts. The gifts should be supported and developed during the learning processes, should be enriched during the practice and only then gifts could turn into talents[10].

These Different Appearances of Giftedness

Ordinary gifted children. The description of gifted students is based of the characteristic of general behavioral, learning, and creative features given by Blum[11]. Gifted children's behavior differs from that of their age-mates because many of them learn to read early, with better comprehension of the nuances of language. Usually they learned to read before entering school and often read widely, quickly, and intensely and have large vocabularies. They are extremely curious about objects, ideas, situations, or events. They may read a great deal on their own, preferring books and magazines written for children older than they are. That could be the reason why they are better able to construct and handle abstractions and have well-developed powers of conceptualization and synthesis. Quite often they pick up and interpret nonverbal cues and can draw inferences that other children need to have spelled out for them. Gifted children like to learn new things, are willing to examine the unusual, and are highly inquisitive, what is more, they learn basic skills better, more quickly, and with less practice. They often take great pleasure in intellectual activity, exhibit an intrinsic motivation to learn, find out, or explore and are often very persistent and they tackle tasks and problems in a well-organized, goal-directed, and

---

[9] J.F.Feldhusen & F.A.Jarwan, *Identification of gifted and talented youth for educational programs*. In K.A.Heller, F.J.Mönks, R.J.Sternberg, & R.F.Subotnik (eds.), *International handbook of giftedness and talent,* 2nd ed. Oxford, UK: Elsevier 2000, p.273.

[10] M.Aleksandrovich & H.Zoglowek, Has the teacher of the gifted to be gifted? About characteristics and competencies of teachers for gifted and talented students. In O. Holz & R. Seebauer: Interactive and Competence-orientated Education. Hamburg: Dr.Kovac, 2012.

[11] M.W.Blum, *Parents of gifted children. a minibibliography on readings for parents and teachers of gifted children.* ERIC Clearinghouse on Handicapped and Gifted Children, Association Dr., Reston, VA, 1985.

efficient manner. At the same time, sometimes they can work independently at an earlier age and can concentrate for longer periods. While working they often have seemingly boundless energy, which sometimes leads to a misdiagnosis of hyperactivity.

In everyday life they show keen powers of observation and a sense of the significant; they have an eye for important details, because often they attack complicated material by separating it into components and analyzing it systematically. They have a large storehouse of information about a variety of topics, which they can recall quickly and they are quick to spot inconsistencies, readily grasp underlying principles and can often make valid generalizations about events, people, or objects. That is why also they are sometimes skeptical, critical, and evaluative.

Gifted children's creative abilities often set them apart from their age-mates. They are fluent and flexible thinkers, able to generate possibilities, consequences, or related ideas. This flexibility makes then also original thinkers, seeking new, unusual, or unconventional associations and combinations among items of information. They are studding showing intellectual playfulness and well developed fantasize and imagination. As a result they can also see relationships among seemingly unrelated objects, ideas, or facts. And this ability makes them elaborate thinkers, producing new steps, ideas, responses, or other embellishments to a basic idea, situation, or problems. They can be less intellectually inhibited than their peers are in expressing opinions and ideas, and they often disagree spiritedly with others' statements. They often are aware of their own impulsiveness and irrationality, and they show emotional sensitivity also to beauty and are attracted to aesthetic values[12].

Gifted students with learning difficulties. This group of children may display asynchronic development and very different characteristics from each other (Hishinuma & Tadaki, 1996; Willard-Holt, 1999; Ruban & Reis, 2005; Baum, Cooper & Neu, 2001 Aleksandrovich, 2012). So, a group with reading disabilities may have high verbal or visual-motor aptitude, well developed creativity, boredom with grade level or below grade level reading, variable scores on achievement tests in reading sections, improved performance with compensation strategies. Students with math disabilities may display high verbal aptitude, possible creativity, boredom with grade level or below grade level math, variable scores on achievement tests in math sections, improved performance with compensation, low tolerance for frustration with rote-drill math tasks, possible inattention, and unrealistically high or low self-concept[13].

---

[12] M.W.Blum, *Parents of gifted children. a minibibliography on readings for parents and teachers of gifted children.* ERIC Clearinghouse on Handicapped and Gifted Children, Association Dr., Reston, VA, 1985.
[13] E.Hishinuma & S.Tadaki, Addressing diversity of the gifted/at risk: Characteristics for identification. Gifted Child Today, 1996, Sep/Oct, p.25-50.

Gifted students with learning difficulties often have a propensity for advanced content, often they can be obsessed with learning everything about one specific topic and in school they often know about it more than the teacher and at a higher level of complexity (see Table 1). They also have a desire to create original products. They enjoy abstract concepts and playing with the abstract. They show nonlinear learning styles, for example writing is a problem but calculations come easily[14].

Table 1. Characteristics of Gifted Students with Learning Disabilities

Characteristics Which Hamper Identification as Gifted	Characteristic Strengths
Frustration with inability to master certain academic skill Learned helplessness General lack of motivation Disruptive classroom behavior Perfectionism Supersensitivity (e.g., to criticism, to feeling of others) Failure to complete assignments Lack of organizational skills Careless in one's work Demonstration of poor listening and concentration skills Deficiency in tasks emphasizing memory and perceptual abilities Low self-esteem Unrealistic self-expectations Absence of social skills with some peers (e.g., can be aggressive and defensive in relationships)	Advanced vocabulary use Exceptional analytic abilities High levels of creativity High levels of productivity (particularly in the area of interest) Advanced problem-solving skills Ability to think of divergent ideas and solutions Specific aptitude (artistic, musical, or mechanical) Wide variety of interests Good memory Strong critical-thinking skills Unusual ability to see interrelationships among ideas and concepts Extraordinary reasoning skills Task commitment Desire for knowledge, desire to explore and discover Sense of humor A variety of special abilities

Source: L.M.Ruban & S.M.Reis, *Identification and Assessment of Gifted Students With Learning Disabilities.* Theory Into Practice, 2005, 44, 2, p.117, from http://educationinaminute. com/bogota/Resources/Articles/Ruban%20and%20 Reis.pdf date: 13/03/2013

Characteristics Similar in Giftedness and ADHD. Research indicates that in many cases, a child is diagnosed with ADHD when in fact the child is gifted and reacting to an inappropriate curriculum[15]. Among the characteristics of students with ADHD often mentioned poorly sustained attention and, as a result, diminished persistence on tasks not having immediate consequences, often shift from one uncompleted activity to another. They also show

[14] S.M.Baum, C.R. Cooper & T.R.Neu, Dual differentiation: An approach for meeting the curricular needs of gifted students with learning disabilities. Psychology in the Schools, 2001, 38 (5), p.477-490.
[15] J.T.Webb & C.J.Maker, *ADHD and children who are gifted.* ERIC EC Digest E522, 1993.

variability in task performance and time used to accomplish tasks. These students are impulsive with poor delay of gratification. They are more active, restless than other children and often talk excessively and interrupt or intrude on others. It also happens because of difficulty adhering to rules and regulations. They can often lose things necessary for tasks or activities at home or school and may appear inattentive to details. They are highly sensitive to criticism. In everyday life problem behaviors exist in all settings, but in some are more severe[16].

The key to distinguishing between ADHD and giftedness is the pervasiveness of the *"acting out"* behaviors. If the acting out is specific to certain situations, the child's behavior is more likely related to giftedness; whereas, if the behavior is consistent across all situations, the child's behavior is more likely related to ADHD. It is also possible for a child to be both gifted and ADHD[17].

Similarities Between Asperger Children and Gifted Children. In the literature mentioned about seven characteristics common to gifted children and to children with AS. The first one, verbal fluency or precocity is common to both, and both may have excellent memories (Levy, 1988; Frith, 1991; Clark, 1992; Silverman, 1993). The second, both may evidence a fascination with letters or numbers and enjoy memorizing factual information at an early age. The third, both may demonstrate an absorbing interest in a specialized topic and may acquire vast amounts of factual information about it[18]. The fourth and fifth, they may annoy peers with their limitless talk about their interests and ask endless questions or give such lengthy and elaborately specific responses to questions that it seems they are unable to stop. The six it is hypersensitivity to sensory stimuli. The seventh, AS children may have a special deep interest the same as gifted children have their *"passions"*[19]. Both these groups are described as experiencing uneven development, particularly when cognitive development is compared to social and affective development at a young age (Hollingworth, 1942; Altman, 1983; Asperger, 1991).

For to distinguish normal giftedness from twice exceptionality we have to take into account the distinguishing criteria which are listed in Table 2.

[16] R.A.Barkley, Attention deficit hyperactivity disorder: A handbook for diagnosis and treatment. New York: Guilford Press, 1990; S.Cline & D.Schwartz, Diverse populations of gifted children. NJ: Merrill, 1999; J.T.Webb & C.J.Maker, ADHD and children who are gifted. ERIC EC Digest E522, 1993.

[17] C.Bainbridge, *Dual Exceptionalities Gifted and Disabled from, 2012,* http://giftedkids.about.com /od/giftedandld/a/gt_and_ld.htm date: 13/03/2013.

[18] A.Klin & F.R.Volkmar, *Guidelines for parents: Assessment, diagnosis, and intervention of Asperger Syndrome.* Pittsburgh, PA: Learning Disabilities Association of America, 1995.

[19] P.Torrance, *Gifted children in the classroom.* New York: MacMillan, 1965; G.Betts & J.Kercher, *Autonomous learner model: Optimizing ability.* Greeley, CO: ALPS, 1999.

Table 2. Proposed Criteria to Differentiate Ordinary Gifted Children from Twice Exceptional Children

Differentiating Characteristic	Ordinary Gifted Child	Gifted Child with Asperger's Syndrome	Gifted Child with ADHD	Gifted Child with Physical Disabilities	Gifted Child with Visual Impairment	Gifted Child with Hearing Impairments	Gifted Child with Learning Disabilities
Speech	Normal, but may have language of older child	Pedantic, seamless speech May be able to talk extensively on a topic of interest, but have difficulty with more practical tasks	Often talk excessively Often interrupt or intrude on others	If developed then normal, but may have own language or language of older child	Superior verbal communication skills and vocabulary	Symbolic language abilities (diff. symbol system) Development of speech-reading skills without instruction Early reading ability	Advanced vocabulary
Attention	Very good, if disturbance exists, it is usually external	Poor, and disturbance is internal	May appear inattentive to details Poorly sustained attention Diminished persistence on tasks not having immediate consequences Often shift from one uncompleted activity to another	Development of compensatory skills	Excellent ability to concentrate	Delays in concept attainment	Difficulties with sequential tasks
Memory	Excellent memory	Excellent factual memory espe-	Normal, but may have diffi-	Superior memory Often have impres-	Superior memory often as compen-	Excellent memory	Difficulty with memo-

		cially good for the events from the prticular field of interest	culties with memorization connecting with lack of concentration and attention deficit	sive store of knowledge	satory skill		rization, computation, phonics, and/or spelling Keen visual memory, spatial skills
Learning abilities	Well developed and determinate by the field of interests	The drive to perform well at school if given a supportive and inclusive environment	Difficulty adhering to rules and regulations Often lose things necessary for tasks or activities at home or school	Advanced academic skills Possible limited achievement due to pace of work	Fast rate of learning Ease in learning	Nontraditional ways of getting information	Exceptional ability in geometry, science, arts, music
Cognitive abilities	Excellent, especially in the field of interests	Average or above-average intelligence	Variability in task performance and time used to accomplish tasks	Curiosity, insight Exceptional problem-solving skills Rapid grasp of ideas Cognitive development that may not be based on direct experience Possible difficulty with abstractions	Sometimes slower rate of cognitive development than sighted students Advanced problem-solving skills Braille	Ingenuity in solving problems High reasoning ability Superior performance in school Use of problem-solving skills	High abstract reasoning ability Good mathematical Good problem-finding and -solving skills Reasoning ability Comprehension of complex systems
Creativity	Well developed and sometimes	Sometimes very well developed Expertise in their	Have well developed divergent thinking,	Creativity in finding alternate ways of communicating	Creative production or thought that may progress	Rapid grasp of ideas Wide range of	Imaginative and creative Insightful

	present unusual and unexpected problem-solving approaches	chosen topic of interest – although this can become difficult in social situations as they may only talk about one topic	have original ideas and creative achievement	and accomplishing tasks	more slowly than sighted students in some academic areas	interests	Wide variety of interests
Motivation	Usually inner achievement motivation	A narrow field of interests which are exterminating the motivation to act	Impaired adherence to commands to regulate or inhibit behavior in social contexts	Motivation to achieve	Motivation to know	Self starters Intuition	Unreasonable self expectations Often, failure to complete assignments
Organizational skills and behaviour	In the response to routines may passively resist, but will often go along	Difficulty in forming friendships, playing alone or with older children & adults Very low tolerance for change, agitation, aggression	More active, restless than other children Problem behaviors exist in all settings, but in some are more severe	Ability to set and strive for long-term goals Persistence, patience	Very well developed ability to organize the nearest environment	Ability to function in the regular school setting Possibly on grade level Enjoyment of manipulating environment	Distractibility and/or disorganization
Motor Clumsiness	Not characteristic of most gifted children	50-90 % of Asperger children manifest	Often manifest	Not characteristic and manifest only in the connection to the disability	Not characteristic	Not characteristic	Not characteristic
Emotions	Perfectionism	Highly sensitive to criticism	Highly sensitive to criticism Impulsivity, poor delay of gratifi-	Self-criticism and perfectionism Greater maturity than age mates	Perfectionism Great persistence	Perfectionism Super sensitivity	Perfectionism Super sensitivity

			cation				
Humour	Engages in socially re-ciprocal hu-mor	Can do word play, but typically doesn't under-stand humor that requires social reciprocity	Usually under-stand humor	Good sense of hu-mor	Good sense of humor	Good sense of humor	Sophisticated sense of hu-mor Grasp of metaphors, analogies, satire
Stereotypes	Not a charac-teristic	May be present	May be present	May be present	Not a characteris-tic	Not a charac-teristic	Not a charac-teristic
Prepared on the basis Aleksandrovich, 2012, Barkley, 1990; Cline, 1999; Webb & Latimer, 1993; Baum, Owen, & Dixon, 1991; Silverman, 1989; Cline & Schwartz, 1999; Whitmore & Maker, 1985; Willard-Holt, 1994; Cline, 1999; Whitmore & Maker, 1985; Whitmore & Maker, 1985.							

Teachers for the Gifted

The analysis of the characteristics of gifted children provides us to the idea of the analysis of the competencies and characteristics of the teachers for the gifted. "The competencies and characteristics attributed to excellent teachers have begun to assume almost Herculean proportions. Teachers need professional expertise in subject matter and pedagogy. Teachers with deep conceptual understanding of their subject area ask higher level questions, better engage students, and enable students to apply and transfer knowledge" [1]. This assertion seems to right, but in reality it has to hold true for any other teacher. Therefore it will be interesting to have a look on the special list of characteristics and competencies of teachers of the gifted. Feldhusen presents a well-known list of "main characteristics and competencies of teachers of the gifted"[2].

Characteristics of Teacher of the Gifted

Is highly intelligent

Has cultural and intellectual interests

Strives for excellence, high achievement

Is enthusiastic about talent

Relates well to talented people

Has broad general knowledge

Competencies of Teachers of the Gifted

Has knowledge of the nature and needs of the gifted

Can identify gifted and talented students

Can develop (or select) methods and materials for use with the gifted

Is skilled in teaching higher thinking abilities, including creativity and problem solving

Is adapted at questioning techniques

Is skilled in facilitating independent research

Can direct individualized learning and teaching

Can work with culturally different talented youth

Is skilled in counseling gifted and talented youth

Source: G.A.Davis & S.B.Rimm, *Education of the gifted and talented.* Bosten: Allyn and Bacon, 1998, pp.42-43.

[1]L.J.Croft, *Teachers of the Gifted: Gifted Teachers*. In N.Colangelo & G.A.Davis (eds.), *Handbook of Gifted Education.* Boston: Allyn and Bacon, 2003, p.558.

[2] J.F.Feldhusen, *A case for developing America's talent. How we went wrong and where we go now*. Roeper Review, 1994, 16, pp.231-233

Also other lists or overview of teacher's characteristics and competencies (cf. e.g. Gallagher, 2000; Landvogt, 2001; Vialle & Quigley, 2002; Croft, 2003; Chan, 2010) do not differentiate substantially from these. It is quite obvious that the conclusions of the various researchers nearly inevitably lead to the combination of personality traits, knowledge and skills, professional attitudes and teaching approaches and strategies[3]. And therefore it seems the most productive to put the focus on teacher behavior and not as much on characteristics. This is also mostly according to Gagné's pedagogical approach that not static personality characteristics contribute to improvement of giftedness, but active promoters or catalysts.

So, we can conclude that for the teachers of the gifted it is not necessary to be gifted themselves, but they have to be able to adapt their general teacher competences, attitudes and teaching approaches to the special needs of the gifted children. It is possible to evaluate the traits of the teacher in such a way: "One looks back with appreciation to the brilliant teachers, but with gratitude to those who touched our human feelings. The curriculum is so much necessary raw material, but warmth is the vital element for the growing plant and for the soul of the child"[4]. Only in this way they can meet the requirements of their special tasks with gifted children. This includes in the final analysis also a changing of the role for the teacher. Teachers of the gifted have to be predominantly (a) counselors, who have to support the gifted children in their development, in better understanding of their abilities, (b) coordinators, who have to serve the gifted children with a formal and informal development program, and (c) consultants, who have to fight and to advice other colleagues to the advantage of the gifted[5].

Work with Gifted Children: Teaching Tips

Gifted students as well as gifted students with disabling conditions remain two groups of underserved and understimulated youth[6]. Development of the teachers and parents knowledge about inconsistencies of abilities and *"asynchrony"* of giftedness development it is a fist step in understanding of exceptionality of gifted students. The second important, from our point of view, step it is to focus on suggestions any teacher can use in the classroom to aid their gifted students and promote their achievement in positive ways. Teaching gifted children it is a challenge and teaching children who are twice exceptional it is twice challenging. The

[3] Cf. W.Vialle & S.Quigley, Does the teacher of the gifted need to be gifted? In D. Eyre, Gifted and Talented Education. Abingdon: Routledge, 2001.
[4] C.G.Jung, *The Gifted Child*, In Collected works of C.G. Jung, Vol. 17, Princeton University Press, 1979.
[5] Cf. L.J.Croft, *Teachers of the Gifted: Gifted Teachers.* In N.Colangelo & G.A.Davis (eds.), *Handbook of Gifted Education.* Boston: Allyn and Bacon, 2003.
[6] S.Cline & D.Schwartz, *Diverse populations of gifted children.* NJ: Merrill, 1999.

following strategies provide a framework for addressing the specific learning needs of children who are twice exceptional.

Students who are gifted with disabilities are often holistic learners who learn best when instruction assists them in creating relationships among ideas. Teachers can facilitate instruction by:

- Teaching skills within concepts
- Teaching from essential understandings and essential questions
- Using advance organizers to illustrate overarching concepts and themes.

Students who are twice exceptional are often visual learners, using mental pictures to process information and recall details. Instruction that communicates a concept as an idea or thought supported by multisensory activities enhances success.

Twice exceptional students are often motivated by higher-level thinking rather than making a grade. Motivation increases when teachers:

- Engage them in abstract thinking and problem solving
- Pre-assess their skills in order to compact the curriculum, thereby eliminating unnecessary work, work they have already mastered
- Integrate creative thinking and problem solving
- Use compacting to *"buy time"* for independent work[7].

Among the strategies provide a framework for addressing the specific learning needs of children who are twice exceptional the most important once are the following:

1. Teach students to appreciate individual differences. For all students in a class to accept the presence of differentiation opportunities, teachers need to be willing to spend time helping all students understand and appreciate individual differences.

2. Be aware that many students who have learning difficulties are global learners who prefer visual and tactile-kinesthetic formats for learning success.

3. Always teach content by teaching concepts first and details second. Make sure students see the big picture before they try to learn its pieces.

4. Teach students how to set realistic short-term goals and to take credit for reaching those goals, even if they represent only a partial amount of the entire task.

5. Teach in a way that ties past learning to new content. In order for students to learn and generalize new skills, they must be able to connect the new learning to something they already know.

[7] J.Campanelli. & C. Ericson, *Twice Exceptional Guide*. USA: Ohio Department of Education, 207, pp.37-38.

6. Immerse all the senses in learning activities. Use musical chants, raps, rhymes, or rhythms for students who respond to those methods.

7. Provide specific instruction in organizational techniques.

8. Find and use any available technology that will improve a student's productivity.

9. Allow students to take tests in separate, supervised environments so they can either read the test aloud to themselves or have someone else read it to them[8].

Conclusion

Children who are twice exceptional are those who are gifted and who also have some disabilities like ADHD, Asperger's Syndrome, a learning disability, an emotional disturbance, sensory disability such as hearing or vision impairment, or a physical disability. So the teaching situation is complicated, as the abilities of gifted students often mask their disabilities, and, in turn, their disabilities can disguise their giftedness. An aim of a professional teacher in this situation is to support students and allow them to achieve maximum of their potential.

Bibliography

Aleksandrovich, M. & Zoglowek, H. *Has the teacher of the gifted to be gifted? About characteristics and competencies of teachers for gifted and talented students.* In O. Holz & R. Seebauer: *Interactive and Competence-orientated Education.* Hamburg: Dr.Kovac, 2012.

Anthony, T., Baldwin, L., Bianco, M., Bieber, B., Busby, B., Cornier, J., Franklin-Rohr, Ch., Medina, J., Miller, A., Muir, Sh., Pereles, D., Thurman, K., Trail, B., Worner, M. *Twice-Exceptional Students Gifted Students with Disabilities*. Denver, Colorado, 2009.

Asperger, H. Autistic psychopathy in childhood. In U. Frith: *Autism and Asperger Syndrome* London: Cambridge University Press, 2009, pp. 37-92.

Bainbridge, C. *Dual Exceptionalities Gifted and Disabled from*, 2012, http://giftedkids. about.com_/od/giftedandld/a/gt_and_ld.htm date: 13/03/2013.

Barkley, R.A. *Attention deficit hyperactivity disorder: A handbook for diagnosis and treatment.* New York: Guilford Press, 1990.

Barron, J., & Barron, S. *There's a boy in here.* New York: Simon and Schuster, 1992.

[8] S.Winebrenner, *Teaching gifted kids in the regular classroom* (2nd ed.). Minneapolis: Free Spirit, 2000, pp.133-135.

Baum, S. M., Cooper, C. R., & Neu, T. R. *Dual differentiation: An approach for meeting the curricular needs of gifted students with learning disabilities.* Psychology in the Schools, 2001, 38 (5), pp. 477-490.

Baum, S.M., Owen, S.V., & Dixon, J. *To be gifted & learning disabled.* Mansfield Center, CT: Creative Learning Press, 1991.

Betts, G., & Kercher, J. *Autonomous learner model: Optimizing ability.* Greeley, CO: ALPS, 1999.

Blum, M.W. *Parents of gifted children. a minibibliography on readings for parents and teachers of gifted children.* ERIC Clearinghouse on Handicapped and Gifted Children, Association Dr., Reston, VA, 1985.

Brody, L. E., & Mills, C. J. *Gifted children with learning disabilities: A review of the issues.* Journal of Learning Disabilities, 1997, 30 (3), 282-286. from http://www.ldonline.org /indepth/gifted date: 03/03/2013

Campanelli, J. & Ericson, C. (2007). *Twice Exceptional Guide.* USA: Ohio Department of Education, 106 p.

Chan, D.W. *Characteristics and competencies of teachers of gifted learners: the Hong Kong student perspective.* Roeper Review 2010, 33, 3, 160-169.

Clark, B. *Growing up gifted.* New York: MacMillan, 1992.

Cline, S., & Schwartz, D. *Diverse populations of gifted children.* NJ: Merrill, 1999.

Coggins, S.A. *Asynchronous Development and Gifted Children*, 2009, http://www.brighthub.com/ education/special/articles/28354.aspx date: 23/09/2010

Croft, L.J. *Teachers of the Gifted: Gifted Teachers.* In N.Colangelo & G.A.Davis (eds.), *Handbook of Gifted Education.* Boston: Allyn and Bacon, 2003.

Davis, G.A. & Rimm, S.B. *Education of the gifted and talented.* Bosten: Allyn and Bacon, 1998.

Dewey, M. *Autistic eccentricity.* In E. Schopler & G. B. Mesibov (Eds.): *High Functioning Individuals with Autism.* New York: Plenum Press, 1992, pp. 281-288.

Farmer, D. *Meeting the Needs of Gifted Students in the Regular Classroom,* 1997, http://austega.com/gifted/9-gifted/21-whatis.html date: 01/03/2013

Feldhusen, J.F. *A case for developing America's talent. How we went wrong and where we go now.* Roeper Review, *1994,* 16, pp. 231-233.

Feldhusen, J.F., & Jarwan, F.A. *Identification of gifted and talented youth for educational programs.* In K.A.Heller, F.J.Mönks, R.J.Sternberg, & R.F.Subotnik (eds.), *International handbook of giftedness and talent* (2nd ed.). Oxford, UK: Elsevier, 2000, pp. 271-282.

Frith, U. Asperger and his syndrome. In U. Frith (Eds.): *Autism and Asperger Syndrome.* London: Cambridge University Press, 1991, pp.1-36.

Gagné, F. *Transforming gifts into talents: the DMGT as a developmental theory*. High ability studies, 2004, 15, (2), 119-147.

Gagné, F. *From gifts to talents: The DMGT as a development model*. In R.J. Sternberg & J.E. Da-vidson (Eds.): *Conceptions of giftedness*. New York, NY: Cambridge University Press, 2005, pp. 98-119.

Gardner, H. *Multiple Intelligences: the theory in practice*. New York: Basic Books, 1993.

Gifted Students: Recommendations For Teachers, http://www.udel.edu/education/masters/psychology/handbook/recommendations/GiftedStudents.doc date: 13/03/2013

Gillberg, C. *Autism and autistic-like conditions: Subclasses among disorders of empathy*. Journal of Child Psychology and Psychiatry and Allied Disciplines, 1992, 33, 813-842.

Heller, Kurt A. I*nternational Handbook of Giftedness and Talent* - Second Edition; Elsevier Science Ltd., Oxford, 2000.

Hishinuma, E., & Tadaki, S. *Addressing diversity of the gifted/at risk: Characteristics for identi-fication*. Gifted Child Today, Sep/Oct, 1996, pp. 25-50.

Hollingworth, L. S. *Children above 180 IQ Stanford-Binet: Origin and development*. Yonkers-on-Hudson, NY: World Book, 1942.

Jung, C.G. *The Gifted Child*, In Collected works of C.G. Jung, Vol. 17, Princeton University Press, 1979.

Klin, A. *Asperger Syndrome*. Child and Adolescent Psychiatry Clinic of North America, 1994, 3, pp. 131-148.

Klin, A., & Volkmar, F. R. *Guidelines for parents: Assessment, diagnosis, and intervention of Asperger Syndrome*. Pittsburgh, PA: Learning Disabilities Association of America, 1995.

Landvogt, J. *Affecting eternity. Teaching for talent development*. Roeper Review 2001, 23, pp. 190-196.

Levy, S. *Identifying high-functioning children with autism*. Bloomington, IN: Indiana Re-source Center for Autism, 1988.

Limont, W. *Uczeń zdolny: jak go rozpoznać i jak z nim pracować*. Gdańsk: GWP, 2005.

Neihart, M. *Gifted children with Asperger's Syndrome*. Gifted Child Quarterly, 2000, 44, 4, pp. 222-230.

Parker, J.P. *NAGC standards for personnel preparation in gifted education. A brief history*. Gifted Child Quarterly 1996, 40, pp.158-164.

Reber, A., S. *Penguin dictionary of psychology*. London: Penguin Books, 1995.

Rourke, B. *Nonverbal learning disabilities: The syndrome and the model*. New York: Guil-ford Press, 1989.

Ruban, L.M. & Reis, S.M. *Identification and Assessment of Gifted Students With Learning Disabilities.* Theory Into Practice, 2005, 44, 2, 115–124, from http://educationinaminute.com/bogota/Re-sources/Articles/Ruban%20and%20Reis.pdf date: 13/03/2013

Schopler, E., & Mesibov, G. B. (Eds.). *High-functioning individuals with autism.* New York: Plenum Press, 1992.

Silverman, L.K. *Invisible gifts, invisible handicaps.* Roeper Review, 1989, 12, 1, 37-42.

Stronge, J.H. *Evaluating What Good Teachers Do.* Larchmont, NY: Eye on education, 2010.

Svanberg, R. & Wille, H.P. *La stå! Læring – på veien mot den profesjonelle lærer.* Oslo: Gyldendal, 2009.

Vialle, W. & Quigley, S. *Does the teacher of the gifted need to be gifted?* In D. Eyre, *Gifted and Talented Education.* Abingdon: Routledge, 2002.

Webb, J.T. & Maker, C.J. *ADHD and children who are gifted.* ERIC EC Digest E522, 1993.

Whitmore, J.R., & Maker, C.J. *Intellectual giftedness in disabled persons.* Rockville, MD: Aspen, 1985.

Willard-Holt, C. *Recognizing talent: Cross-case study of two high potential students with cerebral palsy.* Storrs, CT: National Research Center on the Gifted/Talented, 1994.

Willard-Holt, C. Dual exceptionalities, 1999, LD Online, Retrieved September 9, 2006 from http://www.ldonline.org/article/5888 date: 10/03/2013

Winebrenner, S. *Teaching gifted kids in the regular classroom* (2nd ed.). Minneapolis: Free Spirit, 2000.

Winebrenner, S. *Teaching Strategies for Twice-Exceptional Students.* Intervention In School And Clinic, 2003, 38, 3, 131-137.

Wing, L. *Manifestations of social problems in high-functioning autistic people.* In E. Schopler & G. B. Mesibov (Eds.): *High functioning individuals with autism.* New York: Plenum Press, 1992, pp. 129-142.

Herbert Zoglowek
Pomeranian University in Slupsk, Poland
University of Tromsø - Norwegian Arctic University, Alta, Norway

GIFTED CHILDREN AND UNIFIED SCHOOL IN NORWAY – IMPOSSIBILITY OR FRUITFUL LIAISON?

Summary

Giftedness and Unified School are the central terms in this article. Is it possible for gifted children to get the right and necessary stimulation in a Unified School system, or does the thought of equality and the principle of egalitarianism not allow the promotion of children, who have special abilities? The pedagogical approaches of inclusion and adapted teaching open up all possibilities, but nevertheless giftedness miscarries in the Norwegian Unified School system. This article is a description of the actual situation in Norway and a discussion of possible reasons and facilities for alteration.

Introduction

This article is a discussion of two at the first appearance incompatible pedagogical concepts: giftedness and egalitarianism. How meets an egalitarian pedagogical idea as the Unified School system in Norway children, who are special academically gifted? The article is structured that first the two central terms will be explained. It will be given in broad outline a short history of the Norwegian Unified School *(enhetsskole)*, and, in general lines, a description and discussion of giftedness. Then the main chapter presents the situation of gifted children in the Norwegian school system today, which is following of a discussion, whether and how the Unified School can meet gifted children.

The Norwegian education system

The Norwegian education policy is characterized by an advanced ambition to balance adverse circumstances, factors and impacts for all people who are living in Norway. All should be equal that means equivalent or egalitarian. This ideology about human beings and their development has a long tradition in Norway, even if the meaning and the realization of this ideology have changed through the times. The actual situation in school policy is mainly characterized with the keywords including school *(inkluderende skole)* and adapted teaching *(tilpasset opplæring)*. "The school shall have room for everybody and teachers must therefore have an eye for each individual learner. The mode of teaching must not only be adapted to subject and content, but also to age and maturity, the individual learner and the mixed abilities of the entire class. The pedagogical design must be pliable enough to permit the teacher to meet the pupils' differences in ability and rhythm of development with kindness and ease. Rules of conduct alone are not sufficient to transmit care and consideration. The teacher must make use of the variations in pupils' aptitudes, the diversity in the classroom, and the heterogeneity of the school as resources for all-round development as well as the development of all"[1]. Lastly in a public report from 2006 the department of education has underlined this vision: "Everybody should have the same opportunities for developing themselves and their gifts. A society characterized by community and equality provides the best opportunities for the individuals' possibilities to realize their own individual life projects"[2].

The Unified School is the basic of the Norwegian education system. The educational policy has followed in more than hundred years these basic thoughts that the school has to be a common and equal school for all children, regardless of gender and social layers, of geographical location and ethnicity, of any disabilities or maybe other idiosyncrasies.

Already in the first school law in 1739, it is mentioned as an explicit aim that the school education should be for each and every. However, the way how to handle the individual starting situations and differences was seen in different approaches, and it should last for another 250 years until Norway got in 1998 a common law for all children, which obliged all schools to cultivate and to give an adapted education for all[3].

A look into the Norwegian school and curriculum history gives an understanding of today's situation. As already suggested the distinct characteristic of the Norwegian educational system is the Unified School *(enhetsskole)*. The first compulsory education, since the middle of the 1700s, was extremely influenced by the Christianization, and was unequal in many respects. But just after introduction of parliamentarism in Norway, the first Prime Minister, Johan Sverdrup, proclaimed 1884 the political vision of "[...] a common school for all children, irrespective of social layers, geographical location, gender, ethnical group or many of the idiosyncrasies that pupils may have"[4]. That can be referred to as the beginning of the idea of the Norwegian Unified School, but nevertheless, it took some decades before a com-

[1] Kirke-, utdannings- og forskningsdepartement, Læreplanverket for den 10-årige grunnskolen. Oslo: Ministery of Education, 1997, p.19.

[2] Kunnskapsdepartement. St.meld.nr.16 (2006-2007) "...og ingen stå igjen". Oslo: Ministry of Education, 2006, p.7; translation of the author.

[3] A.Askildt & D.Johnsen, Spesialpedagogiske røtter og fagets utvikling i Norge. In E. Befring & R. Tangen: *Spesialpedagogikk.* Oslo: Cappelen Akademisk Forlag, 2008.

[4] P.Østerud & J. Johnsen (Eds.), *Leve skolen. Enhetsskolen i et kulturkritisk perspektiv*, Oslo: Oplandske Bokforlag, 2003 p. 149, translation of the author.

mon compulsory school of seven years became a reality in 1920. The first curriculum in the 1920th had two editions, one for urban schools and one for rural schools, but both were honeycombed with the idea of the Unified School. From that time still nearly the end of the last century the political governance was strong in the Labor party, and the Unified School was never a discussion point at the social democratic authoritatively political agenda.

From special schools to adapted education

Already in the middle of the 1800s special schools were established in Norway with the aim "to give an education for disabled children and youth, who were falling out of the school and society context"[5]. Then the act for special schools came in 1951, and this was the basic for public special schools differentiated and specialized for different disabilities. In the aftermath of long and deep social- and educational-political debates about integration and segregation of disable children, in 1975 the act for special schools was repealed and the new act for basic school formalized a common basic school for all children in Norway. The school policy in social democracy's mind and ideology consolidated the Unified School. "The same opportunities should be valid for all children and youth of different socioeconomic conditions, for children and youth form the rural and the urban parts, for practical capable children as well as mental gifted pupils[6]. With that said integration became a key word in the school policy since 1975. Another term also came up in the new curriculum in 1974[7]: adapted education (*tilpasset opplæring*). The term itself was new, but not the meaning. Adapted education was known before as e.g. "differentiation". Since 1994, over the course of the Salamanca declaration[8], the term "inclusion" came up on the international educational agenda. Inclusion is understood as a broader term, which refers to the experience of affinity, appreciation and social relationship[9]. "The fundamental principle of the inclusive school is that all children should learn together, wherever possible, regardless of any difficulties or differences they may have. Inclusive schools must recognize and respond to diverse needs of their students. (...) This should include educational disabled and gifted children, street and working children, children from remote or nomadic populations, children from linguistic, ethnic or cultural minorities

---

[5] K.Skogen, *Spesialpedagogikk: En innføring*. Oslo: Universitetsforlaget, 2005, p.35-36, translation of the author.
[6] A.O.Telhaug, Skolen mellom stat og marked. Norsk skoletenkning fra år til år 1990-2002. Oslo. Didaktika Norsk Forlag, 2002, p.12, translation of the author.
[7] KUF: Kirke-, utdannings- og forskningsdepartement. Mønsterplan for grunnskolen. Oslo: Aschehoug, 1974.
[8] UNESCO. The Salamanca statement and framework for action on special needs education: adopted by the world conference on special needs education : access and quality. Paris: UNESCO, 1994.
[9] E.Befring, Skolen for barnas beste. Oppvekst og læring in eit pedagogisk perspektiv. Oslo: Det Norske Samlaget Aschehoug, 2004.

and children from other disadvantaged or marginalized groups"[10]. With the agreement to the Salamanca declaration this position was also noticed more clearly in the Norwegian school policy and the new curriculum in 1997[11] react to these kinds of obligation. But in the first instance, the formulation was very generally and giftedness was not explicit named. Also in the Education act from 1998 it is rather wide formulated: "Education should be adapted to the abilities and prerequisites of every pupil"[12] .

Equality, inclusion and adapted education are the superordinate principles in the Norwegian School system. There is consensus and conformance that children are unequal, that they have unequal preconditions, and that an equal offer for all gives not an equivalent offer.

The actual situation: Curriculum K'06

The history of the Norwegian education during the whole last century has shown that the compulsory school was dominated by the ideology of a collectivistic development, dominated by the ideal of providing education for all, eliminating of social differences, end securing equality between different groups. Not only in aims and content, also the main methods and criteria for evaluation were very strongly influenced by this collectivistic thinking, which e.g. can be shown in group work, pupil's influence on school decision, or the moderate way in giving marks or grades. But the voices of critic on this system became more and louder during the nineties, and the political perspective, at least also caused by a few research reports (Hofset, 1970; Welle Strand & Tjeldvoll, 2002; Birkemo, 2002; Hagenes, 2009; Skogen & Cosmovici Idsøe, 2011) and the mediocre ranking on international tests, has started to change. When in 2001 the social democrat government was replaced by a right-centered government, one of the first actions of the new government was to abandon the Unified School and to complement – some would say to compensate – the collectivistic characteristics by individualistic moments, and at least also by market mechanism[13]. Already the penultimate curriculum from 1997 suggested in the "aims of education" (*formålsparagrafene*) a kind of opening, when it is written about the importance of creating a balance between individual and collective interests, "where the individual should have the opportunity to develop according to their own particular qualifications within the scope of community considerations"[14].

---

[10] UNESCO. The Salamanca statement .....

[11] KUF: Kirke-, utdannings- og forskningsdepartement. *Læreplanverket for den 10-årige grunnskolen*. Oslo: Ministery of Education, 1997.

[12] http://www.lovdata.no/all/tl-19980717-061-001.html#1-2. Checked july 30th, translation of the author.

[13] A.Welle-Strand & A.Tjeldvoll, The Norwegian unified school – a paradise lost? *Journal of Education Policy,* 2002, vol 17, no. 6., Taylor & Francis, pp.673-686.

[14] G.Imsen, Elevens verden. Innføring i pedagogisk psykologi. Oslo: Tano, 2008, p.132

Gifted and talented children

Giftedness is a not quite clear defined term. Many decades the IQ was the one and only unitary manner to decide and to describe giftedness, today, however, it is an insight by mutual agreement that giftedness means much more than to have a high IQ. To be gifted is a more complex synopsis and co-action of several abilities. These must not be always the same. Johnsen (2004) emphasizes that gifted children exhibit a potential for high performance in special spheres or fields, or in general: "The term 'gifted and talented' when used in respect to students, children, or youth means students, children, or youth who give evidence of high performance capability in areas such as intellectual, creative, artistic, or leadership capacity, or in specific academic fields, and who require services or activities not ordinarily provided by the school in order to fully develop such capabilities"[15].

Renzulli was the first, who tried to describe the complex giftedness in a model, which shows the different influence factors, in the so-called Ring Model (1978). Today exist several models. The main distinctive feature in the theoretical description and discussion of giftedness is the focus either on achievement-orientated or factor models, which assess giftedness because of certain achievements, or on cognitive models, which evaluate giftedness because of learning abilities. Most known are today Carroll's Three Stratum Theory (1996), Sternberg's Triarchic Theory (1985), Gardner's Multiple Intelligences Modell (1993), as well as Mönks' Triade Model (1992) and Gagné's Differentiated Model of Giftedness and Talent (2005).). The model of Mönks, which looks most actually in the intention of this article, should be redescribed here.

Mönks' Multi-factorial Model of Giftedness

In addition to Renzulli's three internal spheres Mönks and his colleagues (1992) subjoin in his model three external spheres. The social environment gets a special status as an important factor for to evolve giftedness. Above all the family, the friends/peers and the school, and that means first and foremost the teacher, are exposed as the essential external promoter for the improvement of giftedness.

[15] S.K.Johnsen, *Identifying Gifted Students: A Practical Guide.* Waco, Texas: Prufrock, 2004, p.388

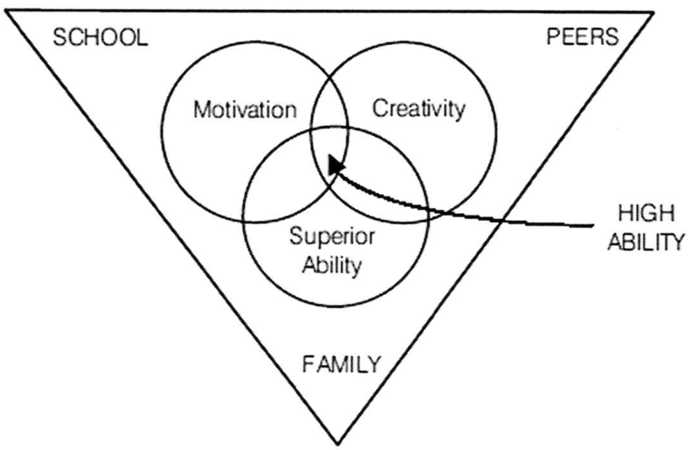

Figure 1: The Multi-factorial Model of Giftedness by Franz J. Mönks (1992)

The main point, which this model wants to emphasize, is that giftedness is not just given. Gifted behavior is not a state or a static situation, it is rather more the result of the functional interaction of individual gifted aptitudes and the targeted promoting influence of the environment. Only, when these named six components intertwine and are playing together, it is possible for the gifted child to transfer his/her high abilities in corresponding to high achievement. Thereby it is underlined that the social context forms the main interaction opportunities for the gifted children to meet and learn from other people, and although it is not possible to choose the family, a child has the freedom to choose the peers and to influence the choice of the school. Figure 1 shows the six components and their correspondence for to stimulate the gifted abilities.

Are gifted children children with special needs?

It is to underline that there are often only small differences between gifted children and "normal" children, but the specific occurs in special task or situations[16]. In general there are central components as excellent language skills, thirst for knowledge, learning capacity, logical reasoning, memory, energy, concentration ability and endurance. All these abilities find expression in competencies such like creativity, humorous sense, critical sense and

[16] M.Aleksandrovich, Интеллектуальные операции старших дошкольников в норме и с особенностями психофизического развития: сравнительный анализ. Münster: LIT Verlag, 2012.

autonomy and self-reliance[17]. Differences often are shown in the behavior, that means how they handle with their special abilities, how they manage their competencies. Betts and Neihart[18] have worked out six profiles of the gifted and the talented, which they label as:

Type I: The successful

In this group there are the most of gifted students. They have learned the system, are usually identified for placement in programs for the gifted, and are often characterized by they will "make it in their own". Overall it can be said that these children have a positive self-concept because they have been affirmed for their achievements.

Type II: The challenging

They are divergently gifted, challenge the parents and teachers, and do not conform to the system, respectively they have not learned to use it to their advantage. They often do not get affirmation of their talents and abilities, are struggling with their self-esteem and possess a more negative self-concept.

Type III: The underground

In this group there are mostly female students, who try to hide their giftedness in order to feel more safe and included with a non-gifted peer group. They feel often insecure and anxious, they react on the expectations of the parents and the teachers with increasing resistance and denial.

Type IV: The dropouts

Here it shows a possible escalation of type III. The students are angry because the adults and the system have not met their needs for many years and the feel rejected. As a result they are also angry with themselves because the feel that they cannot manage alone and they do not get adequate support or challenge. School seems therefore irrelevant and they try to find other realms, dropping out emotionally, mentally and physically.

Type V: The double-labeled

The students in this group are probably most difficult to identify. Often they are handicapped in a way, and the focus on the weakness covers the special abilities, so that they did not nurtured their strength or talents. They may feel discouraged, frustrated, rejected or isolated and both their own behavior and the reaction of the others put them on a bad circle, where they cannot come away.

---

[17] K.Skogen & E.Cosmovice Idsøe, *Våre evnerike barn – en utfordring for skolen*. Kristiansand: Høyskoleforlaget, 2011, 55 ff

[18] G.T.Betts & M.Neihart, Profiles of the Gifted and Talented. In D. Eyre: *Gifted and Talented Education.* Vol.IV. London and New York: Routledge, 2009, 190 ff.; K.Skogen & E.Cosmovice Idsøe, *Våre evnerike barn.....*, 89 ff.

Type VI: The autonomous learner

This type is very like type I, but unlike them, who try to do as little as possible, they students of this group are more active. They try to use the system to create new opportunities for themselves. They do not work for the system, but they make the system work for them. The students are independent, are well respected, have a high self-esteem and a positive self-concept.

The description of the different types shows very obvious that giftedness is not necessarily an ability, which is only positive and gives the children a prerequisite for happiness, satisfaction and success in life. Both the improvement of the specific gift or talent and also negative aspects, which occurs often because of or in addition to the giftedness, need special attention. With other words: gifted children have special needs. The authors of the referred research summarize their typology with the conclusion: "By looking closely at the behavior and feelings of gifted and talented youth, better educational programming may be developed to meet their special diversified needs"[19].

How to meet the special needs?

With the concept "adapted education" it is already named one approach for specialized and individualized teaching. Skogen & Cosmovici[20] mention, with reference to George (1997), five elementary pedagogical principles, which have to be use for to utilize the learning and developing potential of the children optimally. The methods or the learning approach has

- to attach weight to logic and comprehension;
- to be flexibly enough to meet the child's individual requirements and needs;
- to proceed in a learning climate, which gives all the time stimulations for the child;
- to have a progression, which is adapted to the child's prerequisites;
- to take more care to the child's need than to the prestige of the school or the adults.

To look more precisely to these points, it is dashy that they are in reality relevant for all children, for all students. Therefore it can be concluded that the demands for adapted education are relevant for all students, selfsame that the teaching-learning situation has to be built up in greatest possible way on

- student's subject-specific level of knowledge;
- student's learning capacity according to tempo and quantity;
- student's preference about the way to learn.

---

[19] G.T.Betts & M.Neihart, Profiles of the Gifted and Talented.... p.194.
[20] K.Skogen & E.Cosmovice Idsøe, *Våre evnerike barn....*, p.56.

It seems that it is very easy just to follow the "normal rules" and the pedagogical demands, which are useful for all students, for to satisfy also the needs for gifted students. To take adapted education serious means to find an adapted approach for the gifted, too. And for the most there are two adaptations, which can be already very successful: higher tempo and enrichment[21]. On the other hand, every teacher knows that these adaptations are not quite so easy to realize in teaching situation. But that is the challenge, which every teacher has to adopt with respect to every student.

Gifted children in the Norwegian Unified School

"Everybody should have the same opportunities for developing themselves and their gifts. A society characterized by community and equality provides the best opportunities for the individuals' possibilities to realize their own individual life projects"[22]. With these words the Norwegian government expresses the vision of an equal that means equivalent personal development and education. The Norwegian education policy promises no more, no less than to balance adverse circumstances, factors and impacts for all people who are living in Norway. "The same opportunities should be valid for all children and youth of different socio-economic conditions, for children and youth from the rural and the urban parts, for practical capable children as well as mental gifted pupils"[23]. These are hopeful, but also challenging words, but the department of education is also conscious of problems: "The starting point of today's compulsory education is that education should be adapted to all pupils. That is the way compulsory education should be organized to include all. The educational system is, however, put to a hard press in this process, and there are difficulties related to its adaptation in regards to the weaker pupils and challenges related to the academically gifted pupils"[24]. Indeed, the demands of the average pupils are more or less easy to meet, but how to manage the weaker pupils and how to manage the gifted pupils. Even the topic is now several decades on the agenda of the educational policy and the named keywords Including School and Adapted Teaching underline the importance, the Norwegian pedagogical approach to these both problem groups – weaker pupils and gifted children – can not be more different.

---

[21] Cf. F.J.Mönks & I.H.Yppenberg, Begavede barn. En veiledning for foreldre og pedagoger. Oslo: Abstrakt, 2008.

[22] KD: Kunnskapsdepartement (2006): St.meld.nr.16 (2006-2007) "...og ingen stå igjen". Oslo: Government, 2006, p.7, translation of the author.

[23] A.O. Telhaug, *Skolen mellom stat og marked. Norsk skoletenkning fra år til år 1990-2002*. Oslo. Didaktika Norsk Forlag, 2002, p.12, translation of the author.

[24] NOU (2003). Norges offentlige utredninger 2003:16 *I første rekke. Forsterket kvalitet i en grunnopplæring for alle.* Oslo: Government, p.83

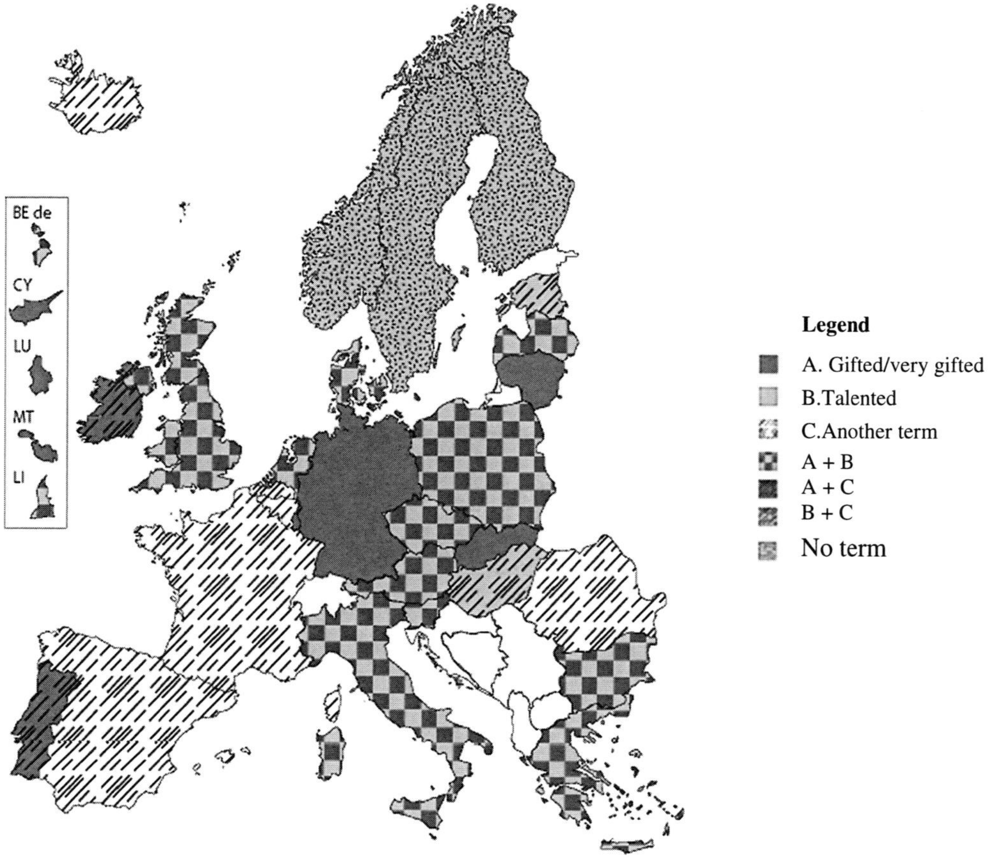

Figure 2. Official terminology using to describe exceptionally gifted children and youth, 2005/2006
Source: Eurydice 2008, p.8

Rightly recent research shows that the situation of weaker pupils has improved; here it is possible to say the Norway is leading by example. But on the other hand it is to notice that there is nearly no adapted approach to gifted children. Even worse it looks that the gifted children are neither a topic on the educational policy agenda nor a special pedagogical theme[25]. The gifted children are scarcely visible in the Norwegian school, and therefore nearly not existent. Some voices are even more critical in their description of the situation at Norwegian schools, when they conclude that it is not well accepted to be exceptional gifted. Cosmovici Idsoe e.g. emphasizes that the first step has to be to change the fundamental attitude towards gifted children, and that the mentality has to be altered that it is allowed to be gifted[26]. It is to notice that the

[25] Cf. Skogen, K. & Cosmovice Idsøe, E. (2011). *Våre evnerike barn – en utfordring for skolen*. Kristiansand: Høyskoleforlaget, p.48
[26] Olsen, T. B. (2011). Er det lov å være flink. *univers* 2, pp.16-17

term "giftedness" in official educational papers and in pedagogical debates pretty much never is used. This phenomena Norway shares uniquely in Europe only with the two other Scandinavian states Sweden and Finland, as it is visible in figure 2.

It is to notice that the problem of gifted children in Norway is first and foremost not to search or to find in the didactic or methodic approach, the problem is rather the attitude to giftedness at all: the attitude of the teacher, the intention of the educational policy and the mindset of the society at all. Even if there have been some changing in the last decade, it still looks that special attention and support for gifted children is regarded as unwelcome elitism[27].

Despite of the official policy and explicit formulations in education law – e.g. education law paragraph 1-3 about adapted teaching for all pupils, or paragraph 5 about special education for these pupils, who cannot get enough gain of the ordinary teaching (lovdata, 2008) – it looks that gifted children don't get enough attention. Paragraph 5 is used extremely seldom in connection with gifted children. 25% of pupils have difficulties to follow active the teaching[28], 7% of pupils have need for special education[29]. In a white paper from education ministry it is emphasized that the understanding of individualized education is very broad, that "special needs find expression in a lot of different ways and include a much bigger group than these, who get special offers"[30]. But the 2-5% of children in Norway[31], who are gifted, are not more concrete and special named, and therefore they cannot get any form for support.

Skaalvik & Skaalvik[32] show in a survey that nearly 50% of the students with good or very good marks in average in secondary I school and more than 50% in secondary II school, are not satisfied with the adapted education. They say that the teaching is not adequate to their professional level. Of course, good marks are not necessarily a criterium for giftedness, but nevertheless these results give some indications for unsatisfactory situation also in this group of students, who can and who want more. In a way it is also characteristically in this research report that this group is not deeper discussed, the focus and the argumentation lie again only on the weaker students and their needs.

"In our country we have had an egalitarian culture that means that one should not be conspicuous in order to gain an advantage, coupled with a deeply ingrained consideration for

[27] K.Skogen, *Spesialpedagogikk: En innføring*. Oslo: Universitetsforlaget, 2005
[28] NOU (Norges offentlige utredninger). *Rett til læring*. Oslo: Ministry of Education, 2009, p.20, translation of the author.
[29] http://www.nhf.no/ index.asp?id=66602.
[30] NOU (Norges offentlige utredninger). *Rett til læring* ...., p.33, translation of the author.
[31] K.Skogen & E.Cosmovice Idsøe, *Våre evnerike barn* ..., p.14
[32] E.M.Skaalvik & S.Skaalvik, På vei mot en inkluderende skole? In *Spesialpedagogikk 71, 2006,* nr.2, p.10.

the weakest in society. These elements are instrumental in explaining why we do not have any traditions for special development programs for the most gifted pupils"[33].

Conclusion

First it is to state that there is a lack of extensive and comprehensive research of giftedness and gifted and talented students in school. The works in hand are mostly masterworks of teacher students, which are case studies or have just a limited representative status (e.g. Straube, 2003; Simonsen, 2006; Geeske, Otter den Hollander 2007; Adams, 2008). Nevertheless it is possible on the basic of official documents and research reports to formulate some indications, which are very clear at two moments: on the one hand, the education act and other documents from the ministry of education express explicit and clear the intention that *all* students should have adapted education, which is individual and professional liable. On the other hand gifted children are neither a theme in the curriculum for teacher training education nor a specialty in pedagogical and special pedagogical studies. It can be concluded that the idea of the Unified School is implanted very strong and deep in the Norwegian education culture. Through nearly one century of social democratic government the egalitarian thoughts in development and education have influenced the school system, the teacher education, the teaching methods and the evaluation system. It has been some revisions, reforms and changes during this period, which has improved the situation for the weak and in any way handicapped pupils. So, today one can say that Norway has probably one of the most human, stress less, and social- and pupil-orientated school education system. They take care for all children with diseases and problems and improve their individuality, but the disadvantage is, that the average is the aim. Children, who are under the level, get a lot of support to reach the average line, but the children, who are already over the level, cannot develop and improve in the same way. They are not seen, and if so, there is not enough knowledge how to support and to improve these children.

Here is to name one reason for this situation: the teacher. According to the models of Mönks and Gagne, the teacher is one of the most important factors in supporting and developing gifted children. The big deficiency, however, is that the teachers in any school type in Norway are not prepared to meet gifted children. The teachers have no competence to observe and to identify the gifted children, they have no competence to teach the gifted children and they have no competence to support the gifted children according to their special needs. Apart

[33] G.Imsen, *Elevens verden. Innføring i pedagogisk psykologi.* Oslo: Tano, 2008, p.342, translation of the author.

from these "can not" arguments there are also some "don't want" reasons, which can be e.g. such misunderstandings that "good students will manage all by themselves" and also a apprehension of elitism, which means implicit that special offers for the gifted can lead to egoism and individualism, which are on the expense of social relations and the sense for collective responsibility[34].

In the description of different types of gifted children it was also shown negative aspects of to be gifted, that gifted children are not necessarily also successful, felicitous and happy children. It is also to distinguish between students who achieve very well and students who are gifted. Especially when gifted children do not get the attention for their giftedness and talents, they maybe suffer with their giftedness, and therefore they often show bad or strange behaviour. In this case, when the behaviour is not adequate, then it is possible that they get special offers. But these offers are not according to their needs and cannot satisfy the necessities.

Sport is the only exception, where talented children get systematic support for to extend and to intensify their abilities, in all other realms the e.g. art, musician or academically gifted children have to find and to go their way alone. Some of them succeed nonetheless but there is also a great number, those who don't succeed. The Unified School in Norway takes care for all children with diseases and problems and improve their individuality, but it is not a good climate for developing of gifted children.

Bibliography

Adams, J. *Tall Poppies in Two Education Systems - Cut, Conserved or Cultivated?* How do contextual factors influence the official educational approach towards gifted and talented children? Masterwork. Oslo: University, 2008.

Aleksandrovich, M. *Интеллектуальные операции старших дошкольников в норме и с особенностями психофизического развития: сравнительный анализ.* Münster: LIT Verlag, 2012.

Aleksandrovich, M. & Zoglowek, H. *Has the teacher of the Gifted to be Gifted? About Characteristics and Competencies of Teachers for Gifted and Talented Students.* In O. Holz & R. Seebauer: *Interactive and Competence-orientated Education.* Hamburg: Dr.Kovac, 2012.

Askildt, A. & Johnsen, B. *Spesialpedagogiske røtter og fagets utvikling i Norge*. In E. Befring & R. Tangen: *Spesialpedagogikk.* Oslo: Cappelen Akademisk Forlag, 2008.

[34] Cf. K.Skogen & E.Cosmovice Idsøe, *Våre evnerike barn...*, p.63

Betts, G.T. & Neihart, M. *Profiles of the Gifted and Talented.* In D. Eyre: *Gifted and Talented Education.* Vol.IV. London and New York: Routledge, 2009.

Birkemo, A. *Læringsmiljø og utvikling*, Oslo: Pedagogisk forskningsinstitutt, 2002.

Befring, E. *Skolen for barnas beste. Oppvekst og læring in eit pedagogisk perspektiv.* Oslo: Det Norske Samlaget Aschehoug, 2004.

Carroll, J. B. *The three-stratum theory of cognitive abilities*. In D.P.Flanagan, J.L.Genshaft et al., *Contemporary intellectual assessment: Theories, tests, and issues*. New York, NY, USA: Guilford Press, 1997, p. 122-130.

Gagné, F. *From gifts to talents: The DMGT as a development model*. In R.J.Sternberg & J.E.Davidson (eds.): *Conceptions of giftedness,* New York, NY: Cambridge University Press, 2005, pp. 98-119.

Gardner, H. *Multiple Intelligences: The Theory in Practice*. New York: Basic Books, 1993.

Geeske Otter den Hollander, M. *Evnerike elever". Hvordan blir "evnerike elever" ivaretatt i en norsk og i en nederlandsk skole?* Masterwork. Oslo: University, 2007.

Hagenes, T. *Begavede barn i norsk grunnskole: hvordan opplever foreldrene barnas og sitt eget møte med skolen?* Masterwork. Oslo: University, 2008.

Hofset, A. *Evnerike barn i skolen.* Oslo: Universitetsforlage, 1970.

Imsen, G. *Elevens verden. Innføring i pedagogisk psykologi.* Oslo: Tano, 2008.

Johnsen, S. K. *Identifying Gifted Students: A Practical Guide.* Waco, Texas: Prufrock Press, Inc., 2004.

KD: Kunnskapsdepartement *St.meld.nr.16 (2006-2007)* "…og ingen stå igjen". Oslo: Government, 2006.

KUF: Kirke-, utdannings- og forskningsdepartement. *Mønsterplan for grunnskolen.* Oslo: Aschehoug, 1974

KUF: Kirke-, utdannings- og forskningsdepartement *Læreplanverket for den 10-årige grunnskolen*. Oslo: Ministery of Education, 1997.

Mönks, F. J. *Development of the gifted child: The issue of identification and pro-grammimg*. In F.J.Mönks & W.Peters, *Talent for the future*. Mastricht: Assen, 1992, pp. 191-202.

Mönks, F. J. & Yppenberg, I. H. *Begavede barn. En veiledning for foreldre og pedagoger.* Oslo: Abstrakt, 2008.

Olsen, T. B. *Er det lov å være flink. univers* 2, 2011, pp.16-17

NOU. Norges offentlige utredninger 2003:16 *I første rekke. Forsterket kvalitet i en grunnopplæring for alle.* Oslo: Governmen, 2003.

NOU. Norges offentlige utredninger. *Rett til læring.* Oslo: Ministry of Education, 2009.

Østerud, P. & Johnsen, J. (Eds.). *Leve skolen. Enhetsskolen i et kulturkritisk per-spektiv*, Oslo: Oplandske Bokforlag, 2003.

Renzulli, J. S. *What Makes Giftedness? Reexamining a Definition*. In: *Phi Delta Kappan*, 60 (3), 1978, pp. 180-184, 261.

Simonsen, L. M. *Evnerike elever - "skolelysene som ikke blir tent?"* : en kvalitativ studie av tilpas-set opplæring for evnerike elever på 9.trinn i faget matematikk. Masterwork. Oslo: University, 2006.

Skaalvik, E. M. & Skaalvik, S. På vei mot en inkluderende skole? In *Spesial-pedagogikk 2006, 71,* nr.2, pp.4-17.

Skogen, K. *Spesialpedagogikk: En innføring*. Oslo: Universitetsforlaget, 2005.

Skogen, K. & Cosmovice Idsøe, E. *Våre evnerike barn – en utfordring for skolen*. Kristian-sand: Høyskoleforlaget, 2011.

Sternberg, R. J. *Beyond IQ: A Triarchic Theory of Intelligence*. Cambridge: Cambridge Uni-versity Press, 1985.

Straube, E. D. *Enhetsskolens glemte barn: en studie om tilrettelegging av undervisning for evne-rikeelever i grunnskolen*. Masterwork. Oslo: University, 2003.

Telhaug, A. O. *Skolen mellom stat og marked. Norsk skoletenkning fra år til år 1990-2002*. Oslo. Didaktika Norsk Forlag, 2002.

UNESCO. *The Salamanca statement and framework for action on special needs education: adopted by the world conference on special needs education: access and quality*. Paris: UNESCO, 1994.

Welle-Strand, A. & Tjeldvoll, A *The Norwegian unified school – a paradise lost?* Journal of Education Policy, vol 17, no. 6. Taylor & Francis, 2002, pp.673-686

Zoglowek, H. *Gifted and Talented Children in Unified School – A Provocation in the Norwe-gian Education System?* In M. Aleksandrovich & B. Kolakowska: *Uczen zdolny jest wsrod nas*. Olsztyn, 2013.

Lovdata (15.05.08) Opplæringslova § 1-2. Formålet med opplæringa:
http://www.lovdata.no/all/tl-19980717-061-001.html#1-2. Checked july 30th.
http://www.nhf.no/index.asp?id=66602 Checked 2012, may12th)

Anna Babicka-Wirkus

Pomeranian University in Słupsk, Poland

SELF-EXPRESSION IN SCHOOL – A WELCOME OR NEGATED NOTION?

Summary

In educator's critical reflection on the education process, the issue of self-expression is of great importance because it is one of the basic conditions for the human subjectivity to take form. Respect for the right to self-expression is especially crucial for adolescents because of the fact that during this period of human development, expressing oneself freely constitutes a significant predictor of identity development. The ability and readiness to express one's opinions, thoughts and emotions in a conscious, critical and responsible way is extremely important in the process of reaching maturity independently. Respect for the right to self-expression also constitutes means of comprehension and evaluation of other people's words and actions. It is also one of the pillars of a civil society which rests on a strongly developed public sphere. This sphere, in turn, is constituted on a social discourse within the framework of which every person can express their opinions and confront them with the opinions of others. School, as an educational institution and, at the same time, as a propagator of the dominant culture, tries to deal with the issue of students' expression in many ways. Usually, however, it does not create conditions that would make their self-expression possible. It is done both deliberately and unknowingly. Violating or limiting free expression causes the emergence of resistance which might or might not be of developmental character.

Introduction

In critical pedagogical reflection upon the process of education, the issue of self-expression holds a significant place as one of the basic conditions for shaping subjectivity of a young person. The ability and readiness to conscious, critical and responsible expression of one's opinions, thoughts and emotions constitute an essential element in the process of maturation[1]. The importance of free expression for achieving full humanity is so great that it has been included in two fundamental documents concerning human and children's rights. These documents are the *Universal Declaration of Human Rights* (UDHR) and the *Convention on the Rights of the Child* (CRC). At their premise, these acts of international law guarantee pro-

[1] M. Czerepaniak-Walczak , *Między dostosowaniem a zmianą. Elementy emancypacyjnej teorii edukacji*, Szczecin: Wydawnictwo Naukowe US 1994, p.59

tection and recognition of the right to self-expression in every signatory country. However, numerous scientific studies on the observance of the Universal Declaration of Human Rights or the Convention on the Rights of the Child show the alarming state of respecting the right to self-expression as well as other rights included in these documents in Poland[2].

School, as an education institution, as well as a promoter of the leading culture, attempts to tackle the issue of student expression. Most frequently, however, school fails to provide conditions enabling their self-expression, both unconsciously and on purpose.

In this article I attempt to present the importance of the right to self-expression for the development of a person as an autonomous subject. My considerations are embedded in the context of assumptions of critical pedagogy.

Self-expression and critical pedagogy

The Polish term *autoekspresja* (self-expression) is a combination of the words ***auto*** and ***ekspresja*** (expression). According to Słownik Wyrazów Obcych (Dictionary of Foreign Words), ***auto*** derives from the Greek word *autós*, which means self, one's own, self-[3]. The word ***ekspresja*** (expression) has Latin etymology. It derives from *expressio*, which means *the action of squeezing out, the action of manifesting a feeling*; or from *exprimere*, which means *to press out, clearly utter, express, present.* By *expression* we understand manifesting feelings and inner experiences[4]. As one of very few dictionaries defining pedagogical terminology, Słownik Pedagogiczny (Pedagogical Dictionary) formulates *expression* as „external manifestation of thoughts, emotions, and experiences of a person. One can distinguish verbal, facial, movement and artistic expression. Unconscious expressive reactions sometimes constitute a valuable source of information on emotional experiences of the observed person (...)"[5]. It ought to be stressed here that, taking into account the assumptions of critical pedagogy, expression is a state of manifesting opinions, experiences in line with the requirements of the leading culture, which are often internalised. Such expression may destroy a person's individuality, as it limits it to set frames in which a person should function, and often gives a false

[2] Cf. Research conducted by the Helsinki Foundation for Human Rights e.g. E. Czyż. *Prawa ucznia w szkole. Raport z badań*, www.bezuprzedzen.org/doc/Prawa_ucznia_w_szkole_HFPCz.pdf, J. Ciechanowski, E. Czyż, E. Szewczyk, *Prawo do nauki. Raport z monitoringu*, 2002, www.hfhrpol.waw.pl/publikacja-2-14-pl.html.
S. Hart, C. P. Coheb, M. F. Erickson, M. Flekkøy, *Prawa dziecka w edukacji,* trans. S. Pikiel, Gdańsk: Gdańskie Wydawnictwo Psychologiczne, 2006

[3] *Słownik Wyrazów Obcych. Wydanie Nowe*, ed. E. Sobol, Warszawa: Wydawnictwo Naukowe PWN, 1995, p. 93

[4] Ibidem, p. 279

[5] Ekspresja, in: *Słownik Pedagogiczny*, ed. Cz. Kupisiewicz, M. Kupisiewicz Warszawa: Wydawnictwo Naukowe PWN, 2009, p.44

sense of agency. Construed in this way, expression manifests itself in the processes of mimicry, emulation[6] or resistance understood as a protest of an individual, acceptable by institutions of authority[7].

Self-expression, on the other hand, is a process in which a human is able to use his or her *own voice,* becomes a causal agent, who does not fit the pattern imposed by the leading culture[8]. He or she becomes different from others who uncritically obey the authority. The importance of the term was aptly described by R. W. Emerson: *The man is only half himself, the other half is his expression*[9].

The Webster Dictionary defines self-expression as expression of one's individuality, usually in a creative way[10]. Individuality means one's character or a characteristic which is typical or unique to a given person. It is a quality which distinguishes one person from another. Individuality may also be viewed as a sum of all characteristic features of an individual[11].

Self-expression is expression of one's own thoughts and feelings. It is accomplished by words, choices or actions[12]. Expression of oneself is achieved through real or symbolic signs, which is always accompanied by constant verification of other's understanding of the message conveyed. Should the need arise, the manner of expression may be changed. The reception of feedback on the transmitted message is significant for the process of *becoming* a person[13]. Acts of expressing oneself which satisfy the Habermasian validity claim[14] are not only an opportunity for self-evaluation, but also a motive for change, which manifests in a modification of self-expression forms, so that they are understandable to recipients[15]. Self-

---

[6] *Emulation* is an action aimed at approximating the model. Read more in:
T. Szkudlarek, *Wiedza i wolność w pedagogice amerykańskiego postmodernizmu*, Kraków: Oficyna Wydawnicza „Impuls", 2009.

[7] Ibidem, p.168-170

[8] M. Fine, *Silencing and Nurturing Voice in an Improbable Context. Urban Adolescents in Public School*, in: *Critical Pedagogy, the State and Cultural Struggle*, eds. H. Giroux, P. McLaren. New York: State University of New York Press , 1989, p. 152-170

[9] R. W. Emerson, *The Poet*
http://www.vcu.edu/engweb/transcendentalism/authors/emerson/essays/poettext.html, 02.03.2011

[10] Self-expression, http://www.websters-online-dictionary.org/definitions/self-expression?cx=partner-pub-0939450753529744%3Av0qd01-tdlq&cof=FORID%3A9&ie=UTF-8&q=self-expression&sa=Search#922, 13.02.2011

[11] Individuality, http://www.websters-online-dictionary.org/definitions/individuality?cx=partner-pub-0939450753529744%3Av0qd01-tdlq&cof=FORID%3A9&ie=UTF-8&q=individuality&sa=Search#922, 13.02.2011

[12] H. S. Kim, D. Ko, *Culture and Self-Expression*, University of California Santa Barbara, www.psych.ucsb.edu/labs/kim/Site/.../Kim%26Ko.Frontier.pdf, 12.02.2011

[13] R. May, *O istocie człowieka*, Poznań: Wydawnictwo Rebis, 1995, p.33

[14] Validity claims are: truthfulness, effectiveness, comprehensibility, sincerity. Read more in: J. Habermas, *Teoria działania komunikacyjnego*, v. I, trans. A. M. Kaniowski. Warszawa: Wydawnictwo Naukowe PWN, 1999.

[15] M. Czerepaniak-Walczak, *Prawo do autoekspresji jako szansa doświadczania samego siebie*,
in: *Doświadczanie wartości samego siebie w procesach edukacyjnych*, ed. A. M. Tchorzewski, Bydgoszcz: Wydawnictwo Uczelniane WSP w Bydgoszczy, 1997, p.105

expression constitutes an act of conscious expressing of oneself, whereas expression may bear signs of unconscious verbal or motor behaviours.

Expressing oneself is often a form of opposing the prevailing logic of dominance. This contestation may take place within the boundaries permissible by the authority and, then, assume a form of resistance, which could be defined as a process of inverting externally defined meanings, that is, to use P. McLaren's term, symbolic inversion[16]. In the case of this kind of resistance, it is only possible to obtain a certain margin of freedom accepted by the leading culture. Authority creates pretence of negating such resistance behaviours, hence allowing an individual a false sense of agency and freedom[17].

A different category of the above described resistance is emancipatory resistance. It fails to contain within the *margin of otherness* allowable by authority, since it frees from domination. According to H.A. Giroux, emancipatory resistance is not based on defiance. It does not negate domination or reject institution. Neither does it consist in inverting elements within the same structure. This resistance is based on critical consciousness[18] and civil courage, which is construed by the author as the ability to express disagreement to the domination of prejudice and subjugation by authority[19]. Resistance should provide theoretical opportunities for self-reflection and a fight for public interest and empowerment of an individual[20]. The categories essential in this approach to resistance are: intentionality, consciousness, common sense, as well as the nature and value of non-discursive behaviour[21]. Resistance behaviours understood in this way are developmental in character and help an individual achieve full maturity. As resistance, P. McLaren defines all student behaviours of symbolic, historical nature as well as the symptoms of experienced behaviours. They oppose authority, validity and the dominance of the school culture over so-called *street culture*, which is typical of students[22].

Conscious resistance may develop in students emancipatory competence, which constitute a combination of critical thinking, courageous speaking and responsible accepting of the consequences of one's own actions. It includes three correlates: innovativeness, emancipa-

---

[16] P. McLaren, *The Ritual Dimension of Resistance: Clowning and Symbolic Inversion*, "Journal of Education", 1985, vol. 167, nr 2

[17] T. Szkudlarek, *Wiedza i wolność..., op.cit.*, p.177

[18] H. A. Giroux, *Reprodukcja. Opór i akomodacja*, trans. P. Kwieciński, [in:] *Edukacja i strefa publiczna. Idee i doświadczenia pedagogiki radykalnej*, eds. H. A. Giroux, L. Witkowski, Kraków: Oficyna Wydawnicza "Impuls", 2010, p.133-137

[19] H. A. Giroux, *Teoria krytyczna i racjonalność w edukacji obywatelskiej*, trans. P. Kwieciński, A. Nalaskowski, in: *Edukacja i strefa publiczna.., op.cit.* p.182

[20] H. A. Giroux, *Reprodukcja. Opór i akomodacja..., op.cit.*

[21] *Read more* in: H. A. Giroux, *Theory and Resistance in Education. Towards a Pedagogy for the Opposition*, Bergin & Garvey, 2001.

[22] P. McLaren, *Schooling as a Ritual Performance: Towards a Political Economy of Educational Symbols and Gesture,* Rowman & Littlefield, Inc. 1999, p.146

tory rationality and courage. The first correlate contains in the capability for alternative behaviour, especially in a new situation. The second one entails the ability of an individual to free themselves from self-imposed limitations, as well as from the fossilised social forces and institutions. The third correlate manifests itself in readiness to bear the consequences of one's decisions and actions[23].

Expressing oneself is also connected with the category of responsibility for the manner and content of this expression. Responsibility constitutes an expression of becoming aware of the implications of one's actions, as well as the readiness to bear the consequences[24]. Responsibility construed in this way sets the boundaries of one's self-expression. Expressing oneself constitutes a critical project of an emancipated individual, who is conscious of his or her own subjectivity, as well as subjectivity of others.

The category of self-expression is of particular importance to youth. In adolescence, people are especially sensitive to any attempts at colonisation and oppression. Young individuals perceive themselves as the central object of interest of others, therefore they attach special importance to the content and form of expressing their own opinions and emotions. Adolescents do not want to differ from their peers and, at the same time, have the need to be different[25]. For this reason, considering the issue of respecting self-expression in school is of great importance.

The category of self-expression in legal perspective

The significance of self-expression to achieve full humanity was noticed by the authors of the two above mentioned documents (UDHR and CRC), which are important for an individual. The right to freedom of expression is explained, first and foremost, as a person's right to his or her position as an individual. The roots of this right can be traced back to the Western social, political and philosophical thought, which assumes that the adequate goal of a person is to pursue one's character and potentiality as a human being[26].

The discussed right is stated in articles 12, 13, and 14 of the *Convention on the Rights of the Child*, and in article 19 of the *Universal Declaration of Human Rights*. According to these regulations, a child has the right „to express (…) views freely in all matters affecting the

[23] M. Czerepaniak-Walczak, *Pedagogika emancypacyjna. Rozwój świadomości krytycznej człowieka*, Gdańsk: Gdańskie Wydawnictwo Psychologiczne, 2006, p.131-134
[24] Ibidem, p.114
[25] P. S. Kaplan, *Educational Psychology for Tomorrow's Teacher*, St. Paul: West Publishing Company 1990, p. 194-195
[26] T. I. Emerson, *Towards a general theory of the first amendment. Faculty Scholarship Series*, Paper 2796, 1963, http://digitalcommons.law.yale.edu/fss_papers/2796, 12.03.2011

child" (article 12 of CRC) as well the freedom of expression, which must include freedom "to seek, receive and impart information and ideas of all kinds, regardless of frontiers, either orally, in writing or in print, in the form of art, or through any other media of the child's choice" (article 13 of CRC). Article 14, on the other hand, states that a child has the right to freedom of thought, conscience and religion. The right to self-expression is also guaranteed in article 19 of the Universal Declaration of Human Rights, which states that "everyone has the right to freedom of opinion and expression; this right includes freedom to hold opinions without interference and to seek, receive and impart information and ideas through any media and regardless of frontiers".

In Poland, the freedom of expression is also guaranteed in the Constitution. Article 54 section 1 states that "the freedom to express opinions, to acquire and to disseminate information shall be ensured to everyone".

Including the freedom of self-expression in the above mentioned acts manifests its importance for the development of a human as an individual who is able to express his or her own experiences and reflections connected with his or her subjective existence. The ability to express oneself constitutes a rudimentary predictor of the process called, in the emancipatory theory of education, independent maturation[27].

The right to self-expression grows in importance in the period of adolescence, when free self-expression is particularly significant. It is a difficult period, however a crucial one in terms of forming identity of a human being[28]. For this reason, respecting the right of adolescents' self-expression, in particular by adults, but also among peers, creates possibilities to enrich experiences of self-expression, as well as to develop one's communicative competence and the ability to use symbolic meanings. Respecting this right is also a means of understanding and evaluation of others' words and actions[29].

However, school, as an institution reproducing the leading culture, fails to favour self-expression of students. This situation is caused by employing mechanisms such as silence training and ignoring differences. School day routine fails to allow students independent self-expression, for it forces them to speak, write and behave according to the established rules. If a teacher allows students self-expression, its boundaries are precisely determined. Perfect examples of such routinized and imitative methods of school work are guessing the thoughts of the poem's persona or educating students to solve tests, that is developing the ability to fit the

[27] M. Czerepaniak-Walczak, *Prawo do autoekspresji ..., op.cit.*, p.106
[28] Cf.: I. Obuchowska, *Drogi dorastania. Psychologia rozwojowa okresu dorastania dla rodziców i wychowawców*, Warszawa: Wydawnictwo Szkolne i Pedagogiczne, 1996.
[29] M. Czerepaniak-Walczak, *Prawo do autoekspresji ..., op. cit.*, p.107

answer key. The described actions favour colonisation of a young person and, therefore, deprive him or her of the capability for rational argumentation. Lack of rational dialogue between teachers and students is a cause of subjugation of young people and *squeezing* them into the standards imposed by the leading culture.

School life consists not only of formal situations, but also informal ones. Self-expression occurs during the latter, when, out of the teacher's sight, that is during breaks or in toilets and changing rooms, students give vent to their self-expression, which was supressed during the lesson. It frequently manifests in obscene writings, drawings or utterances. These products usually bear characteristics of symbolic inversion rather than conscious resistance which would meet Habermasian validity claims. It is yet another significant reason for respecting the right to self-expression in school. Students should be taught such ways of self-expression which do not impede the freedom and dignity of other people.

It should be stressed that the right to freedom of self-expression falls into the category of *soft rights*[30], proposed by M. Czerepaniak-Walczak. This group includes such rights whose breach do not result in penal sanctions. They usually function in relationships between adults (parents, teachers) and children. Frequently, those who break or impede children's right to self-expression boast their concern for the child's development.

The described right is particularly troublesome in the child[31]-adult relationship. It raises questions about the boundaries of self-expression which could or should be set for a young person. Adults impeding this right leave themselves open to a charge of censorship on young people and may cause attempts to circumvent these limitations and, therefore, perpetuate double identity of a child. On the other hand, however, unrestrained use of this right may lead to negative social phenomena, such as vulgarity in expressing views or self-mutilation in forms of tattoos or scarification[32].

Concluding remarks

According to the principles of critical pedagogy, school is a place of presenting cultural opposites, where one can learn about the world, as well as interrelations and development of phenomena. School also teaches the ability of discussion, understood as achieving

[30] M. Czerepaniak-Walczak, *Źródła i aspekty profesjonalnej refleksji nauczyciel,*. Toruń: Wydawnictwo EDYTOR, 1997, p.71

[31] According to art. 1 of CRC a child means every human being below the age of 18 years.

[32] M. Czerepaniak-Walczak, *Prawo do autoekspresji ..., op. cit.*,p.107

consensus. It is a place where violence and resistance clash[33]. Education in school creates in students a specific image of the world and the society. The process of teaching and educating students allows them to recognise their possibilities and learn patterns of behaviour in situations of conflict and oppression. It also enables students to acquire abilities of emancipating themselves and predicting consequences of their states[34]. School teaches how to be free and helps recognise chances to emancipate and become aware of the scope of risk involved in the use of the achieved rights. It also develops the capability for being a subject in a democratic society[35], whose essence is celebration of differences.

However, the described above vision of school significantly differs from its real image. For school presents as a place of promoting the leading culture, whose aim is to spread unification and subordination. Under the slogans of freedom, equality and brotherhood, it educates enslaved and egoistic individuals. To achieve that, school employs techniques of *silence training* and *ignoring differences*. In order to make necessary modifications in this state of affairs, introducing strategies of emancipatory pedagogy to the system of education seems to be essential. These strategies entail "making people able to make use of their voice, express their own view of the world, articulate their interests– and do it in a manner which helps them achieve real emancipation from institutionally imposed definitions of situations, in order to overcome structural limitations in the process of learning[36]. H.A. Giroux's postulate clearly indicates the importance of freedom of self-expression for the development of an individual as a critically thinking and acting subject. However, in order to reach such level of children and youth education which follows the principles of emancipatory pedagogy, one must take into account the need to transform the training of teachers, who, from passive communicators of values and norms of the leading culture, would become transformative intellectualists.

Self-expression in school is a welcome notion, however only as long as it is contained within the boundaries determined by the oppressive structures. Nevertheless, it should be pointed out that this usually small margin of freedom allows students to manifest resistance behaviours, which violate, for example by means of symbolic inversion, the fossilised rules and principles of school life, and, therefore, expose their arbitrariness. It causes damage in

[33] E. Bilińska-Suchanek, *Opór wobec szkoły. Dorastanie w perspektywie paradygmatu oporu,* Kraków: Oficyna Wydawnicza „Impuls", 2003, p.26
[34] M. Czerepaniak-Walczak, *Między dostosowaniem a zmianą..., op. cit.*, p.77
[35] Cf. E. Bilińska-Suchanek, *Opór wobec szkoły..., op. cit.*
[36] H. A. Giroux, *W kierunku nowej sfery publicznej*, in: *Nieobecne dyskursy, p. I*, ed. Z. Kwieciński, Toruń: Wydawnictwo Uniwersytetu Mikołaja Kopernika, 1991, p.60

these structures and may lead to their destruction and replacement of old rules with new ones. As I mentioned before, school is an arena of constant fighting and representatives of the dominant and dominated structures constantly impose the established order on the remaining participants of the system.

Bibliography

Bilińska-Suchanek E., *Opór wobec szkoły. Dorastanie w perspektywie paradygmatu oporu*, Oficyna Wydawnicza „Impuls", Kraków 2003.

Czerepaniak-Walczak M., *Między dostosowaniem a zmianą. Elementy emancypacyjnej teorii edukacji*, Wydawnictwo Naukowe US, Szczecin 1994.

Czerepaniak-Walczak M., *Pedagogika emancypacyjna. Rozwój świadomości krytycznej człowieka*, Gdańskie Wydawnictwo Psychologiczne, Gdańsk 2006.

Czerepaniak-Walczak M., *Prawo do autoekspresji jako szansa doświadczania samego siebie*, w: *Doświadczanie wartości samego siebie w procesach edukacyjnych*, red. A. M. Tchorzewski, Wydawnictwo Uczelniane WSP w Bydgoszczy, Bydgoszcz 1997.

Czerepaniak-Walczak M., *Źródła i aspekty profesjonalnej refleksji nauczyciel,* Wydawnictwo EDYTOR, Toruń 1997.

Fine M., *Silencing and Nurturing Voice in an Improbable Context. Urban Adolescents in Public School*, [w:] *Critical Pedagogy, the State and Cultural Struggle*, red. H. Giroux, P. McLaren, State University of New York Press, New York 1989.

Giroux H. A., *Reprodukcja. Opór i akomodacja*, tłum. P. Kwieciński, w: *Edukacja i strefa publiczna. Idee i doświadczenia pedagogiki radykalnej*, red. H. A. Giroux, L. Witkowski, Oficyna Wydawnicza "Impuls", Kraków 2010.

Giroux H. A., *Teoria krytyczna i racjonalność w edukacji obywatelskiej*, [w:] *Edukacja i strefa publiczna. Idee i doświadczenia pedagogiki radykalnej*, red. H. A. Giroux, L. Witkowski, Oficyna Wydawnicza "Impuls", Kraków 2010.

Giroux H. A., *Theory and Resistance in Education. Towards a Pedagogy for the Opposition*, Bergin & Garvey, 2001.

Giroux H. A., *W kierunku nowej sfery publicznej*, [w:] *Nieobecne dyskursy, cz. I*, red. Z. Kwieciński, Wydawnictwo Uniwersytetu Mikołaja Kopernika, Toruń, 1991.

Habermas J., *Teoria działania komunikacyjnego*, t. I, przekł. A. M. Kaniowski, PWN, Warszawa, 1999.

Hart S., Coheb C. P., Erickson M. F., Flekkøy M., *Prawa dziecka w edukacji,* przekł. S. Pikiel, Gdańskie Wydawnictwo Psychologiczne, Gdańsk, 2006.

Kaplan P. S., *Educational Psychology for Tomorrow's Teacher*, West Publishing Company, St. Paul, 1990.

May R., *O istocie człowieka*, Wydawnictwo Rebis, Poznań, 1995.

McLaren P., *Schooling as a Ritual Performance: Towards a Political Economy of Educational Symbols and Gesture,* Rowman & Littlefield, Inc., 1999.

McLaren P., *The Ritual Dimension of Resistance: Clowning and Symbolic Inversion*, "Journal of Education", 1985, vol. 167, nr 2.

Obuchowska I., *Drogi dorastania. Psychologia rozwojowa okresu dorastania dla rodziców i wychowawców*, Wydawnictwo Szkolne i Pedagogiczne, Warszawa, 1996.

Słownik Pedagogiczny, red. Cz. Kupisiewicz, M. Kulisiewicz, Wydawnictwo Naukowe PWN, Warszawa, 2009.

Słownik Wyrazów Obcych. Wydanie Nowe, red. E. Sobol, Wydawnictwo Naukowe PWN, Warszawa, 1995

Szkudlarek T., *Wiedza i wolność w pedagogice amerykańskiego postmodernizmu*, Oficyna Wydawnicza „Impuls", Kraków, 2009.

Notegrafia

Ciechanowski, J., Czyż, E., Szewczyk E., *Prawo do nauki. Raport z monitoringu*, 2002, http://www.hfhrpol.waw.pl/publikacja-2-14-pl.html

Czyż, E. *Prawa ucznia w szkole. Raport z badań*, http://www.bezuprzedzen.org/doc/Prawa_ucznia_w_szkole_ HFPCz.pdf

Emerson, R. W., *The Poet* http://www.vcu.edu/engweb/transcendentalism/authors/emerson/essays/poettext.html

Emerson, T. I. (1963). Towards a general theory of the first amendment. *Faculty Scholarship Series*, Paper 2796, http://digitalcommons.law.yale.edu/fss_papers/2796

Individuality, http://www.websters-online-dictionary.org/definitions/individuality?cx= partner-pub-0939450753529744%3Av0qd01-tdlq&cof=FORID%3A9&ie=UTF-8&q= individuality&sa=Search#922

Kim, H. S., Ko, D., *Culture and Self-Expression*, University of California Santa Barbara, http://www.psych.ucsb.edu/labs/kim/Site/.../Kim%26Ko.Frontier.pdf.

Barbara Kędzierska
Pedagogical University of Krakow
Agnieszka Kędzierska
Free University of Berlin

MEDIA AS CATALYST OF INNOVATIVE EDUCATION

Summary

The most important area of the activity of each society is the education, which in fundamental way determines the pace its development and the quality of its members life. Since ages teachers, playing the role of master and the basic source of the information, were the most important in the process of education. Rapid technological development of the information and communication techniques in recent decades has changed form and meaning of the two main forms of the human's activity which decide on the scope and effects of his actions – communication and the access to the information, which not only forces change of the role of teachers and puts in front of them up till now unknown challenges, but as well rises the need for implementation within education methods, which include episodic and hypertext information transfer as well as revolutionary possibility of the media, new media and new new media.

Media context of contemporary education

Everyday life filled with media and virtual reality rivaling with the real world can not make education to be inert to the changes taking place in the cognitive process of modern man. Universal access to information and omnipresent, various in content and form, media message does not make us to constantly seek information because they are looking for us, and sometimes even attack. The basic competence today has become the resistance to the accidental excess of information incentives and the ability to critically analyze them and make wise selection. In accordance with the principle of 80/20, also known as the principle of Pareto[1], if we can properly select 20% of the information coming to us, they will be able to make 80% contribution into achieving our objectives and targets. Today, in a globalizing world, we gain

[1] The rule 80/20 (or "80 for 20") also called the rule of Pareto, is a result of the observation, which was conducted and published by Vilfredo Pareto about 100 years ago. This Italian scientist observed, that 80% of goods is in the posses of only 20% of the society. (Pareto did not invent " Pareto's rule" nor "80/20 rule" he only spotted the proportion)

autonomy, which can become our threat if it is not integrated with the responsibility increasingly conditioned by the skills of critical analysis and selection of information coming to us. Pervasive culture of immediacy, eye-catching advertisements or distorted media coverage will cease to be a threat if we will be able to critically monitor the situation. Information literacy of teachers and parents is essential in a responsible and effective training and education.

They are a prerequisite for adequate personal performance in life, work and subsequent learning, essential in a knowledge society and guarantee more flexibility in the labor force, allowing it to adapt more quickly to constant changes in an increasingly interconnected world. Key competences are a major factor in innovation, productivity and competitiveness and they contribute to the motivation and satisfaction of workers and the quality of work. They should be transferable and therefore applicable in many situations and contexts and multifunctional in that they can be used to achieve several objectives, to solve different kinds of problems and to accomplish different kinds of tasks[2].

Media message, which often exaggerates social pathologies, promotes consumerism and decreases the level of artistic standards through the dominance of popular culture[3] can be a carrier of information, however, also important, real and current, on the basis of which learners actively grow and develop their knowledge, acquire skills and qualifications. Modern education can not therefore ignore or resign from the media coverage but the media should be adequately integrated in innovative methods and forms, adapting them to the new circumstances. Media fulfill more and more functions (informative (multi-code), educational (means – method), culture-forming, simulating, tool (in the process of learning, at work, when playing or in communication) and offer three kinds of experience which refer to three – system representation of the world according to Jerome S. Bruner cognitive learning theory:

- action based experience refer to enactive representation,
- image based experience refer to iconic representation,
- language based experience refer to symbolic representation.

Full integration of ICT and media in education requires a four-step approach: emerging approach, applying approach, integrating approach and tansforming approach.

Emerging **-** this approach is linked with a school in the beginning stages of ICT development. The school begins to purchase, or has had donated, some equipment and software. In this initial phase, administrators and teachers are just starting to explore the possibilities

[2] Recommendation of the European Parliament and of the Council, of 18 December 2006, on key competences for lifelong learning [Official Journal L 394 of 30.12.2006]

[3] S. Juszczyk, *Człowiek w świecie mediów elektronicznych,* Katowice 2000, s. 87.

and consequences of adding ICT for school management and the curriculum. The school is still firmly grounded in **traditional, teacher-centred practice.** In this approach an ICT-curriculum is indicated that increases the basic skills and awareness of the uses of ICTs. This curriculum assists movement to the next approach if so desired.

Applying - this approach is linked with a school in which new understanding of the contribution of ICTs to learning has developed. In this approach administrators and teachers use ICTs for tasks already carried out in school management and in the curriculum. Teachers largely dominate the learning environment. In this approach the school best chooses an ICT-curriculum that increases **the use of ICTs in various subject areas with specific tools and software**. This curriculum assists movement to the next approach if so desired.

Integrating - this approach is linked with a school that now has a range of technologies both in laboratories, classrooms and administrative offices. The school staff explore new ways in which ICTs change their personal productivity and professional practice. The ICT-curriculum begins to merge subject areas to reflect real-world applications.

Transforming - This approach is linked with a school that has used ICTs to creatively rethink and renew school organisation. ICTs become an integral though invisible part of daily personal productivity and professional practice. The focus of the curriculum is now learner-centred and integrates subject areas in real-world applications. ICTs are taught as a subject area at the professional level and incorporated into all vocational areas. **The school has become a centre of learning for the community.**

Dynamic development of ICT focus recently around mobile technologies, what results in a steady increase in the number of users of this type of media in all areas of social activity. The most commonly used media in private, educational or professional activities are (beyond mobile phones and smartphones) social media, represented by Facebook or Twitter and all kinds of blogs and forums. The next generation of ICT tools offers us more efficient and attractive method of acquiring, processing, presentation and storage of information. Quickly forgotten floppy discs emerged as CD-ROMs, DVDs or USB sticks. And today number of supporters of work, study and research *in the cloud* (figure 1) is constantly increasing.

Research Tools in the Cloud:

- LinkedIn, Research Gate, NING, DL,
- Recommendersystems (People- Ressource-Tagging)
- Mendeley, Delicious, Dropbox, iCloud, Drive, BibTeX
- SVN, Repository,Tortoise, Trac, AAN
- Facebook, Blog, WiKi, Pushpin, Gingko

Tools for Teaching in the Cloud:

- e-Portfolio, e-Learning Platforms, Podcasts
- MOOCs
- PINGO, Twitterwalls
- Mobile Learning, PLME (Simple, Soboleo)
- Social Learning Networks (Chat, FM, Skype)

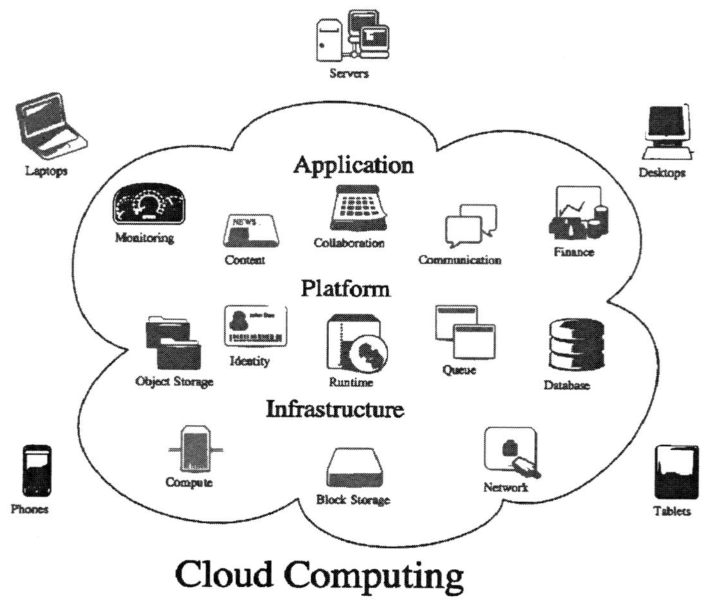

Figure 1. Cloud Computing

Subsequent generations of media described as *new* or *new new media* find quickly their place in the daily activities of not only young people but those active ones. Used every-day, they unconsciously modify the way we function, the way we think of learning and they stimulate new ways of cooperation and training.

The role of ICT in innovating teaching methods

Nowadays, technology compromises an indispensable part of our life. Young people are spending more time chatting through social networks then in the real life. For many, especially for those who decided to leave their fatherlands (for work, travel or else), internet became the most effective and fastest tool for communication with the beloved ones. Technology is entering all aspects of our lives and thereby changing the way we communicate, inform ourselves, buy, sell, etc. Education, especially formal education, is being relevantly influenced by technology, especially by the use of computers and internet. Nowadays, when information is easily available for everyone, the role of a teacher undergoes significant transformation. Educators need to adjust to their new role and learn how to use the potential technological development brings to them.

Information and communication technology (ICT) understood as unified communication tools (i.e. radio, television, cellular, computers, etc.) is playing an especially crucial role in the education of the “y generation”[4]. In contradiction to the generation x[5] (people who started using technology in their adult life for a very first time, discovering the world of e-mails, websites and social networks) generation y became accustomed to the communication with their peers through different social networks like Facebook, Flickr, Linkedin and so on. Internet, therefore, is for them not just a source of an information or a tool for efficient communication (e-mails), but it is becoming “an answer to all needs”. Presented above graph shows that about 83% of the y-generation representatives is actively using social networks and about 80% of them is active on portals like Hulu, Youtube or Video. The only common aspect for both generations are search engines and e-mails (about 90% of both generation is claiming to be using them).

For generation 'Y' it is natural to use social networks as well as video portals for learning. Facebook is full of groups devoted to different fields of science. And the more controversial the groups are the more visitor and comments they have. Today, when the available information is overwhelming, one has to learn how to filtrate it and how to choose the most valuable and accurate one. Hence, the educational methods and approach needs to change. We need to recognize that the role of the teacher, as it is much different from the one he had while working with generation x. Of course introduction of the computer to all fields of education is bringing both: benefits and threats. Confucius said: 'I hear and I forget. I see and I believe. I do and I understand'. That is where computers and multimedia learning[6] are of very much use. Various programs have been developed to visualize the theory being though by teachers. We can travel through the whole world within few seconds. Biology and cells science is no longer a black magic, as by means of different specialized software we are able

---

[4] Generation Y – teenagers, often called 'echo boomers', who had constant contact to technology during their youth, therefore they are completely relying on the technology, which compromises one of the most important aspect of their lives. Due to the demand of the generation Y various aspects of everyday life had to change (i.e. the hiring systems, university applications, etc.)

[5] Generation X – so called 'post-World War II baby boom'. In 1961 Douglas Coupland has written a book where he described the x-generation in many details.

[6] Multimedia learning is described by Dr.V.S.Damodharan and Mr.V.Rengarajan Faculty (from Business Studies Department, Higher College of Technology Sultanate of Oman) as an interactive learning process where teacher, student and multimedia are working together.

to build models and see what is normally not visible for human eyes. On the other hand though, the usage of computes is causing many questions about inclusion and exclusion, justice, decrease in the hand-writing of pupils, etc. Perhaps, it might be even harder for parents to help children with their homework (as generation X is not always fit with ICT and newest technologies), but through social media and learning platforms students are able to get in contact with peers from all over the world (even work in groups) as well as sometimes to get in contact with the teacher and ask for a hint how to solve hard homework.

Nevertheless, despite small threats and neuralgic aspects for consideration ICT is putting education on a next level, is enhancing the cognition and meta-cognition, is bringing pupils from all over the world together enabling the exchange of information as well as is supporting teachers in undertaking a new role. Role of a guide, of one that will show the right direction and will teach how to choose the correct and real information, but not the role of 'the only source of knowledge'. Generation Y is also demanding new, innovative, teaching methods. Methods, which put upon all available tools and which prepare graduates for the demanding and very competitive labor market.

In further part of this article we would like to firstly introduce the notion of innovating teaching methods and next present few (in our opinion most relevant) innovating teaching methods and the importance ICT has for their implementation and effectiveness.

Innovating teaching methods (ITM)

Noorifashar M. (2013) in his articles about innovative teaching methods cites the example of late 90s when the multimedia system was introduced for the very first time and what resulted in over 95% more satisfactory results. These example, support the hypothesis that by adopting innovative ideas and approach more students will be able to cross the bridge and learn advanced topics, i.e. complex mathematics theories, in much more enjoyable manner. Also the very positive responses from the students prove that the multimedia extension is an effective means of reinforcing the learning process, particularly for those students who are not able to take advantage of the traditional (face-to-face) mode of delivery.[7]

The learning pyramid proposed by Dale E. (1969) highlights the difference between passive and active learning, between what we read and what we do. Dale states that things we learn only by reading, after two weeks, stays in our memory only in 10%, whereas if we learn by saying or doing (that includes simulations and etc.) we remember it in 90%. It seems to be

[7] M. Nooriafshar, *The use of innovating teaching methods for "maximizing' the enjoyment from learning mathematical concepts*, International Journal of Mathematics Teaching and Learning, 2013.

a strong argument speaking in a favor of ITM, methods that involve learners in an active and responsible action, that are much more effective and contribute in much greater extend to the creation of well educated and prepared graduates securely entering the labor markets.[8]

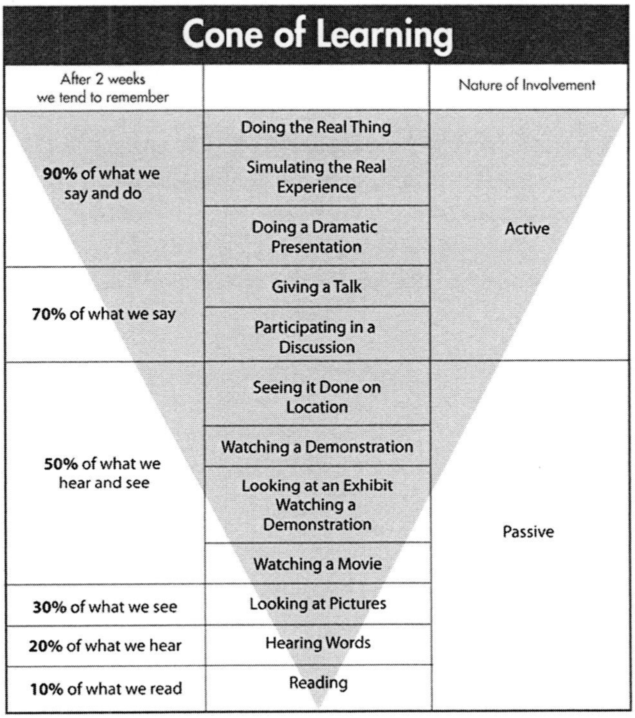

Figure 2. Corner of learning adapted from Dale (1969)

Source: www. http://uclass.in/909

Generally speaking one could say that ITM, as a teaching methods, are concentrating on discussion rather then on a lecture (frontal teaching). It is more important to learn how to learn then to memorize definitions and rules. It is a methodological approach that affects all senses. To do so it involves all: text, images, audio, video, animation and etc. ITM is shaping team spirit, teaching learners how one should work in groups in regard to achievement of a common goal, but at the same time ITM strengthens self-confidence of individuals, enabling therefore, individual action, initiative and responsibility for own actions. ITM should be always

[8] E.Dale *Audiovisual methods in teaching*. New York: The Dryden Press, 1969.

conducted within student-centered approach. Biggs J. (1999, p. 118) differentiates three types of teaching-learning activity and corresponding forms of learning (see table 1 below).

Biggs shows here, that when learning process is self-controlled, though it is much more demanding, it is more effective and it is shaping valuables skills. According to Biggs such an approach results not only with generic and content study skill, but most importantly with metacognitive learning skills, thereby prepares young people, fresh graduates to enter the labor market and constantly strive for social change and improvement of the surrounding.[9]

Being convinced about the importance of the role ICT plays in the teaching-learning process we present below chosen ITM methods (they main methodological approach) and explain the role of ICT in their implementation and effectiveness.

Table 1. Teaching-learning activities

Teacher-controlled	**Forms of learning**
lecturer, set texts	reception of selected content
think-aloud	demonstrate conceptual skills
questioning	clarifying, seeking error
advance organizer	structuring, preview
concept mapping	structuring, overview
tutorial	elaboration, clarification
laboratory	procedures, applications
excursion	experiential knowledge, interest
seminar	clarify, presentation skills
Peer-controlled	**Forms of learning**
various groups	elaboration, problem-solving, metacognition
learning partners	resolve differences, application
peer teaching	depends, whether teacher or taught
spontaneous collaboration	breadth, self-insight
Self-controlled	**Form of learning**
generic study skills	basic self-management
content study skills	information handling
metacognitive learning skills	independence and self-monitoring

[9] J. Biggs. *Teaching for Quality Learning at University: What the Student Does*. Higher Education, 1999, 40 (3), pp 374-376.

Self-regulated learning

Self-regulated learning (SRL) is a methodological approach which concentrates on strategies referring to actions and processes, directed at the acquisition of information and skills, which involve agency, purpose, and instrumentality perceptions by learners. According to Zimmermann (Zimmerman 1990), SRL enclose 3 most important dimensions: metacognitive, motivational and behavioral.[10] In SRL very important is the self-orientated loop, with a strong focus on the self-evaluation process.[11] SRL learners put much importance on the evaluation of their learning progress. Therefore, self-regulated learning demands both will and skill. SRL puts emphasis on how student selects, organizes and creates proper learning environment. Hence, students who show outstanding motivation achieve particular academic achievements. Education should help students to be aware of their thinking: they must be strategic and direct their motivation toward valuable goal as well as they should learn how to be their own teachers.[12] Learners are distinguished by theirs awareness of strategic relations between regulatory processes and learning processes as well as they make use of those strategies (metacognitive, motivational, behavioral) to achieve academic goals. SRL learners view acquisition as a systematic and controllable process, and try to accept greater responsibility for their achievements outcomes.[13]

Most importantly SRL students: a) know how to use cognitive strategies (repetition, elaboration and organization) and therefore are able to transform, organize, elaborate and recover information, b) know how to plan, control and direct their mental processes, c) maintain motivational beliefs and adaptive emotions (self-efficacy), d) know how to create and structure favorable learning environments, e) show effort for the participation in the control and regulation of academic task.[14][15][16][17].

---

[10] B.J. Zimmermann *Self-regulated learning and Academic Achievement: An Overview*. Educational Psychologist, 1990, 25 (1), pp.3-17.

[11] M. Torrano, G. Fermin, M.C. Gonzalez. Torres *Self-regulated learning: Current and Future Directions*. Electronic Journal of Research in Educational Psychology, 2013, 3, 27.

[12] M. Torrano, G. Fermin, M.C. Gonzalez. Torres *Self-regulated learning: Current and Future Directions*. Electronic Journal of Research in Educational Psychology, 2013, 3, 27.

[13] D.H. Schunk, B.J. Zimmermann. *Self-Regulated Learning and Academic Achievement: Theoretical Perspectives*. Routledge, 2012.

[14] D.H. Schunk, B.J. Zimmermann *Self-regulated learning: From Teaching to slef-reflective Precice*. Guilford Press, 1998.

[15] B.J. Zimmermann *Self-regulated learning and Academic Achievement: An Overview*. Educational Psychologist, 1990, 25 (1), pp.3-17.

[16] D.H. Schunk, B.J. Zimmermann. *Handbook of Self-Regulation of Learning and Performance*. Educational Psychology Handbook. Taylor & Francis, 2011.

[17] D.H. Schunk, B.J. Zimmermann. *Motivation and Self-Regulated Learning: Theory, Research, and Applications. Routledge*, 2012.

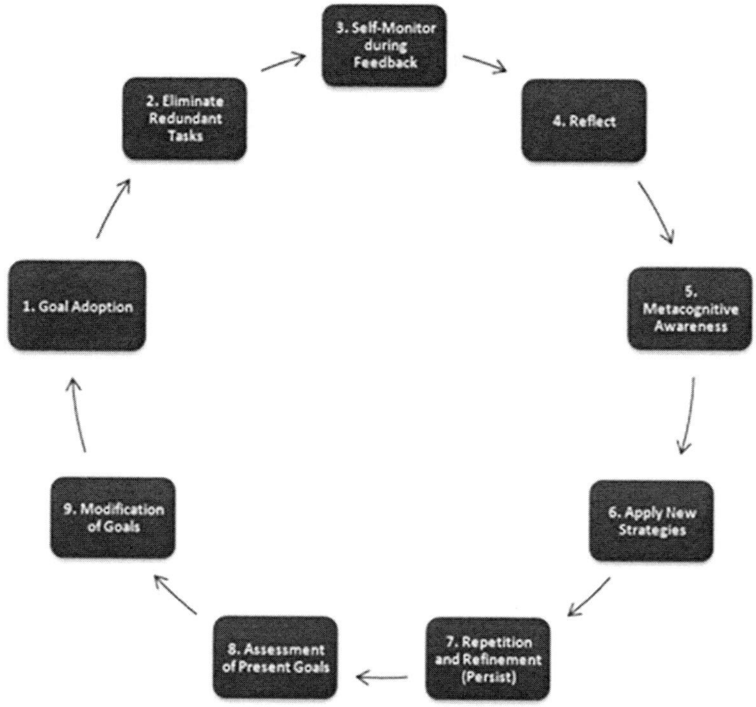

Figure 3. Model of Self-Regulated Deliberate Flow
Source: http://motivatedmusician.com/

ICT in SRL

Self-regulated learning leaves much space for the usage of the information and communication techniques (ICT). Currently, there are many available tools on the market which can help students to organize their learning process and their knowledge (i.e. programs for creation of mind maps). Ambitious students, eager to expand their knowledge, can take advantage of e-learning course widely available on internet. Thanks to ICT and Internet a student attending an university in Europe without problems or effort can take part in e-course being organized i.e. by the Harvard University in USA. That allows students to precisely direct and shape their education and allows them to be competitive and well prepared for labor market.

Students functioning in technically enhanced learning environments (TELEs) build up their ability to self-regulate.[18] Bender also shows that students that had access to TELE improved their SRL abilities in much greater extend.

[18] T. Bender. *Discussion-based Online Teaching to Enhance Student Learning: Theory, Practice, and* Assessment. Stylus Publishing, 2003.

Problem-based learning (PBL)

Problem-based learning is an active learning style, where students acquire theirs knowledge by finding solutions to problems they are being presented to. Barrows (2012) defines PBL as a student-centered learning process, where learning is happening in small groups (preferably 6-10 peers), where teachers are undertaking the role of a guide or tutor not a dictator and where the learning process is always happening around some problem (problem is the stimulator of the learning process as well as of the cognitive process). In PBL the acquisition of the new knowledge is happening through self-directed learning. Nevertheless, meetings in groups and and using the group as a learning tool is the clue activity of this methodology. Students should constantly relate their knowledge to the given problem. Once learners manage to solve first problem another one is provided, which base on the previous one and should motivate students to deepen their knowledge on a given topic. An important factor for this methodology is constant access to different sources of knowledge (library, lectures, seminars, etc.) so that learners have all necessary tools to solve the problem.[19][20][21]

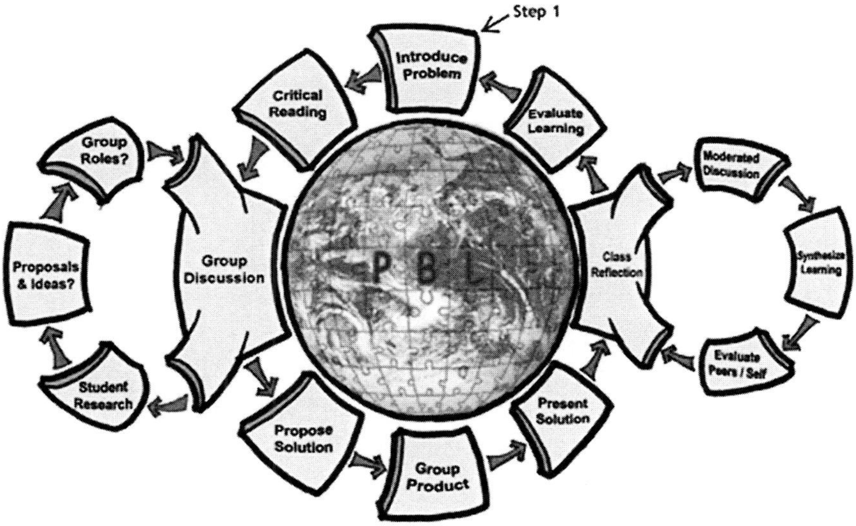

Figure 4. Model of Problem-based learning

Source: http://www.vcu.edu/cte/resources/nfrg/11_07_problem_based_learning.htm

---

[19] M. Savin-Baden. *Facilitating Problem-Based Learning: Illuminating Perspectives.* McGraw-Hill International, 2003.

[20] M. Savin-Baden. Wilkie K. *Problem-based learning Online.* McGraw-Hill International, 2006.

[21] M. Savin-Baden. *A Practical Guide to Problem-Based Learning Online*. Routledge, 2007.

ICT in PRL

Already from it's assumptions problem-based learning can be successful only when access to different sources of knowledge is given. Students will not be able to find solutions to difficult problems without necessary information and best practice examples. Through ICT learners are able to communicate and ask for advices on the possible solution to given problem experts from all over the world, they can use forums, start a Facebook group, Skype with peers from other countries and learn about their experience.

Figure 5. Inquiry-Based Learning, IBL (enquiry-based learning)
Source: http://www.inquirylearn.com/

The popularization of the 'learning by doing' philosophy contributed to the development of Inquiry-Based Learning (IBL). IBL is a student-centered approach[22] , it is a very active process that invites all learners to take initiative and participate in the learning process.[23] [24] IBL is proposing to students to find their personal understanding of reality.[25]

Inquiry-Based Learning is a learning 'by researching', students should get a life-long insight into research as a method of creation of the new knowledge and learning. In IBL

[22] D. Kember. *A reconceptualisation of the research into university academics' conceptions of teaching*. Learning and Instruction, 1997, 7, 255-275.
[23] G. Gibbs. *Learning by Doing: A guide to teaching and learning methods*. Further Education Unit, Oxford Brookes University, Oxford, 1988.
[24] M. Healey, J. Roberts, Ed. *Engaging students in active learning: case studies in geography, environment and related disciplines.* Cheltenham: University of Gloucestershire, Geography Discipline Network and School of Environment, 2004.
[25] J. Bruner. *Acts of Meaning*. Cambridge, Mass.: Harvard University Press, 1990.

students are responsible for defining the central parts (aspects) of the curricula, which teacher has chosen as a subject for the course. Therefore, student must find, evaluate and use the source of information available for the subject. A very important aspect of IBL is the assessments or learners. Each practitioner of IBL should maintain learning portfolios, prepare reports from each step of the learning process and in the end attend traditional examinations. Grading conducted by teachers should reflect the contract fulfillment of learners.

ICT in IBL

Inquiry-based learning, as a methodology concentrating on research, demands a constant access to news scientific articles, journals, conferences, etc. Certainly, students practicing IBL can go to libraries, attend conferences and talk to scientists from their local environment. However, just by taking advantage of the online journals, online conference proceeding, recorded talks of known scientists from all over the world (i.e. at TED) learners can get an in-depth understanding of the topic and acquire required knowledge.

At the same time, ICT can simplify the assessments for teachers (i.e. by implementation of the e-portfolio as a learning portfolio of students taking part in their courses). In that way the process of grading and evaluation might take less time, can be more personalized (as each student will have his/hers profile) and can leave much more freedom to teachers, who will be able to assess students in best for them time (not as before, only during the consultation hours).

Conclusions and roadmaps

Technological development has always resulted in accelerating the development of societies, but it was impossible to predict the consequences of Internet's appearance in our reality. Common access to information and electronic forms of communication radically changed the way we function and form professional, social and educational activities. The added value of new media in education will be complete if they will integrate the innovative teaching methods that take into account episodic, hypertext transfer of information and mobility based on various forms of communication during synchronous and asynchronous time.

Bibliography

Azer S. *Navigating Problem Based Learning.* Elsevier Health Sciences, 2008.

Baldwin L. P. *Active Learning in Higher Education.* SAGE Journal, 2012.

Bender T. *Discussion-based Online Teaching to Enhance Student Learning: Theory, Practice, and Assessment.* Stylus Publishing, 2003.

Biggs. J. *Teaching for Quality Learning at University: What the Student Does*, Higher Education, 1999, 40 (3), pp 374-376.

Bruner, J. *Acts of Meaning*. Cambridge, Mass.: Harvard University Press, 1990.

Chiu C., Salili F., Hong Y. *Multiple Competencies and Self-Regulated Learning: Implications for Multicultural Education Tom 2* Research in Multicultural Education and International Perspectives Series, 2001.

Dale E. *Audiovisual methods in teaching*. New York: The Dryden Press, 1969.

De Grez L., Valcke M., Roozen I. *How effective are self- and peer assessment of oral presentation skills compared with teachers' assessment?* SAGE Journal, 2012.

Dettori G., Persico D. *Fostering Self-regulated Learning Through ICT.* IGI Global, 2011.

Edmonds A., Amy H., Patricia R. *Inquiry-Based Learning Using Everyday Objects: Hands-On Instructional Strategies That Promote Active Learning in Grades 3-8.* Corwin Press, 2003.

Futrak E. M., Seidel T., Iverson H., Briggs D. C. *Experimental and Quasi-Experimental Studies of Inquiry-Based Science Teaching: A Meta-Analysis.* Review of Educaitonal Research, 2012.

Gibbs G. *Learning by Doing: A guide to teaching and learning methods*. Further Education Unit, Oxford Brookes University, Oxford, 1988.

Healey, M., Roberts, J., Ed. *Engaging students in active learning: case studies in geography, environment and related disciplines.* Cheltenham: University of Gloucestershire, Geography Discipline Network and School of Environment, 2004.

Hmelo-Silver C. E., Golan Duncan R., Chinn C. A. *Scaffolding and Achievements in Problem-Based Learning and Inquiry-Learning: A Response to Kirschner, Sweller, and Clark.* Educational Psychologist, 2007, 42 (2), pp. 99-107.

Juszczyk S. *Człowiek w świecie mediów elektronicznych,* Katowice, 2000.

Kedzierska B., *Kompetencje informacyjne w kształceniu ustawicznym,* Warszawa, 2007.

Kember, D. *A reconceptualisation of the research into university academics' conceptions of teaching*. Learning and Instruction, 1997, 7, 255-275.

Kuhlthau C., Maniotes L., Caspari A.: *Guided Inquiry: Learning in the 21st Centaury"*, Greenwood Publishing Group, 2007.

LearningLab DTU, UDTU H18, Activating Teaching Methods.

Muchacka B., Szymański M. (red.), *Szkoła w świecie współczesnym.* Kraków 2008.

Nageswari K. S., Malhotra A. S., Kapoor N., Kaur G. *Pedagogical effectiveness of innovative teaching methods initiated at the Department of Physiology, Government Medical College, Chandigarh.* Department of Physiology, Government Medical College, 2004, 28, pp. 51-58.

Poikela E, Nummenmaa A.R. *Understanding Problem-Based Learning.* University of Tempere, 2006.

Recommendation of the European Parliament and of the Council, of 18 December 2006, on key competences for lifelong learning. Official Journal L 394 of 30.12.2006.

Savin-Baden M., Wilkie K. *Problem-based learning Online.* McGraw-Hill International, 2006.

Savin-Baden M. *A Practical Guide to Problem-Based Learning Online.* Routledge, 2007.

Savin-Baden M. *Facilitating Problem-Based Learning: Illuminating Perspectives.* McGraw-Hill International, 2003.

Schunk D.H., Zimmermann B. J. *Self-regulated learning: From Teaching to slef-reflective Prectice.* Guilford Press, 1998.

Schunk D.H., Zimmermann B.J. *Handbook of Self-Regulation of Learning and Performance. Educational Psychology Handbook.* Taylor & Francis, 2011.

Schunk D.H., Zimmermann B.J. *Motivation and Self-Regulated Learning: Theory, Research, and Applications.* Routledge ,2012.

Schwartz P., Webb G., Mennin S. *Problem-Based Learning: Case Studies, Experience and Practice.* Routledge, 2011.

Spronken-Smith R. *Experiencing the Process of Knowledge Creation: The Nature and Use of Inquiry-Based Learning in Higher Education.* New Zealand.

Torrano M., Fermin G., Gonzalez Torres M. C. *Self-regulated learning: Current and Future Directions.* Electronic Journal of Research in Educational Psychology, 2013, 3, 27.

Vilonen K. M., Zitting E., Krause A. O. I. *The use of activating teaching methods in an industry course on chemical processes.* European Society for Engineering Education, 2009.

Woods D. R. *Problem-based learning: how to gain the most from PBL.* D.R. Woods, 1994.

Zimmermann B. J. *Self-regulated learning and Academic Achievement: An Overview.* Educational Psychologist, 1990, 25 (1), pp.3-17.

Zimmermann B.J., Schunk D.H. *Self-Regulated Learning and Academic Achievement: Theoretical Perspectives.* Routledge, 2012.

NOTES ABOUT THE AUTHORS

Krystyna Duraj-Nowakowa - *Professor, the Head of the Department of Pedology at the Ignatianum University, Cracow, Poland. She has a very wide field of scientific interests, which concentrates around several disciplines: Methodology of the Scientific Research in Pedagogy, Pedology, Pedagogy of High School as well as Social Pedagogy. She is the author of 23 books and co-author of 13, the author of more then 300 scientific articles, reports and esseys.*

Irina Surina - *Professor, the Dean of the Faculty of the Social Sciences and the Head of the Department of Sociology at the Pomeranian University, Slupsk, Poland. Her scientific interests concentrate around questions of sociology of young people, sociology of education, ethnosociology and ethno- and social pedagogy. Author of three monographs, seven textbooks and scripts and co-author of six monographs in Russian language, editor of several scientific books concerning the questions of Social Pedagogy, as well as the author of numerous articles in Polish, Russian and Ukrainian language.*

Bogdan Gębski - *Professor, the Head of the Department of Pedagogy at the Higher Pedagogical School in Warsaw, filial in Szczecin. His field of interests is Sociology and Methodology of Social Research. He was one of the participants of the grant of the University in Greifswald: Kulturelle Unterschiede in der subjektiven Gesundheit: Stresserleben, Sinnerleben und Burnout von estnischen, polnischen und deutschen Studenten.*

Karolina Zaniewska - *MA of Pedagogy. Her main scientific interests are Social Pedagogy and Sociology of Youth as well as Pedagogy of High School. Nowadays she is working as Lecturer at the Department of Social Work at the Pomeranian University, Slupsk, Poland.*

Kazbek Gaysanov - *PhD, Doctor of Sociology. His main scientific interests are Sociology, System of National Values of Youth, as well as National and Global Models of Modern Universities. Nowadays he is working at the Pomeranian University, Slupsk, Poland.*

Henryk Porożyński - *PhD, Doctor of Pedagogy. His main scientific interests are History of Upbringing and Comparative Pedagogy. Nowadays he is working at the Department of History of Education and Upbringing at the Pomeranian University, Slupsk, Poland.*

Ewa Murawska - *PhD, Doctor of Pedagogy. Her main scientific interests are forming of adolescents' identity, identity of the teacher, as well as the phenomenon of power and resistance in educational relations. Nowadays she is working as Assistant Professor at the Department of General Pedagogy and Basics of Education at Pomeranian University, Slupsk, Poland.*

Julitta Nowak - *PhD, Doctor of Sociology, the Dean of the Szczecin filial of the Higher Pedagogical School in Warsaw. The field of her scientific interests spreads from Sociology to Social Pedagogy and Social Work.*

Roma Kwiecińska - *PhD, Doctor of Pedagogy. Her main scientific interests accomulating in the field of Social Pedagogy and ways of the support of the development of children* *and youth with special need. Nowadays she is working as Assistant Professor at the Institute of Sciences about Education at Pedagogical University of Cracow, Poland.*

Jolanta Rybska-Klapa - *PhD, Doctor of Pedagogy, the Head of the Lab of Psychological and Pedagogical Help and Methodogy Advices at the Pedagogical University of Cracow, Poland. Her main scientific interests are Psychologycal and Pedagogical Support and Consulting of Children and Teachers.*

Maria Aleksandrovich - *PhD, Doctor of Psychology, Associate Professor and the Head of the Department of Psychology at Pomeranian University, Slupsk, Poland and the Guest Professor at the Finnmark University College, Alta, Norway. Author of 3 books and over 50 scientific articles. She is a member of the International Society of Studying of Behavioral Development (ISSBD), member of the European Council of High Abilities (ECHA), member of the American Psychological Association (APA).*

Herbert Zoglowek - *PhD, Doctor of Philosophy, Master of Pedagogic. Since 1992 he is working as Associated Professor at the Finnmark University College in Alta, Norway. Since 2007 guest lecturer at the University of Education in Ludwigsburg, Germany. Since 2010 professor II at the Pomeranian University in Slupsk, Polen. His main teaching and research fields are professionalism of P.E. teacher, didactics of ball games and experimental education. In these subjects he is author of three books and a plenty of articles and chapters in books.*

Anna Babicka-Wirkus - *PhD, Doctor of Pedagogy. Her main scientific interests are Qualitative Social Research, Quantitative Social Research, Pedagogy and Education, Sociology, Cultural Anthropology, Pedagogy and Statistical Software. Nowadays she is working at the University of Szczecin.*

Barbara Kędzierska - *Professor, Director of the Institute of Sciences about Education at the Pedagogical University of Cracow, Rector's Plenipotentiary responsible for IT in Didactic Process, Rector's Representative for Co-operation with Region Malopolska Municipal Administration in teachers education and development. She is also Co-ordinator of the National Group of Representatives of all Pedagogical Universities and Colleges in Poland for the issues of Didactic Process Computerisation (the Group's activities included development of the IT Framework Curriculum for Pedagogical Universities and Colleges) as well as director of European Centre for Lifelong Learning And Multimedia Education (PUK (ECKUM)).*

Agnieszka Kędzierska - *She got her MA at the University of Science and Technology in Cracow and toady she is working at the Freie Universität in Berlin. The field of her scientific interests is Social Science, Qualitative Social Research, Environmental Engineering, Quantitative Social Research, Pedagogy and Academic Writing. She is a member of such organizations as Junior International ESD Experts Network, Berliner Inno-Kreis, InnovationLab, and Environment for Environment / Środowisko dla Środowiska.*

Erziehungswissenschaft

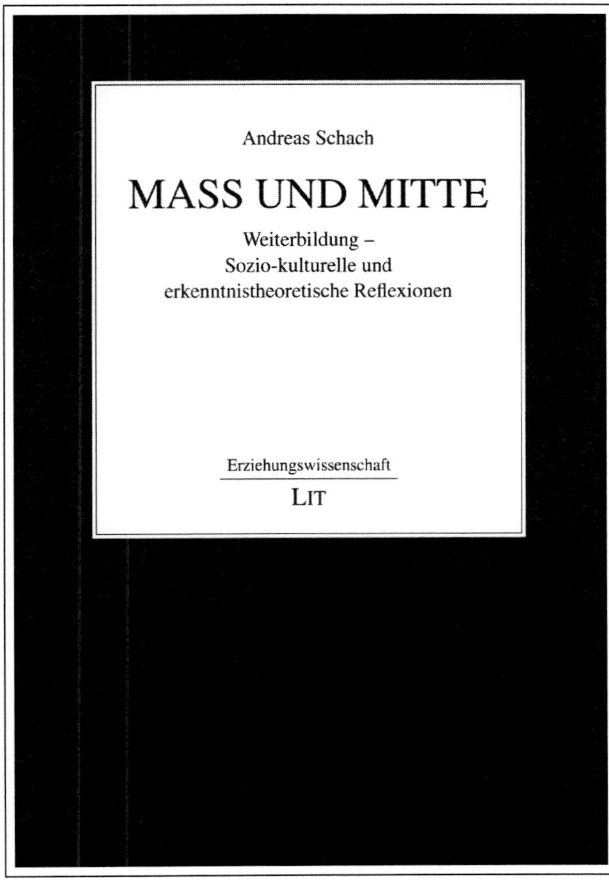

Andreas Schach
Maß und Mitte
Weiterbildung – Sozio-kulturelle und erkenntnistheoretische Reflexionen
Wie selbstverständlich bleibt Weiterbildung in Hinblick auf kritische Fragen aus kultureller, erkenntnistheoretischer oder politischer Sicht? Der Autor formuliert keine erziehungswissenschaftlich-methodische Monographie. Er thematisiert anders gelagerte Problemfelder. Der Zirkel der Betrachtung ist weit geöffnet, um eine kritische Reflexion bestehender Grundaxiome der Weiterbildung zu initiieren.
Bd. 68, 2013, 384 S., 39,90 €, br., ISBN 3-643-11986-5

Erziehungswissenschaft

Marian Louise Giffhorn

Kann sich die Schule selber helfen?

Erziehungswissenschaft LIT

Marian Louise Giffhorn

Kann sich die Schule selber helfen?

Kann sich die Schule selber helfen? Die Studie über ein neurophysiologisches Übungsprogramm belegt positive Auswirkungen auf das Lernverhalten bei Schulkindern.

Schulkinder zeigen heute andere und mehr Auffälligkeiten als in zurückliegenden Zeiten. Dies zeigt sich in ausgeprägtem Maße in dem Lernverhalten von Kindern. Das sensomotorische Übungsprogramm zeigt Möglichkeiten und Auswirkungen für den Schulunterricht.

Mit Erfahrungsberichten von Lehrern und Eltern sowie einem Bericht von Dr. Carsten Queißer über die Jugendmedizin heute und die Auswirkungen von Stress auf Gesundheit und Bewegung.

Bd. 69, 2013, 128 S., 24,90 €, br., ISBN 978-3-643-12142-4

LIT Verlag Berlin – Münster – Wien – Zürich – London

Auslieferung Deutschland / Österreich / Schweiz: siehe Impressumsseite